BRITISH PRISONERS OF THE KOREAN WAR

British Prisoners of
the Korean War

S. P. MACKENZIE

OXFORD
UNIVERSITY PRESS

UNIVERSITY PRESS

Great Clarendon Street, Oxford, OX2 6DP,
United Kingdom

Oxford University Press is a department of the University of Oxford.
It furthers the University's objective of excellence in research, scholarship,
and education by publishing worldwide. Oxford is a registered trade mark of
Oxford University Press in the UK and in certain other countries

British Library Cataloguing in Publication Data
Data available

Library of Congress Cataloging in Publication Data
Data available

ISBN 978–0–19–965602–8

Printed in Great Britain by
MPG Books Group, Bodmin and King's Lynn

For Jacques Loeb

Acknowledgements

This book could not have been written without the patient assistance of the staff of the following archives and libraries: the British Library; the Imperial War Museum; the Labour History and Archives Centre, Manchester; the National Archives, Kew; the National Archives and Records Administration, Archives II, College Park, Maryland; the National Archives of Australia; the National Army Museum; the Soldiers of Gloucestershire Museum; the State Library of Victoria; and the inter-library loan department of Thomas Cooper Library, University of South Carolina. Crown copyright material is reproduced under Class Licence Number C2006000011 with the permission of OPSI and the Queen's Printer for Scotland. Thanks go to Elbie Bentley for producing a version of a Crown copyright Ministry of Defence map. All reasonable effort has been made to contact the holders of other copyrighted materials reproduced in this book. Any omissions will be rectified in future printings if notice is given to the publisher. Thanks are also due to the anonymous readers of various portions of this work, and to my OUP editor, Stephanie Ireland. Any errors that remain are, perforce, my responsibility as author.

Contents

List of Abbreviations

AI9	British military intelligence organization concerned with POWs
CPGB	Communist Party of Great Britain
CPV	Chinese People's Volunteers
GI	slang for US soldier
IWMDD	Imperial War Museum, Department of Documents
IWMDS	Imperial War Museum, Department of Sound
LHASC	Labour History Archive and Study Centre, People's History Museum, Manchester
MGB	Ministry for State Security, Soviet secret service
NAA	National Archives of Australia, Series A2151, Item KB1073/11G
NAM	National Army Museum, Chelsea
NARA	National Archives and Records Administration, Archives II, College Park, Md.
RAMC	Royal Army Medical Corps
RM	Royal Marines
RMA	Royal Military Academy
SIS	Secret Intelligence Service (MI6)
SLV	State Library of Victoria, Melbourne
TNA	The National Archives, Kew
USAF	United States Air Force
USMC	United States Marine Corps

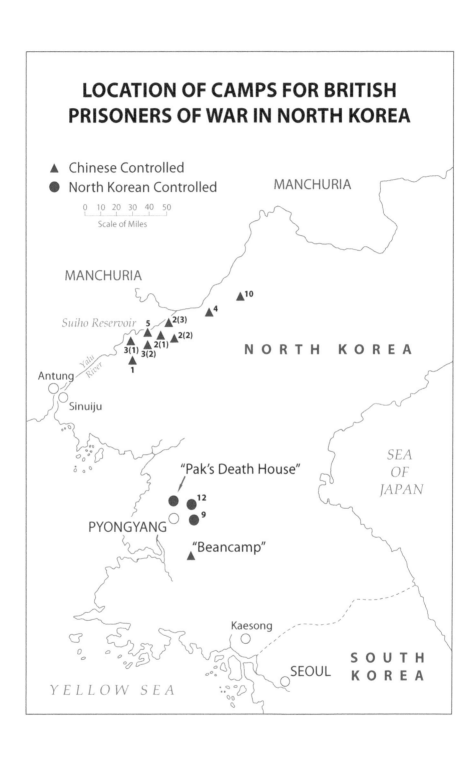

LOCATION OF CAMPS FOR BRITISH
PRISONERS OF WAR IN NORTH KOREA

▲ Chinese Controlled
● North Korean Controlled

0   10 20 30 40 50
Scale of Miles

MANCHURIA

MANCHURIA

NORTH KOREA

Suiho Reservoir   5   ▲2(3)
                    ▲   ▲4   ▲10
         ▲   ▲2(2)
Yalu River 3(1) ▲2(1)
              ▲   3(2)
Antung   ▲1

Sinuiju

SEA
OF
JAPAN

"Pak's Death House"

PYONGYANG   ●   ●12
            ○   ●9

"Beancamp" ▲

Kaesong   ○

YELLOW SEA

SEOUL   ○

SOUTH
KOREA

Introduction

My supervisor asked me to read the regulations to the POWs. It began 'Dear students.' I was very surprised, and asked why, because to me they were prisoners and we were their captors. But my supervisor said, 'Yes, they are students, and you are instructors.'

Qian Meide, camp translator[1]

For much of the twentieth century, books on prisoners of war were the preserve of those who wrote about daring escapes for a general audience; first the participants themselves and then writers who were inspired by their adventures. Indeed the popularity of the genre remains such that new works, especially of the latter kind, are still being published to this day. Over the past two decades or so, though, POWs have also become the subject of a good deal of academic research in the English-speaking world. As one accomplished scholar observed in 2006, 'the number of specialist works on the history of POWs continues to expand',[2] a process that has accelerated down to the present as the myriad issues raised by the Guantánamo Bay detention facility continue to inspire historical reflection.[3] Yet, in spite of the growing academic interest in POWs, British captives taken in the Korean War have been largely ignored.[4]

This holds true for other nationalities too, perhaps the result of a wider tendency to overlook 'the forgotten war';[5] but there are likely several more specific reasons for bypassing the British experience in North Korea, beginning with the issue of scale. Only around 1,000 servicemen of the Crown were held by the enemy as POWs during the Korean War, as against over 194,000 in the First World War and more than 365,000 in the Second World War. There are also comparatively few published recollections. As against the hundreds of printed memoirs by former

---

[1] Qian Meide in *They Chose China* (National Film Board of Canada, 2005).

[2] Neville Wylie, 'Review Essay: Prisoners of War in the Era of Total War', *War in History*, 13 (2006), 233.

[3] See e.g. Robert C. Doyle, *The Enemy in Our Hands* (Lexington, Ky., 2010); Paul G. Springer, *America's Captives* (Lawrence, Kan., 2010). A scholarly overview can be found in Sibylle Scheipers (ed.), *Prisoners in War* (Oxford, 2010).

[4] What discussion of British POWs there is tends to be relegated to small sections of studies devoted to wider aspects of the Korean War: e.g. see Andrew Salmon, *To the Last Round* (London, 2009), 269–300; Peter Gaston, *Thirty-Eighth Parallel* (Glasgow, 1976), 80–3.

[5] For an overview of the limited published literature see Alan R. Millett, *The Korean War* (Washington, DC, 2007).

captives held during the Second World War and the dozens arising from the First World War, less than half a dozen such books by British servicemen captured in the Korean War came out in its aftermath.[6] Just as significantly, any and all surviving Chinese and North Korean records in, respectively, Beijing and Pyongyang, remain under lock and key, as do many files in London.[7] In addition there is the simple fact that—an especially uncomfortable one from the perspective of popular historians drawn to escape narratives of the kind that have dominated trade publishing in relation to POWs—no serviceman made it back to UN lines from the enemy prison camps dotted along the Yalu River.[8]

Over the years, to be sure, there have been a few official and semi-official accounts chronicling the British POW experience in the Korean War. Shortly after the fighting ended the Ministry of Defence published its 'Blue Book', *Treatment of British Prisoners of War in Korea*, a version of which one of the officials involved, Cyril Cunningham, would over forty years later rework into the single comprehensive study of the British experience, *No Mercy, No Leniency*.[9] Moreover, when the two-volume official history *The British Part in the Korean War* appeared in the latter 1990s, its author, Anthony Farrar-Hockley, who had himself been held by the Chinese and North Koreans, devoted a chapter to POWs.[10]

Unfortunately there are some drawbacks to these works. The Blue Book was specifically designed to counter claims made by some of the first men to be released—carefully selected by the Chinese authorities for their pro-communist views and echoing the line taken in communist propaganda—to the effect that captives were treated well and were broadly sympathetic to enemy aims.[11] Though solidly grounded in the experiences of the later returnees,[12] it was perforce not impartial. As the Cabinet Secretary commented in a note to the Prime Minister, while the facts were doubtless accurate 'the tone and presentation of the document is not as objective as one would expect an official publication to be'.[13] The heavily reworked version published at the end of the century was, as its author claimed, a 'more balanced account'; but it too was primarily about 'the mistreatment of the

---

[6] S. J. Davies, *In Spite of Dungeons* (London, 1954); Anthony Farrar-Hockley, *The Edge of the Sword* (London, 1954); Derek Kinne, *The Wooden Boxes* (London, 1955); Dennis Lankford, *I Defy!* (London, 1954); R. F. Matthews, as told to Francis S. Jones, *No Rice for Rebels* (London, 1956).

[7] TNA, WO 208/4015–19, 4024–102 cannot be viewed until the year 2030.

[8] Max Hastings, *The Korean War* (London, 1987), 348—though see J. Graham in Arthur W. Wilson, *Korean Vignettes* (Portland, Oreg., 1996), 281. Hundreds of men did, however, manage to evade or escape before or while being transported to camps. Department of the Army, *U.S. Prisoners of War in the Korean Operation* (Fort Meade, Md., 1954), 288; see e.g. Paul G. Petredis, *Escape From North Korea* (Victoria, BC, 2005); Ward M. Mallar, *Valley of the Shadow* (New York, 1955), 3 ff.; Clay Blair, Jr, *Beyond Courage* (New York, 1955).

[9] C. Cunningham, *No Mercy, No Leniency: Communist Mistreatment of British Prisoners of War in Korea* (Barnsley, 2000); Ministry of Defence, *Treatment of British Prisoners of War in Korea* (London, 1955).

[10] Anthony Farrar-Hockley, *The British Part in the Korean War*, 2 vols. (London, 1995), II, 266–81.

[11] Ministry of Defence, *Treatment of British Prisoners of War in Korea*, v.

[12] Most of what was described in the Blue Book (and indeed in the later iteration authored by Cunningham) can be verified by reading the primary source material (NAA, Parts 1–7).

[13] TNA, CAB 21/4020, Brook to Churchill, 14 December 1954.

British p.o.w.' in Korea.[14] The chapter on POWs in the official history that had appeared a few years earlier, meanwhile, could not escape the limitations of being authored by someone who had himself been tortured by the communists and who relied almost exclusively on the memories of officers and men he knew who had also been branded 'reactionaries' by the Chinese.[15]

There are a number of reasons why, from the perspective of a professional historian who, in contrast to the authors of the works mentioned above, has no personal or institutional connection to what happened, it seems worth taking up the challenge of exploring in detail the British POW experience in the Korean War. The source material now available, at least from the UN side, is much more substantial than it once was. The number of memoirs has grown a little;[16] a significant number of recorded interviews with ex-prisoners can now be listened to;[17] and, most important of all, summaries of their responses to official questioning immediately after their release are now accessible.[18] Moreover, though the number of captives may have been small in comparison to the world wars, prisoners in Korea faced a unique and prolonged test of mind, character, and body: grappling with an intensive and sustained effort by the enemy to change their allegiance and help subvert their government's war effort.[19]

Inevitably, perhaps, popular historians have tended to echo the official tendency after the war to publicly downplay the effectiveness of this campaign.[20] The author of the first postwar narrative of British operations in Korea claimed British POWs 'maintained their loyalty and morale in captivity, and showed proper pride in defying Communist indoctrination and attempts at subversion'.[21] Fourteen years later another officer-turned-writer covering the same subject matter was arguing that British captives had 'flagrantly sabotaged their Communist indoctrination',[22] while

---

[14] Cunningham, *No Mercy, No Leniency*, xv. Like *Treatment of British Prisoners of War in Korea*, Cunningham's book contains no citations, and the author shies away from identifying by name known POW collaborators by using pseudonyms.

[15] See Farrar-Hockley, *The British Part in the Korean War*, II, 293; Farrar-Hockley, *Edge of the Sword, passim*.

[16] See David Green, *Captured at the Imjin River* (Barnsley, 2003); Lofty Large, *One Man's War in Korea* (London, 1988); Henry O'Kane, *O'Kane's Korea* (Kenilworth, 1988); see also IWMDD, E. F. Beckerley memoir, F. E. Carter memoir, R. W. McGuire memoir.

[17] See Select Bibliography.

[18] NAA, Parts 1–7. There are also summaries and questionaires relating to US prisoners that occasionally pertain to British prisoners. NARA, RG 38, 319.

[19] During the Second World War the Japanese had put some effort into pressuring thousands of Indian prisoners captured in Malaya into joining the Indian National Army (Peter Ward Fay, *The Forgotten Army* (Ann Arbor, Mich., 1993)), but showed no interest in suborning their British captives, while the Germans, after trying fitfully and without success to recruit disaffected Irishmen in POW camps (as they had in the First World War), late in the day persuaded a handful of gullible POWs to join the tiny British Free Corps for propaganda purposes (Adrian Weale, *Renegades* (London, 2002)).

[20] See e.g. Ministry of Defence, *Treatment of British Prisoners of War in Korea*, 3–5. Behind the scenes there existed concern that—as proved to be the case with the MI6 officer George Blake—some of those who came back from North Korea and remained in the services might profess to be loyal but in fact had become communist agents while held prisoner. See TNA, WO 32/20495.

[21] C. N. Barclay, *The First Commonwealth Division* (Aldershot, 1954), 191.

[22] Tim Carew, *Korea* (London, 1967), 165.

fourteen years after that yet another author was stating that they had proved 'remarkably resistant' to enemy efforts at undermining their loyalty.[23]

As we shall see, the evidence now available in some respects supports and in other ways undermines this position. The experiences and reactions of British prisoners varied from place to place and over time. In order to understand how British prisoners behaved in Korea, however, we must first grasp how they were perceived by their enemies.

* * *

The responsible officers serving the Democratic People's Republic of Korea, whether from military intelligence, the bureau of politics, or the security police, were ruthlessly utilitarian in their attitude towards captured servicemen. Deaths from exhaustion, starvation, beatings, shootings, and torture were entirely acceptable as long as those who remained served a purpose. The main aim with captured South Koreans was to force them to join the North Korean People's Army.[24] The goals in relation to other UN prisoners included extraction of military intelligence, expending as little as possible in terms of maintenance costs, making sure none were liberated when enemy forces were advancing, using them as slave labour when needed, and employing a selected few as propaganda tools.[25] Keeping men alive and in good health for humanitarian reasons was definitely not among the aims. Thus, of 1,037 Americans taken in the months after the war began in June 1951, only 462 were not dead by October.[26]

As we shall see, a fair number of British captives found themselves in North Korean hands at various junctures, and suffered greatly as a result. The majority of those captured, however, arrived in the main Yalu camps in the period when administrative control was being passed from the North Koreans to 'volunteers' from the People's Republic of China. They too cared little for bourgeois convention regarding POWs—neither regime, for example, recognized the rights of inspection of the International Committee of the Red Cross[27]—and as will become clear they were capable of considerable brutality in certain circumstances. The Chinese communists, however, took a more long-term and expansive view of the ideological utility of UN prisoners.

The Chinese, of course, like the North Koreans (and behind both the Russians) were interested in obtaining potentially useful military information from captives. There also existed, however, a much more ambitious aim that had its origins in the recently concluded civil war in China between the communists and the nationalists.

---

[23] Gaston, *Thirty-Eighth Parallel*, 81.

[24] Hyo-Soon Song, *The Fight for Freedom* (Seoul, 1980), 440; Walter G. Hermes, *United States Army in the Korean War: Truce Tent and Fighting Front* (Washington, DC, 1965), 138.

[25] Cunningham, *No Mercy, No Leniency*, 10–11.

[26] Jeffrey Grey, 'Other Fronts: Resistance, Collaboration and Survival among United Nations Prisoners during the Korean War' in Peter Dennis and Jeffrey Grey (eds.), *The Korean War* (Canberra, 2000), 145. On how badly Americans were treated by the North Koreans see e.g. US Senate, Committee on Government Operations, *Korean War Atrocities* (Washington, DC, 1954); Philip D. Chinnery, *Korean Atrocity!* (Annapolis, Md., 2000), chs. 1–2; Paul McGrath Avery and Joyce Faulkner, *Sunchon Tunnel Survivors* (Branson, Mo., 2008).

[27] Caroline Moorehead, *Dunant's Dream* (New York, 1999), 569–71.

During the struggle Mao had augmented the strength of his forces though adopting a Lenient Policy towards captured troops. Instead of simply being killed or worked to death, these men would be offered the chance of communist re-education and, once enlightenment had been achieved, the opportunity to serve the righteous cause of liberation. When the Chinese took over the task of looking after most POWs from the North Koreans in the spring and summer of 1951 a variant of this Lenient Policy was applied against UN captives. It would be explained to prisoners that instead of being treated as war criminals, which they were, they would be allowed to become pupils in order to understand the way in which they had been duped into fighting on behalf of a rapacious and unjust capitalist system. Manpower was no longer an issue for Mao in the wake of the establishment of the People's Republic of China, but it was confidently expected that through a mixture of carrot and stick UN prisoners could be converted over time to the communist cause and used *en masse* as a potent weapon against enemy public opinion through letters, petitions, and other propaganda forms calling for an immediate end to the war or, later on, condemning the supposed dropping of germ bombs. Once the end of the conflict was in sight, moreover, hard-core converts might be encouraged to develop communist front organizations in the West and thereby advance the cause of world socialism.[28]

Towards this end the Prisoner of War Corps of the Chinese People's Volunteers in late 1950 and on into 1951 laid plans and issued orders concerning the implementation of the Lenient Policy. Questionnaires for captives to fill in involving both military and a lot of personal information were prepared.[29] English speakers were brought in from Shanghai and elsewhere to serve as translators and instructors to engage with what were to be termed students rather than captives.[30] Troops were ordered to smile and shake hands with those who surrendered to indicate their fraternal feelings: 'don't kill or maltreat, don't take personal possessions', Chinese soldiers were admonished. 'If POWs lay down their arms, they are not the enemy.'[31] This was certainly a welcome change from the North Korean tendency to view captives as expendable. ('The North Koreans and Chinese were always arguing about what to do with us', a corporal captured in December 1950 remembered: 'The North Koreans wanted to shoot us. The Chinese wanted to move us north as prisoners.'[32]) It was eventually to become obvious to prisoners, however, that acceptance and cooperation in the learning process were expected in return for such clemency. 'POWs must obey orders or they will be punished', the same instruction went on to stress.[33] It was also to be

---

[28] See Cunningham, *No Mercy, No Leniency*, 12–13, 158; Department of the Army, *U.S. Prisoners of War in the Korean Operation*, 24; US Senate, Committee on Government Operations, *Communist Interrogation, Indoctrination and Exploitation of American Military and Civilian Prisoners* (Washington, DC, 1956), 23 ff.; Raymond B. Lech, *Broken Soldiers* (Urbana, Il., 2000), 187–9.

[29] See Cunningham, *No Mercy, No Leniency*, App. A.

[30] *They Chose China* (National Film Board of Canada, 2005). According to information gleaned by a prisoner who spent some time at the POW Corps HQ at Pyoktong, all students of English in China were required during the war to spend six months on the staff of a camp containing American or British Commonwealth captives. NAA, Part 3, AI9/K/BRIT/320, Tpr R. A. Cocks, 6.

[31] Department of the Army, *U.S. Prisoners of War in the Korean Operation*, 211.

[32] D. McAlister in Wilson, *Korean Vignettes*, 209.

[33] Department of the Army, *U.S. Prisoners of War in the Korean Operation*.

made clear to captives that a 'hostile attitude' would not be tolerated, and that leniency 'has its limitations as regards our enemies'.[34]

British servicemen sent to Korea in 1950, it is important to note, were not trained in how to deal with this kind of thing. Capture was not something that the military authorities wanted men to dwell on, and very little information was disseminated beyond a lecture to a few staff officers about escape and evasion techniques and a couple of talks aboard ship on how to behave in enemy hands to which little attention was paid.[35] As for the political dimension of the conflict, talks and discussions on current affairs, a major feature of the British Army during the Second World War, were discouraged.[36] Matters were not helped by the fact that well over half the men of the first units sent out from the United Kingdom were recalled reservists. These were mostly veterans of the Second World War who felt they had already done their bit for King and Country, and were often bitterly resentful at being called away from established jobs and families in order to be sent to a place almost nobody had ever even heard of.[37] Officers, to be sure, might try and brief their men en route to Korea about why they were going, but as they themselves tended to be rather hazy about world affairs and the origins of the conflict this was not particularly helpful.[38] As Private Sam Mercer of the Glosters ruefully admitted many years later, debating the merits of communism and capitalism 'was something for which none of us were really prepared in any shape or form'.[39]

As it happened, the first British subjects taken by the enemy in the Korean War were not servicemen at all, but rather diplomats, churchmen, and others caught up in the North Korean capture of Seoul. The first servicemen captured a few months later, moreover, were not from the British Army but rather from the Royal Marines. Neither group had been given any guidance as to how to behave if captured.[40] It is to their experiences that we must turn in the next two chapters before examining the fate of the thousand-odd British soldiers captured between 1951 and 1953.

[34] Notes taken on address by Camp 1 Commandant in Farrar-Hockley, *British Part in the Korean War II*, 267.

[35] On lack of attention to the lecture from RSM Jack Hobbs see NAM 1989-05-1-1, Sebastian Mercer; Salmon, *To the Last Round*, 40. On another brief talk by the Intelligence Officer and Adjutant of the Glosters aboard ship see NAA, Part 4, A19/K/BRIT/975 Part II, WOII H. Gallagher, 1; Part 5, A19/K/BRIT/4 Part II, Sgt W.A. Lucas, 1. On the escape and evasion lecture to staff officers see TNA, AIR 40/2622, Code Communication with British PW located in Camps in North Korea, J. B. Ponyz memo, n/d. On COs not being keen to have their men briefed on what to do if captured see Cunningham, *No Mercy, No Leniency*, 162.

[36] See S. P. MacKenzie, *Politics and Military Morale* (Oxford, 1992), ch. 9. Only later on in the Korean War was some effort put into explaining Britain's involvement in the conflict. Leslie Wayper, *Mars and Minerva* (Winchester, 2004), 275.

[37] For reservist unhappiness see e.g. IWMDS, 19047/3, Frank Brodie; 17348/3, Walter Cleveland; 16078/1, James Forward; 20057/1, Alfred Gilder; 15428/1, David Holdsworth; 18819/3, Thomas McMahon; 19051/2, Lawrence Moreton; 16618/1, Cyril Papworth; 09784/1, Kenneth Trevor; NAA, Part 5, A19/K/BRIT/290, Rfn F. Moxam, para 13; J. Gray in Adrian Walker, *A Barren Place* (London, 1994), 72. On the high percentage of reservists see TNA, WO308/42, 29Bde History, 1.

[38] See e.g. NAM 1989-05-163-1, R. Bruford-Davies; IWMDS, 15557/1, G. Temple.

[39] IWMDS, 12605/5, S. Mercer.

[40] On lack of instruction on how to behave as a POW among the Royal Marines see Fred Hayhurst, *Green Berets in Korea* (Cambridge, 2001), 358.

1

The Civilians from Seoul

You are most fortunate to be in the care of people who are concerned about your welfare. Even in the middle of a war against the imperialist Americans, we are able to look after your needs.

North Korean officer[1]

On the face of it, Britain had no obvious interests to protect in Korea in the middle of the twentieth century. The peninsula had been a part of the Japanese Empire prior to 1945, and subsequently had been divided into Soviet and American occupation zones that by the end of the decade had evolved into competing independent regimes north and south of the 38th Parallel which each claimed suzerainty over Korea as a whole. In the early hours of Sunday, 25 June 1950 the communists in the north sought to resolve the issue definitively by launching an invasion of the south. Anxious to contain communist expansion, the Truman administration in the United States quickly and successfully convinced the Security Council of the United Nations—thanks to the absence of the representative of the Soviet Union, who was boycotting proceedings at the time—to authorize collective military action under US command in support of the besieged Republic of Korea. London accepted that, as a Great Power and an ally of the United States, Great Britain was obliged not only to support resolutions at the UN but also do what it could to back up the ground forces immediately committed by Washington.[2]

That it would do so was not clear to the small British community resident in South Korea when the invasion started. Border clashes had become more and more frequent, and it was widely expected that a full-scale war would soon develop. What was not so obvious was what position the Western powers, including Great Britain, would take if and when such expectations were realized, and what this would mean for foreigners living in South Korea. The obvious place for British expatriates to turn was the British Legation in Seoul. Unfortunately the Foreign Office had provided no contingency plans as to what to do in the event of a North Korean drive on the South Korean capital, and the Legation did not possess a radio transmitter of its own. Captain Vyvyan Holt, the British Minister, sent a message through the Cable and Wireless Company that Sunday requesting instructions as to what do in case the capital was threatened, but rightly suspected that any reply

---

[1] Larry Zellers, *In Enemy Hands* (Lexington, Ky., 1991), 70.
[2] Anthony Farrar-Hockley, *The British Part in the Korean War*, 2 vols (London, 1990), I, ch.1.

would take days to arrive. By then events would have likely overtaken whatever advice the Foreign Office might have, and in the event the cable office was abandoned before any reply could be received. Holt and his two subordinates, George Blake and Norman Owen, officially junior diplomats but in fact SIS officers, were on their own.[3]

The first step involved Blake using a jeep to make the rounds of the small British community in Seoul—a mixture of businessmen, missionaries, and their families—suggesting that they congregate at the Legation that evening as a prelude to evacuation. Everyone agreed to leave the capital except churchmen who wished to remain and minister to their flocks: notably Bishop Alfred Cooper, leader of the Anglican community, and Commissioner Herbert Lord of the Salvation Army, who was fluent in Korean. Most, however, soon decided to move into the Legation for safety's sake the following day. By then the first confused reports of the fighting were giving way to a clearer picture in which a North Korean occupation of Seoul became more and more of a certainty. With the American embassy and South Korean government pulling out, Holt had to decide whether to flee or stay. He opted for the latter course, in part because the Legation had no idea where the regime of Syngman Rhee to which he was accredited was heading, but also because Holt, like the rest of the staff, assumed Britain would stay out of the war and the Legation might therefore continue to function once the North Koreans arrived in Seoul. It therefore came 'as a great shock and surprise' when it was reported by the BBC on Tuesday evening that Prime Minister Clement Attlee had committed Britain to military action under the UN flag.[4]

By now it was too late to escape as Seoul was full of communist soldiers. 'We spent that night burning our codes and secret documents in a sheltered corner of the garden in the hope that the bonfire would not attract the attention of the North Korean military', Blake remembered.[5] It did not, and on Wednesday the staff also disposed of the contents of the drinks cabinet for fear of what would happen if a mob broke in and got drunk. All that remained was to wait for the North Koreans to put in an appearance at the gates in what had become an eerily quiet city. On Friday a group of Korean civilians sporting red armbands arrived and, despite protests, drove away the Legation's cars. Then on Sunday, a week after the war had begun, an officer accompanied by two soldiers arrived and politely asked that the Union Jack be lowered in case it attracted the attention of enemy aircraft. Accounts differ as to whether Holt refused to do so or not, but the flag came down in any event.[6] Apart from an unruly band of militiamen who departed once it was

---

[3] See George Blake, *No Other Choice* (New York, 1990), 121–3; TNA, FO 371/184173, FK1581/3. Blake in the late 1990s claimed that London had issued instructions before the war broke out that the Legation was to sit tight and serve as an observation post in the event of a North Korean takeover of South Korea (George Blake, <http://www.pbs.org/redfiles/kgb/deep/interv/k_int_george_blake.htm> (accessed 18 October 2011), 4). This cannot be verified from available records and contradicts the account in his own memoir.

[4] Blake, *No Other Choice*, 123–5; see E. H. Cookridge, *Shadow of a Spy* (London, 1967), 90.

[5] Blake, *No Other Choice*, 125.

[6] See Blake, *No Other Choice*,126; Cookridge, *Shadow of a Spy*, 91; Philip Deane, *I Was a Captive in Korea* (New York, 1953), 79.

clear that the Legation's liquor supply had already been disposed of, the diplomats and missionaries were left alone until 2 July 1950 when everyone was driven to police headquarters and quizzed about their identity—while the Legation was being sacked and South Korean prisoners were simultaneously being beaten up and shot nearby—before being trucked the next day with a couple of other foreign nationals to a camp outside Pyongyang. There they were joined in the following weeks by members of the French diplomatic mission, as well as various other civilian foreigners such as Philip Deane, captured war correspondent for *The Observer*, plus nuns and Christian missionaries of various nationalities and denominations, almost all of whom had experienced rough handling at the hands of the North Koreans. By the time everyone had been assembled there were almost fifty men and women present, many of them elderly.[7]

What turned out to be only a temporary transit camp consisted of two rather battered school buildings surrounded by barbed wire, one occupied by prisoners and the other by the camp guards. According to the recollections of several of the British prisoners, the three small bowls a day of rice with some cabbage were tolerable if monotonous; though it is worth noting some of the American prisoners thought both the quantity and quality of the rations remained completely inadequate. What everyone could agree on was the awfulness of having to deal with a plague of insects, including fleas and lice. The authorities did, however, try and make it possible for internees to keep clean: they were issued with water basins, cakes of soap, toothbrushes, and tooth powder. For the earliest arrivals there were also combs and hand mirrors, along with a steadily diminishing cigarette ration.[8]

On 5 September 1950, ostensibly to protect them from American bombing raids on the North Korean capital, these internees and others from various nations were put aboard a train heading northward to the frontier town of Manpo. The six-day journey was uncomfortable, with the internees confined to a couple of damaged and dilapidated carriages into which food and water were distributed infrequently. The train was also attacked from the air on several occasions by USAF pilots unaware that this was not a troop train. But as the civilians could see from the 500-odd emaciated, dirty, lice-ridden, sick, and poorly clothed US Army prisoners crammed by the dozens into open coal trucks also attached to the train, things might have been a lot worse.[9]

On 11 September the train reached Manpo and the civilians were put up in a couple of run-down buildings that were thought to be either disused barracks or customs sheds from the days of the Japanese occupation. For the internees, whose numbers were soon to reach seventy-four, living conditions under the supervision of North Korean army guards and a sympathetic commandant were entirely

---

[7] Zellers, *In Enemy Hands*, 1–51, 53–4, 56; Philip Crosbie, *Three Winters Cold* (Dublin, 1955), 11–65; Blake, *No Other Choice*, 126–7; Cookridge, *Shadow of a Spy*, 93–7; Deane, *I Was a Captive*, 65 ff.; Philip Deane, *I Should Have Died* (New York, 1977), 3–12, 29–33, 40.

[8] Crosbie, *Three Winters Cold*, 68; Zellers, *In Enemy Hands*, 54; Blake, *No Other Choice*, 127; Cookridge, *Shadow of a Spy*, 97; Raymond A. Lane, *Ambassador in Chains* (New York, 1955), 227.

[9] See Deane, *I Was a Captive*, 86–7; Zellers, *In Enemy Hands*, 59–65.

'reasonable' in the eyes of Blake and his companions. The autumn weather was still comparatively mild, and as Deane explained in his memoir of captivity:

> Judging by the standards of the neighboring villagers, we were living in the lap of luxury, with an egg a day, meat three times a week, sugar, oil. In the afternoon we could bathe in the [Yalu] river and sit for as long as we liked on the sunny beach. We were allowed to go into town shopping with what money the diplomats managed to get out of the guards in exchange for their watches.

As for food, Australian missionary Father Philip Crosbie admitted that 'we had no cause to complain about either the quantity or quality'. There was plenty of rice, dried fish, and vegetable soup to go around. A small tobacco ration was occasionally provided with a kilogram of apples for the non-smokers. There was a partial issue of padded winter clothing to cope with the nights, which were getting colder. Decent medical care was even provided through the efforts of a sympathetic visiting North Korean doctor; and, thanks to illicit contact with a Korean boy who happened to be Christian, it was possible to get an approximate idea of how the war was going.[10]

The news was good. In the second half of September the North Korean forces had been thrown into complete disarray by the American landing far behind their lines at the port of Inchon on the west coast and were retreating fast toward the Yalu with their enemies in hot pursuit. 'Fascinated and overjoyed,' Father Crosbie recalled, 'we began excitedly to calculate how soon the U.N. advance would reach us at Manpo.'[11]

In the second week of October the civilians found themselves on the move, shuffled back and forth on foot or occasionally by truck from one temporary location to another with a two-week respite at Kosan, before being sent back in the direction of Manpo towards the end of the month.[12] Despite clear signs that the Chinese were crossing into North Korea in support of the tottering communist regime of Kim Il-sung, many of the civilians were still hopeful that they would soon be freed. During the Kosan interlude this led to a spontaneous attempt to challenge the hitherto unquestioned authority of the North Koreans. As an American missionary who observed the confrontation later explained:

> We were standing inside the schoolhouse one morning when a guard came in and ordered us all to fall out to do some work. Because of the attitude of the guards, we felt that our rescue was near and did not want to comply. Lord, in his very military manner, walked up to the guard and announced that we were not going to carry out his order. At that, the guard leveled his submachine gun at Lord's chest and repeated the order. The commissioner instantly threw back his shoulders and stuck out his chest, as though to provide a better target. What immediately followed was totally unprecedented in our prison experience. I think it was Danny [Dans, an American

---

[10] Deane, *I Was a Captive*, 88–9; Blake, *No Other Choice*, 128; Crosbie, *Three Winters Cold*, 98; see ibid., 100, 102, 105–6, 108; Cookridge, *Shadow of a Spy*, 97–8; Zellers, *In Enemy Hands*, 66–8.

[11] Crosbie, *Three Winters Cold*, 112.

[12] Ibid. 113–32; Deane, *I Was a Captive*, 89–108; Zellers, *In Enemy Hands*, 77–87.

businessman] who made the first move; nothing was planned, but within two or three seconds there was a general movement among the prisoners in the guard's direction. I felt myself being drawn along with the others…The guard did not know how to respond. Apparently, his orders and training did not cover this sort of prisoner behavior, and he went running out of the room.

The major in command claimed the internees had rioted, but as Larry Zellers noted, 'we were not punished at all for our rather serious breach of discipline'.[13] Indeed, as the internees' perambulations continued, more of the escorting guards were becoming amenable towards their charges as the prospect of imminent capture loomed. A sergeant even supported a foray to make contact with UN forces, and Blake was able to slip away on his own. It quickly became apparent, though, that the Chinese intervention was on a massive scale and that there were North Korean officers determined to carry out their orders at any cost. The plan to link up with friendly troops had to be aborted once the guard sergeant had become convinced that Chinese intervention was tipping the scales the other way; and while Blake was not punished after he was recaptured—perhaps a sign of residual uncertainty about which way the wind was blowing—the appearance of an unrelenting new commander for the civilian and military prisoners in the area, soon to be dubbed 'The Tiger', foreshadowed rough times ahead.[14]

On 31 October this tall, thin figure introduced himself as a major in the North Korean People's Army and announced that the civilians, along with a column of American POWs, would depart the Manpo area and undertake a military-style march. All supporting sticks were taken away on the pretext that they were potential weapons, and when Lord and others protested that the more elderly civilians, some of them sick, would not survive a marching pace he replied: 'Then let them march till they die.'[15]

Several did, along with nearly a hundred US Army prisoners, during the following nine days in one of the most infamous death marches of the war. Daily food consisted of a half-cooked ball of maize at best, clothing was totally inadequate for the steadily worsening weather, and there was often no shelter—or in one instance a single schoolroom into which so many people were packed that several died in the course of the night. Worst of all, The Tiger kept forcing the pace across mountainous country, ordering the guards to shoot those who fell out from illness and exhaustion once the columns had passed and killing at least one US prisoner himself in front of several horrified witnesses. Commissioner Lord, who spoke Korean fluently and served as translator, had the added mental burden of passing on orders he knew would produce suffering and pleading in vain for the lives of those The Tiger had decided should be executed. Nevertheless, as one of the American officers noted, he 'was always trying to cheer us up'. The other clergy did their best to

[13] Zellers, *In Enemy Hands*, 77.

[14] Blake, *No Other Choice*, 128–31; Crosbie, *Three Winters Cold*, 126; Deane, *I Was a Captive*, 101–9; Zellers, *In Enemy Hands*, 79–85.

[15] Crosbie, *Three Winters Cold*, 135; Zellers, *In Enemy Hands*, 84–5; see Robert Kenyon, *Valiant Dust* (London, 1966), 52.

offer spiritual sustenance too, and for this US Army officer at least the civilian group as a whole 'was an inspiration to me'. Why? 'As I watched those old folks climb the mountain ahead of us, I said, "If they can do it, so can I."' Though the half-dozen or so British internees, all starving and suffering from dysentery, managed to survive, by the time the march ended on 8 November at a school in Chunggang-ni ninety-six GIs were dead along with three elderly French nuns. Fifteen others, fatally weakened by the ordeal, would die thereafter, along with a solitary Royal Marine.[16]

Less than a week after arriving at Chunggang-ni the internees were moved on foot to the buildings of another school at Hanjang-ni, where they would remain for several months, initially under the command of The Tiger. Living conditions over the winter of 1950–1 were bad. The accommodation was overcrowded—seven people in a room 9 feet by 9 feet was common—while the wood supply for heating remained inadequate. As for food, it consisted of 600 grams of millet per person per day plus a single cabbage for between ten and thirty-five people made into a watery soup. Everyone was lice-ridden and sickness was rife. Holt and Owen were in a particularly bad way, but luckily their companions did everything they could to keep them alive. 'If it were not for George Blake and Philip Deane I would not have survived even the last leg of the death march', the British Minister declared soon after he was freed in 1953. 'At Hadjang [*sic*] they nursed me and Consul Owen and gave us their rations, although they were themselves sick and hungry.' Despite their deteriorating condition, prisoners were expected to carry stores, grind grain, and carry water.[17]

Camp discipline at Hanjang-ni, moreover, could be quite harsh, as several internees had occasion to discover. As Blake recounted in his memoirs:

> I had to fetch water from the well. This was a chore we all had to take in turns. In normal conditions it was not a very arduous task. One had to carry two buckets on a yoke across one's shoulder and empty them into a large barrel. In the freezing temperatures of the North Korean winter this turned into a real ordeal, however. The rope with which the bucket was hauled up turned into a rod of ice and the sides of the well into ice walls. Going to and from the well, we were accompanied by an armed soldier.

---

[16] Ralph E. Culbertson, 'The Korean War: A Former POW's Story', *Ex-POW Bulletin*, 14(3) (1993), 28; see Zellers, *In Enemy Hands*, 87–123; Blake, *No Other Choice*, 133; Deane, *I Was a Captive*, 110–16; Cooper and Lord in *The Times*, 24 April 1953, 2; 25 April 1953, 3; Kenyon, *Valiant Dust*, 52–60; W. Rountree in Richard Peters and Xiaobing Li, *Voices from the Korean War* (Lexington, Ky., 2004), 221–2; Department of the Army, *U.S. Prisoners of War in the Korean Operation* (Fort Meade, Md., 1954), 91; S. Shinagawa in Louis Baldovi (ed.), *A Foxhole View* (Honolulu, 2002), 72–3; S. Estabrook in Philip D. Chinnery, *Korean Atrocity!* (Annapolis. Md., 2000), 75–6; J. Browning in Donald Knox, *The Korean War: Uncertain Victory* (San Diego, 1988), 332–3; Lane, *Ambassador in Chains*, 234–42; NARA, RG 319, entry 85, box 1029, Phase III summaries for John T. Dunn, Raymond L. Dunning, Frank C. Durant, Vincente Escobar-Torres, John A. Fox, Charles F. Frazer; box 1027, Gerard T. Brown, James A. Cogburn; box 1032, Lawrence A. Herad, Arnos J. Jiron. The Royal Marine, G. I. Ahern, was with 41 (Independent) Commando, the story of which is chronicled in ch. 2. He most likely was left behind by the Chinese because of his wounds and later picked up by the North Koreans.

[17] Holt in Cookridge, *Shadow of a Spy*, 105–6; see Crosbie, *Three Winters Cold*, 176–8; Deane, *I Was a Captive*, 120; Zellers, *In Enemy Hands*, 130–1.

I had been hauling up many buckets and the barrel was nearly full. My hands were so cold that I no longer had any feeling in them so that I could pull up the bucket. I told the soldier that I thought we had enough water, but he said I should fetch more. I refused, saying that I wouldn't and couldn't. He got very angry, shouted at me and started hitting me in the chest with his rifle butt which was very painful. He then took me to the yard outside the peasant hut in which we lived and made me kneel in the snow with my hands behind my back and my head bowed. He called to the others so that I should be an example of what happened to anyone who disobeyed. I don't know how long I remained in that position, but it was certainly more than an hour before he told me I could go inside.[18]

Deane remembered in his memoirs what may or may not have been the same incident. Exhausted, he and Blake had refused to do water duty just in order to allow one of the more influential South Korean internees to do laundry. Then:

The guard ordered George Blake and myself to kneel down in the snow. He accused us of insulting the Koreans, and of not carrying the amount of water laid down in regulations. We replied that it was not so. The guard said he would teach us not to lie, and he beat us with his rifle, kicked us and slapped us. George, who got the worst of it, smiled through the ordeal, his left eyebrow cocked ironically at the guard, his Elizabethan beard aggressively thrust forward. The guard walked away, and some time later—I do not know how much later—he came and told us that if we admitted that we had lied [about not insulting Koreans] he would let us go. The temperature was forty degrees below. We admitted we had lied.

The Tiger punished the guard for hitting them, but not for the accusation of lying or making the pair kneel in the snow.[19]

Perhaps in the toughest position was the man The Tiger treated as the civilians' spokesman, Commissioner Lord. 'More than anyone else in our group', one of the other internees later wrote:

the commissioner displayed outstanding qualities of leadership and a solid grasp of the realities of our situation. No one was his equal in courage, audacity, and resourcefulness when it came to dealing with the Communists. No one else could have done the job as well as he did. No one else would have wanted to try; the job was too dangerous, too demanding, [and] fraught with too many headaches.

This was made clear when Lord was placed in an unheated room. 'I was confronted by the Tiger himself', he later explained, 'and made to kneel in front of him while he started to yell at me and brandish his gun in my face.' The commandant wanted him to 'confess', a task made harder by the fact that he refused to let Lord know what his crime was, and he was confined without heat and with only a single meal of millet seed each day for two weeks with The Tiger threatening him each day and demanding a confession. Only at the end did he explain that the heinous act Lord was supposed to have committed was omitting to tell the commandant of dissension

---

[18] Blake, *No Other Choice*, 133–4. On the ordeal of water carrying duty in winter see also Deane, *I Was a Captive*, 123.

[19] Deane, *I Was a Captive*, 149.

among a certain national contingent, thereby allowing the commissioner to obtain release through admitting his mistake and apologizing.[20]

As if all this was not enough for the internees to cope with, there was also an attempt to instil communist values. This began with a diatribe to both the civilian and military prisoners delivered by The Tiger on the iniquities of life in the capitalist world, the effect of which—like subsequent grossly inaccurate and ignorant statements by more junior North Korean officers to GIs about how poor US living conditions were that flatly contradicted their own experience—was undermined by his assertion that conditions in the United States were filthy because most Americans had toilets inside their houses rather than outside in the fresh air. Most of the enemy effort was put into converting the soldiers, but the missionaries were occasionally subjected to anti-religious lecturers. These, not surprisingly, had little effect. Father William Booth, for example, an American, 'delighted in looking for chinks in [the lecturers'] armor', as one of his fellow missionaries explained, while Commissioner Lord—who 'could verbally slug it out with the best of them'—scored palpable hits when he brought up the fact that figures revered by communists such as Marx and Engels were dead and moldering away in their graves: 'Do you mean to say that there is no other life for such great men?' he would ask, which always seemed to put the lecturer on the defensive. The diplomats and journalists were also occasionally subjected to lectures by earnest North Koreans. They were proffered cigarettes, but once the speakers began to quote from the works of key members of the communist pantheon the assembled group consistently managed to find counter-quotations. Blake, as several of the others recalled, was among the most vocal and arrogant in his ripostes. After that, as Crosbie put it, 'we were left in peace'.[21]

The same could not be said for the GIs, who continued to be subjected to political indoctrination and were in a very bad way indeed. Their rations contained only about half the calorific value needed to sustain life, which meant they were slowly starving to death. Pneumonia and dysentery were rife, and medical care essentially consisted of having prisoners carry those too sick to stand into crude huts known as 'hospitals' where they almost invariably died amidst their own filth. It was true that the British civilians had suffered greatly, but Holt and Owen survived in part because The Tiger recognized their value as hostages and made a special effort to acquire doses of penicillin. They also had the advantage of being allowed a crude chamber pot, whereas the GIs, as an Austrian internee physician observed, despite having pneumonia, 'had to go to the [outside] toilet in their summer clothes in seventy degrees below freezing'.[22] Moreover, while Blake and Deane had been

[20] Kenyon, *Valiant Dust*, 68–71; Deane, *I Was a Captive*, 129–31; see Zellers, *In Enemy Hands*, 141, 185; see also Crosbie, *Three Winters Cold*, 182–3 for a slightly different version of what happened to Lord and why.
[21] Crosbie, *Three Winters Cold*, 180; Zellers, *In Enemy Hands*, 153, 185; see Cookridge, *Shadow of a Spy*, 107–8, 111, 112; Deane, *I Was a Captive*, 143–4; Zellers, *In Enemy Hands*, 144.
[22] Deane, *I Was a Captive*, 146; see ibid., 144–5. When the civilians developed beriberi in January 1951, the authorities were quick to provide them with soybeans, which helped eradicate the underlying nutritional deficiency. Zellers, *In Enemy Hands*, 148.

made to kneel in the snow and struck, neither had suffered permanent injury. Being made to kneel in the freezing cold was routine for GIs, and at least one was so savagely beaten for stealing wood that he died within a couple of days.[23] Unfortunately there was not always great sympathy for the soldiers among the British civilians.

Brave individuals such as Sergeant Tex Kimball and Private Jesse Sizemore who stood up to the guards and paid the price were admired, and those who ascribed the departure of The Tiger as commandant in January to illness would have been impressed to learn that Major John J. Dunn, the Senior American Officer, had been courageous enough to privately complain to some visiting North Korean dignitaries about the commandant's behaviour and thereby help bring about the arrival of a new, less antagonistic commanding officer.[24] There were, as Philip Deane acknowledged, plenty of Americans who 'succeeded in preserving their human dignity'.[25]

Yet even Deane concluded that 'disease and privation' were taking their toll. 'There were G.I.s who would give up a day's food for one cigarette rolled in old newspaper, and—I am sorry, it is true—there were those who bought food at the price of another man's life', he remembered 'There were those who worked in the cookhouse and stole their comrades' food. There were those that stripped their skeletic, dying companions, hours before they died.' Some even went along with communist indoctrination in order to obtain a little more to eat.[26]

George Blake already blamed his predicament on the Americans. 'I am certain that the British government had not intended to join in the war but had been drawn into it by the United States', he commented in his memoirs.[27] His relations with the US internees were not always entirely cordial,[28] and he had no hesitation in generating his own ideas about the 'interesting phenomenon' he was witnessing at Hanjang-ni vis-à-vis the American soldiers. He reckoned that between November 1950 and February 1951 over half the GIs had died while less than 20 per cent of the internees had succumbed. Oblivious to the fact that the civilians were not really living under the same conditions as the soldiers, he ascribed the high GI death rate to a decadent prewar lifestyle. 'These young American boys had been serving in the occupation army in Japan', he argued. 'There they had been used to hygienically prepared food in the army canteens, to their doughnuts and Coca-Cola. They had been pampered with army clubs, PXes and Commissaries.' Having suffered the shock of defeat and capture in Korea, they 'could not cope with the

---

[23] Zellers, *In Enemy Hands*, 147. On conditions among the GIs see e.g. Rountree in Peters and Xiaobing, *Voices from the Korean War*, 222–3.

[24] On the departure of The Tiger see Zellers, *In Enemy Hands*, 143; Crosbie, *Three Winters Cold*, 182. On Tex Kimball see ibid. 179; Zellers, *In Enemy Hands*, 145. On Jesse Sizemore see Deane, *I Was a Captive*, 150. Blake acknowledged that under the new regime conditions did improve somewhat. Blake, *No Other Choice*, 135.

[25] Deane, *I Was a Captive*, 150.

[26] Ibid. 149–50, 145; see also, with reference to problems at the next camp at An-dong, Zellers, *In Enemy Hands*, 160–1.

[27] Blake, *No Other Choice*, 125.   [28] See Zellers, *In Enemy Hands*, 74.

lack of hygiene, the bad food, the cold, the hardships, the separation from their loved ones'. Indeed, they 'were so miserable they just didn't want to live any more and gave up the struggle for survival', thereby becoming 'easy prey to disease and deprivation'.[29]

This sort of analysis, however flawed, was to gain currency among British military prisoners during the war and be the cause of a good deal of perhaps quite needless soul-searching in the United States afterward.[30] Its significance in the context of this chapter rests on what it tells us about the mindset of Blake in the months before he decided that in the ongoing global struggle between American capitalism and Soviet communism he would unhesitatingly work for the latter cause as a double agent.

There was a story going around in the New Year that the peasants whose houses the prisoners occupied had been promised them back before planting season; and for once events seemed to bear out the rumour. At the start of February the journalists and diplomats were transferred to a house in a hamlet pronounced Moo Yong Nee north of Manpo, while the rest of the civilian and military prisoners, numbering over 200 in all, were sent at the end of March to a former Japanese army camp at An-dong, also a border town.[31]

Conditions slowly improved for the internees in both locations in the spring of 1951. Those at An-dong, though still officially issued only about 600 grams of grain per day, were allowed to go searching for edible mushrooms and plants as well as firewood in the surrounding hills, and rations now sometimes included Chinese cabbages, turnips, and leeks.[32] The GIs, meanwhile, in what was officially known as Camp 7, became adept at raiding the storeroom and, after a rocky start, behaved more responsibly toward one another. In the summer, khaki overalls and canvas shoes were finally issued to soldiers and then civilians, along with cotton underwear, toilet soap, and toothpaste and toothbrushes.[33] The much smaller party at Moo Yong Nee suffered from the fact that the guard commander, Lieutenant Pak Yong-see (otherwise known as Fatso), at times skimmed rice from the rations in order to entertain guests; but the prisoners were given a record player that could be made to work, occasionally had access to an ancient

[29] Blake, *No Other Choice*, 134–5. Deane estimated that, looking back to September 1950, over 60 per cent of the GIs had died by the New Year. Deane, *I Was a Captive*, 151. The US Army estimated that about 30 per cent of the men were lost between the second week of November 1950 and the end of March 1951. Department of the Army, *U.S. Prisoners of War*, 91.

[30] On the weaknesses of the 'soft young Americans' thesis see Jeffrey Grey, 'Other Fronts: Resistance, Collaboration and Survival Among United Nations Prisoners During the Korean War' in Peter Dennis and Jeffrey Grey (eds), *The Korean War* (Canberra, 2000), 136–49; see also, regarding the real nature of US Army duty in Japan by 1950, Thomas E. Hanson, *Combat Ready?* (College Station, Tex., 2010).

[31] Crosbie, *Three Winters Cold*, 184–7; Deane, *I Was a Captive*, 156–9; Zellers, *In Enemy Hands*, 154–6. Between early February and the end of March 1951 the main camp was run by the new commandant who replaced The Tiger. Conditions improved. Deane, *I Was a Captive*, 186.

[32] Crosbie, *Three Winters Cold*, 194; Zellers, *In Enemy Hands*, 172, 177.

[33] Crosbie, *Three Winters Cold*, 196; Zellers, *In Enemy Hands*, 169, 160–2.

radio; and rations—including rice, turnips, cabbage and occasionally meat—while monotonous were, as Blake put it, 'sufficient to keep body and soul together'.[34]

The communist authorities, it turned out, had not given up on efforts to convert men to their world-view. At An-dong the POWs were once again subjected to compulsory lectures, which the civilians were also at first required to attend. The camp staff soon changed their minds about this arrangement once it became clear that the missionaries were, as one North Korean put it, 'working against what we are trying to do here'. The internees were thereafter banned from the lectures and on 10 May the men and two of the wives were transferred to a separate house nearby. After that they were generally left alone apart from the occasional propaganda lecture. The atmosphere was one of comparative freedom with the guards no longer resorting to rifle butts or in many cases even escorting foraging expeditions. Most of the more able-bodied male internees now gave some thought to the possibility of escape, but all but one decided the difficulties of crossing hundreds of miles of mountainous terrain as an occidental in an oriental land were too great. The one exception, Danny Dans, was soon recaptured and sent back to the main camp which was surrounded by wire.[35]

The group at Moo Yong Nee does not seem to have been subjected to overt North Korean indoctrination attempts at all. But they were potential prey for more subtle influences. In early August an official from the North Korean foreign ministry arrived and announced that a message had been received from the families of the internees indicating that they were all well 'and were thinking of us', adding that the internees themselves could—for the first time—write short messages for transmission home. This gesture had the effect of reminding the prisoners that there was a world out there passing them by, which in turn exposed uncertainties. 'It was incredibly difficult writing those messages', Deane remembered. 'What can you say after a complete year without news? What can you say to an almost total stranger [his wife] who for months and months has lived a life independent from yours? How can you escape banality? How can you write something useful? Something that might reestablish that contact which perhaps has been broken by separation?'[36]

Even more insidious in terms of effects on morale and outlook were the Russian- and English-language books and magazines provided in the spring. While it was recognized that this was for propaganda purposes—everything was selected to

---

[34] Blake, *No Other Choice*, 135; see Cookridge, *Shadow of a Spy*, 109–10; Deane, *I Was a Captive*, 159–63.

[35] Zellers, *In Enemy Hands*, 169, 177, 178–9, 181; Crosbie, *Three Winters Cold*, 196–7.

[36] Deane, *I Was a Captive*, 175. Capt. Holt, who was unmarried, caused a good deal of confusion in the Foreign Office when his message—'To Westminster Bank, Covent Garden: Please give my sister fifty pounds for theatre tickets'—was received. It eventually emerged through consulting the bank that Holt had indeed been in the habit of passing lump sums of money to his sister to buy theatre tickets, but only after much effort had been expended on trying to discern whatever code message such a cryptic phrase might contain. Ibid. 175–7; Blake, *No Other Choice*, 148. The messages were passed to the British Embassy in Moscow by the Soviet foreign ministry, which the Foreign Office had been pressing to act as intermediary for some time. See TNA, FO 371/92851, FK1893/6, Summary of action taken to secure the release of Mr Holt and other British civilians detained in North Korea, 10 November 1951; *The Times*, 10 September 1951, 4; *Daily Worker*, 10 September 1951, 3.

reflect the party line—the fact that there was nothing else to read meant that repetition slowly began to leave an impression. 'There came a time when I had to stop
reading those books,' Deane admitted, 'to stop practicing Russian because with the
study of language the absurd and constant assertion [that the capitalist world was
doomed] began to leave its mark, began to find an echo, and I felt my thinking
processes becoming tangled, my critical faculties blunted.'[37] Holt, according to
Blake, began to accept the inevitable victory of Soviet-style socialism, while reading and much private thought turned the SIS agent himself, already anti-American,
'from a man of conventional political views, and in the real meaning of the word a
militant anti-communist, into a fervent supporter of the movement I had hitherto
been fighting'.[38]

Taking care to shield his true feelings from his compatriots, Blake in October
1951 wrote a note in Russian asking for an interview with a Soviet official and
passed it to the North Korean guard commander.[39] A month-and-a-half later some
Russian secret service officers established themselves at Manpo and attempted to
talk some of the internees into serving as propaganda tools.[40] The man the internees remembered most was Grigori Kuzmich, a tall, thin officer easily recognized by
his fair head of hair. Despite his comparatively humane and sympathetic manner,
'Blondie' apparently won no converts. When he summoned Holt, for instance,
and asked him so sign a statement condemning the Korean War, the British Minister responded that as a government official he could not possibly put his name to
anything without instructions from the Foreign Office, and for good measure,
after asking for and obtaining pen and paper, wrote out a strongly worded protest
addressed to the Soviet Embassy in Pyongyang against the ongoing internment of
the staff of the British Legation.[41] In Blake's mind these interviews were only a
means of allowing the Russians to talk to him without raising suspicions. Though
'Blondie' was there part of the time, his main interlocutor was Vasili Alekseyevich
Dozhdalev, a bald MGB officer. Blake, it emerged, wanted to turn himself into a
double agent and spy for the Soviet Union on ideological grounds.[42]

On 28 December 1951 the two interned journalists, Philip Deane of *The
Observer* and Maurice Chanteloup of the *Agence France Presse*, were suddenly transferred to the Ministry of the Interior in Pyongyang. They speculated that this was
in order to pressure them into making broadcasts, but the only hints as to why they
were there suggested that they were being held in preparation for being sent home.[43]

[37] Deane, *I Was a Captive*, 173.

[38] Blake, *No Other Choice*, 138; see Blake interview, <http://www.pbs.org/redfiles/kgb/deep/
interv/k_int_george_blake.htm> (accessed 18 October 2011). There are indications that Blake in fact
had already developed far-leftist views prior to the Korean War. See Christopher Andrew, *Defend the
Realm* (London, 2009), 944, n. 25.

[39] Blake, *No Other Choice*, 142–3; Andrew, *Defend the Realm*, 489.

[40] The MGB had been granted unrestricted access by its communist allies to prisoners for intelligence and other purposes. Christopher Andrew and Oleg Gordievsky, *KGB* (New York, 1990), 404.

[41] Blake, *No Other Choice*, 143; Zellers, *In Enemy Hands*, 183; Deane, *I Was a Captive*, 177–83.
'Blondie' was also given the nickname Kuzma Kuzmich, after the character in *The Brothers
Karamazov*.

[42] Blake, *No Other Choice*, 144; Andrew, *Defend the Realm*, 489.

[43] Deane, *I Should Have Died*, 42–3; Deane, *I Was a Captive*, 198.

This may have been the case, as Major General Lee Sang Cho let slip to Vice Admiral Charles Turner Joy at the truce negotiations at Panmunjom a week earlier that 'we are going to release civilians who are not actually POW...and it is, of course, a fact that there are among them also newspaper reporters'.[44] The communists at this stage wanted all interned civilians as well as captured military personnel repatriated without exception, and releasing Deane and Chanteloup (who would likely add their own pens to the coverage of the event and possibly aid the communist cause if they could be turned) might have been part of a plan to force the hand of the UN negotiators on the issue. In the event, however, the UN side preferred to keep the issue of civilian internees and military prisoners separate, and ultimately insisted on the principle of voluntary repatriation after an armistice. In July 1952, therefore, Chanteloup and Deane—who had in any event refused to turn traitor[45]—were sent back to live with the diplomats.[46]

Nine months before, the main civilian group had been moved, this time to a civilian prison on the outskirts of Manpo. Translated from Korean, the name of this place could be either House of Learning or House of Culture; but neither learning nor culture were in ample supply amidst the man-made caves in the hillside that the internees were made to inhabit. 'It was a depressing place', Father Crosbie reflected. 'The dugout in which we lived was cold and damp, and the food was poor, consisting usually of *su-su* [maize] and watery soup.'[47] At one point the rations were reduced from 600 grams per person per day to 450, which was what the Korean convicts—dozens of whom died—were receiving.[48] Thankfully conditions improved in the spring, and in August 1952 the internees were moved again, this time to a number of houses of the outskirts of the village of Ujang.

What turned out to be the last of the camps for the civilians was for the most part run by the Chinese, who by this point in the war had solved their logistical problems and were anxious to leave the impression that they treated captives well. Food was varied and plentiful, summer and winter clothing and footwear was issued, and blankets and quilts were provided: 'we sleep now with a comfort unknown in previous camps', noted Father Crosbie delightedly in his diary. In addition, as Larry Zellers remembered, the internees were issued 'soap, toothbrushes, combs and mirrors.' All this and more, as he noted, left them 'better off than most of the local Korean civilians'.[49]

Though they did not know it at the time, the internees were to spend their final winter in Korea. After Stalin died in early March 1953 the armistice negotiations picked up and the communist authorities decided to agree to an oft-repeated request by the Foreign Office for the release of the British civilians as a gesture of

[44] Allan E. Goodman, *Negotiating While Fighting* (Stanford, 1978), 152.

[45] Deane at least was occasionally pressed—albeit politely—to become a communist agent right up until he was repatriated in 1953. Deane, *I Should Have Died*, 43–6.

[46] Deane, *I Was a Captive*, 98–214. On the progress of the truce talks see Goodman, *Negotiating While Fighting, passim*; Admiral C. Turner Joy, *How Communists Negotiate* (New York, 1955).

[47] Crosbie, *Three Winters Cold*, 203.

[48] Zellers, *In Enemy Hands*, 189.   [49] Ibid. 199; Crosbie, *Three Winters Cold*, 215.

good faith. Thus in the third week of March six Englishmen—George Blake, Anglican Bishop Alfred Cecil Cooper, Philip Deane, Vyvyan Holt, Norman Owen, and Commissioner Herbert Lord—along with Monsignor Thomas Quinlan, who hailed from Ireland—were transported to Pyongyang and treated lavishly in preparation for their trip home aboard the trans-Siberian express and an RAF transport plane sent to collect them from Moscow in April.[50]

The first British subjects to be taken prisoner in Korea, the civilian internees were also the first to get home. 'Coddled by the crew, the doctor and the nurse, airborne at last,' wrote Deane of the flight to RAF Abingdon, 'we began to understand that the dreams [of freedom] we had seen shattered so often had at last come true.' For reasons that his fellow internees would never comprehend, this was also 'the beginning of a new life' of a different sort for George Blake as a double-agent working for the Soviets.[51] Though there was considerable press interest in their experiences, the former internees were circumspect in their responses in interviews after touching down. It had been made clear to them since their initial release that the Panmunjom talks were making real progress. The handful of civilians knew that large numbers of military captives remained in the camps along the Yalu, men whose imminent return—a limited exchange of sick and wounded military prisoners was starting to get under way even as they arrived home and a full-scale swap would follow any armistice—might be jeopardized by a full-blooded condemnation of how they themselves had been handled. 'We would all rather not say much about our treatment in the camps since we do not want to prejudice the chances of others getting out', as Father Quinlan explained.[52]

Holt and his companions had themselves encountered hundreds of captured servicemen, often in bad shape in 1950–1; and by the time they arrived home they also would have known that they were by no means the only Englishmen (or for that matter Irishmen) held in North Korea. The majority had not fallen into enemy hands until the first half of 1951; but within six months of the diplomats and churchmen first finding themselves in North Korean hands roughly four times their number of Royal Marines were being made prisoner by the Chinese.

---

[50] See Deane, *I Was a Captive*, 224–53; Cookridge, *Shadow of a Spy*, 122–9. Crosbie, like the rest of the internees, would be released some weeks later. See Crosbie, *Three Winters Cold*, 219–21. On the Foreign Office efforts to free the internees see TNA, FO 371/92851.

[51] Blake, *No Other Choice*, 149; Deane, *I Was a Captive*, 253. On bafflement at Blake's decision to spy for Russia, revealed years later, see Cookridge, *Shadow of a Spy*, 113.

[52] Quinlan in the *Daily Telegraph*, 22 April 1953, 1; see Holt, ibid. 23 April 1953, 1; see also *Daily Worker*, 23 April 1953, 1; 24 April 1953, 1; 25 April 1953, 1, 3. Deane, not surprisingly, wrote a series of pieces for *The Observer*: see TNA, PREM 11/871.

2

The Marines at Kangyee

We always helped one another. If there were a few occasions where you might be able to steal a bit of food, a few beans, a few grains of rice or something, we tended to share. If we were ever given a cigarette by one of the guards or something we shared it. Even if we were on our own we took it back and we shared it with our friends.

Marine Andrew Condron[1]

Like almost all men in their situation, the two dozen or so Royal Marine commandos who were unlucky enough to become the earliest surviving British military captives of the Chinese did not expect to find themselves in enemy hands. They were not members of the first British units in action in Korea, yet they either perished or endured the longest period of incarceration of anyone captured wearing British uniform.[2] To understand why, a brief supplementary introduction to British military intervention in the Korean conflict is necessary.

The original plan had been to send out just 29th Infantry Brigade Group, the imperial strategic reserve based in the UK. This would take months to accomplish, though, and in the weeks following the North Korean attack the situation in South Korea deteriorated markedly. In the latter part of August, as twin stop-gap measures, a pair of British Army infantry battalions from the Hong Kong garrison were hurriedly shipped northward and work begun in the Admiralty on assembling at speed several hundred trained men from various establishments to form a Royal Marine coastal raiding force, 41 (Independent) Commando.[3] The two infantry battalions were in action almost at once, but owing to the need to rely on US resources in occupied Japan for clothing, weapons, and transport, it was not until October 1950 that the Royal Marines conducted their first coastal raid. This operation, and those that succeeded it, appeared to be modestly successful, but by the following month it looked as if the war was almost over. In the wake of the Inchon landing and the breakout from the Pusan perimeter in September the North Korean People's Army had been thrown back in complete disarray, and with

---

[1] IWMDS, 9693/5, A Condron.
[2] See Peter Thomas, *41 Independent Commando Royal Marines* (Portsmouth, 1990), 56. Two soldiers in the Argylls listed as missing appear to have been captured by the North Koreans in September 1950, but they did not survive long. See G. I. Malcolm, *The Argylls in Korea* (Edinburgh, 1952), 96; Peter Gaston, *Korea 1950–1953: Prisoners of War* (Eastborne, 1976), 26; Philip D. Chinnery, *Korean Atrocity!* (Annapolis, Md., 2000), 52; TNA, WO 208/4005, KWC 667.
[3] Andrew Salmon, *Scorched Earth, Black Snow* (London, 2011), 42, 163.

American, South Korean, and other UN formations in hot pursuit, it seemed only a matter of weeks before the combined forces under the command of General Douglas MacArthur achieved complete victory by driving all the way to the Yalu River.[4]

It was in this context that, in the third week of November 1950, the men of 41 Commando were sent ashore to give what assistance they could as a reconnaissance force for the American 1st Marine Division in what was supposed to be a fairly uneventful north-westerly thrust by X Corps to link up with Eighth Army. By the time the Royal Marines arrived, however, the situation was changing dramatically. Chinese forces had suddenly intervened in Korea en masse, and American marine and army units were forced into a precarious fighting retreat toward the port of Hungnam. The role of the Royal Marines, operating with attached American troops and transport as an ad hoc task force, was now to move north from Koto-ri and reinforce the US garrison at Hangaru. This, however, proved easier said than done. As the hours passed on 29 November, the Chinese, commanding the heights on either side of the road, began to pour rifle, machine-gun, and mortar fire into the column's vehicles and forced the occupants to keep deploying on either side to clear a path.[5]

As evening fell and the danger of American air strikes diminished, the Chinese sprang a number of ambushes, managing to break up much of the task force into sections which were unable to support one another or, in some cases, move forward or rearward on the single narrow road. As the night battle continued some of the Royal Marines, having already seen a fair number of their comrades killed and wounded in what was later dubbed 'Hell Fire Valley', were in serious trouble. While significant elements of the task force were able to reach Hangaru and indeed later engage in a successful fighting retreat with American troops to Hungnam some days later, the Chinese nevertheless managed to isolate and immobilize several pockets of resistance, the largest of which was under the de facto command of Major John N. McLaughlin, USMC. With trucks and jeeps already ablaze, radio contact long lost, casualties continuing to mount, and both medical supplies and ammunition diminishing, when dawn began to break on 30 November with temperatures far below freezing it became painfully clear that time was running out. McLaughlin decided the only option was to accept the repeated calls by the enemy to surrender. Though some of the Royal Marines later professed to have been surprised to learn that this path had been adopted—and indeed one group under the command of Captain P. J. Ovens and Sergeant R. G. Davies refused to accept the decision and slipped away—others could see that to continue fighting was pointless under the circumstances.[6] In all approximately 250 US servicemen were

---

[4] The most recent thorough treatment of this phase of the war can be found in Allan R. Millett, *The War for Korea, 1950–1951* (Lawrence, Kan., 2010), chs. 7–8.

[5] Fred Hayhurst, *Green Berets in Korea* (Cambridge, 2001), 109 ff.

[6] See NAA, Part 3, AI9/K/BRIT/934, Cpl F. Bradle; ibid. AI9/K/BRIT/63, Mne W. E. Brown; Part 5, AI9/K/BRIT/543, Mne P. D. Murphy; Part 6, AI9/K/BRIT/304, Cpl G. R. Richards; IWMDS, 9693/3, A. Condron; 10250/1, E. Curd; 9859/2–3, G. Richards; 13711/1, J. Underwood. On the party that slipped away see NAA, Part 4, AI9/K/BRIT580, Mne J. E. Goodman. On Hell Fire Valley see Hayhurst, *Green Berets in Korea*, ch. 4; James Angus MacDonald Jr, *The Problems of U.S. Marine Corps Prisoners of War in Korea* (Washington, DC, 1988), 32–40.

captured here and elsewhere in the valley, along with twenty-four Royal Marines including five corporals, and a badly wounded Royal Navy sick-berth attendant. The fact that there were no commissioned Royal Marines officers or senior NCOs among those not seriously wounded was to have consequences when it came to coping with indoctrination efforts.[7]

As soon as it was clear that the UN troops were raising their arms above their heads the Chinese soldiers surrounding them leapt up and dashed forward. 'The next thing I know', recalled Marine Andrew Condron, a Chinese soldier 'comes running over and starts shaking me by the hand'. It was quite baffling to men who were worried that they still might be shot.[8] They were disarmed by their grinning captors and marched off westward until they reached a hamlet where they were held overnight. There were occasional instances of personal looting and bad behaviour by the Chinese, but those in charge were clearly making an effort to project the Chinese People's Volunteers as benevolent.[9]

The prisoners were quickly hustled away into the hills and in a day or two started marching northward in two columns towards Kanggye, about 50 miles away as the crow flies but a great deal further on snow-laden foot trails that wound their way through the mountains. Moving only at night or during snowstorms during the day to avoid attracting the attention of American aircraft, it took the main column several weeks to reach its destination. Conditions on the march were extremely taxing. Temperatures regularly dipped to twenty degrees Fahrenheit below freezing even without the wind-chill factor, medical attention for the walking wounded was minimal at best, and there was very little food. The Chinese guards generally did not mistreat their charges, though the same could not be said of the North Koreans when they took over for certain stages. The Royal Marines stuck together and tried their best to help one another, but with frostbite, pneumonia, and dysentery adding to the miseries of constant cold and hunger, many of the walking wounded began to suffer from a fatal erosion of strength.[10]

---

[7] Cyril Cunningham, *No Mercy, No Leniency: Communist Mistreatment of British Prisoners of War in Korea* (Barnsley, 2000), 48–9. The only senior RM NCO present after the party led by Capt. Overy slipped away was Sgt R. H. James, who was wounded and, thanks to the Chinese leaving behind most of those unable to walk, was later picked up by UN forces during the retreat to Hungnam. See NAA, Part 3, AI9/K/BRIT/934, Cpl F. Bradle; see also MacDonald, *U.S. Marine Corps Prisoners of War*, 41.

[8] IWMDS, 9693/3, A. Condron; see ibid. 9859/3, G. Richards; 13711/1, J. Underwood.

[9] On personal looting see e.g. NAA, Part 4, AI9/K/BRIT/530, Mne J. E. Goodman; Part 5, AI9/K/BRIT/543, Mne P. D. Murphy. According to Andrew Condron, the personal items taken from him were later returned. IWMDS, 9693/4, A. Condron. On Chinese efforts to restrain their men from mistreating those they had just been battling with see MacDonald, *U.S. Marine Corps Prisoners of War*, 41. One attempt at benevolence ended badly when the Chinese, having provided some prisoners with hot water, discovered that they had used it to wash rather than—as was meant—to drink. See IWMDS, 9693/4, A. Condron.

[10] See IWMDS, 9693/4, A. Condron; 9859/3, G. Richards; 13711/1, J. Underwood; NAA, Part 3, AI9/K/BRIT/63, Mne W. E. Brown; Part 5, AI9/K/BRIT/543; Mne P. D. Murphy; ibid. AI9/K/BRIT/828, Mne R. Ogle; Hayhurst, *Green Berets in Korea*, 156–9, 196–7; MacDonald, *U.S. Marine Corps Prisoners of War*, 43–4; J. Chapman in Donald Knox, *The Korean War: Uncertain Victory* (San Diego, 1988), 340–1. It was during the march that, among other, the RN sick-berth attendant, D. Raine, appears to have died. See NAA, Part 3, AI9/K/BRIT/934, Cpl F. Bradle.

The destination for nearly 300 UN captives was a string of Korean huts, officially known as Camp 10, dotted for several thousand yards on either side of a track tracing the contours of a valley floor approximately 10 miles north of Kangyee itself. Once there the men were split into two companies, each company into three platoons, and each platoon into five squads, with roughly one Chinese guard or overseer for every two captives.[11] The prisoners were no longer exposed to the elements, but the squad huts were not furnished except for straw mats and there were no washing facilities inside or out. Jammed together, men soon found themselves crawling with lice and other parasites. 'It's amazing what the human body can put up with', Andy Condron later reflected. There was only a limited quantity of hot water to drink, shared out 'very, very carefully', he also recalled,[12] while food continued to be inadequate both in quality and quantity, usually consisting of sugar-bowl size portions of gruel made from sorghum, radishes, ground beans, or millet and cracked maize morning and evening: 'it was really horrible', remembered Marine John Underwood.[13] On Christmas Day pork and chicken were promised, but this treat turned out to be merely a few tiny pieces of meat boiled in a soup pot meant to feed over 200 men.[14] Despite low morale the Royal Marines prided themselves on sticking together and helping one another, not least by sharing their meagre rations with the sick. Seven of the latter nevertheless died in the winter of 1950–1 through lack of adequate nutrition and medical care while the rest remained in very poor shape.[15]

It was under these conditions that the Chinese began to apply their Lenient Policy. At various points after capture it had been explained in broken English to the prisoners that despite their criminal behaviour in coming to Korea and killing innocent men, women, and children, it was understood that they were merely tools of imperialism, dupes who would now be given the opportunity to learn and appreciate the righteousness of communism. This baffled many listeners at the time—terms such as 'proletarian' were entirely alien[16]—but they were happy enough to discover they were not to be shot.[17]

[11] NARA, RG 38, entry 1051 (a), Case Files of POWs—Korean War, box 27, Phase III Questionnaire, Robert C. Messman, p. 18; box 35, Ernest R. Reid.

[12] IWMDS, 9693/3, A. Condron.

[13] Ibid. 13711/1, J. Underwood; see MacDonald, *U.S. Marine Corps Prisoners of War*, 65; J. DeLong, <http://www.koreanwar-educator.org> (accessed 13 November 2010), 7.

[14] Hayhurst, *Green Berets in Korea*, 221; J. Chapman in Knox, *The Korean War*, 342.

[15] On the Royal Marines helping one another see e.g. IWMDS, 9693/4; 9859/3, G. Richards. On the sick and the dying see e.g. NAA, Part 3, AI9/K/BRIT/63, Mne W. E. Brown. On inadequate medical care see also MacDonald, *U.S. Marine Corps Prisoners of War*, 66–8. On low morale see Hayhurst, *Green Berets in Korea*, 221. On the seven dead—plus a solitary marine from the initial group who died in North Korean hands—see ibid. 282.

[16] See e.g. IWMDS, 9693/3–4, A. Condron.

[17] See e.g. NAA, Part 4, Mne J. E. Goodman. For the benefit of those who had not been told already, the Lenient Policy was outlined by the commandant of Camp 10 shortly after the main group of prisoners arrived. Department of the Army, *U.S. Prisoners of War in the Korean Operation* (Fort Meade, Md., 1954), 215; see also e.g. NARA, RG 38, entry 1015 (a), Case files of U.S. POW's during the Korean War, John N. McGlauchlin phase II questionnaire, question 21 response.

The Chinese, though, were very serious in their effort to win hearts and minds. Either before or after arriving in Camp 10 everyone was presented with a questionnaire or autobiographical form which asked for name, rank, unit, and—puzzlingly—civilian job, home address, and a great deal of information about the captive's family, especially material possessions and political beliefs. The Chinese already appeared to know about 41 Commando, and there seemed no harm in filling out the rest of the form, which seemed to suggest that information as to their condition would be passed back home and sometimes contained questions about the type of livestock owned which seemed laughable. What was not understood was that the Chinese aimed to build up a detailed picture of their captives' socio-economic status and thereby decide which prisoners, from a class and age point of view, would be most susceptible to communist indoctrination.[18]

The educational programme, supervised by fifteen two-person teams of translators and political aides, was carried out every morning and afternoon through mandatory political discussions in individual huts among groups of eight to twelve men conducted by squad leaders picked by the Chinese as most likely to be sympathetic to the outlook they were trying to foster. There were also compulsory lectures most days for all the prisoners held in an unheated barn, the contents of which—'about the imperialists, the capitalists, how we were their running dogs, we were the tools of our capitalist friends and the Chinese did not hold any grudge against us because we had been duped into following the capitalist line', as John Underwood recalled—would form the subject matter of a quiz the next day.[19]

Despite the effort put into it by the Chinese, the political programme at Kanggye was not terribly effective in terms of producing true conversions to the anticapitalist cause. During the lectures Major McLaughlin, working through five NCOs, covertly issued orders that Americans were to stick together and resist the Chinese, instructions that achieved some success among the US Marines.[20] As for the Royal Marines they, like many of their American cousins in the US Army and USMC, had great difficulty understanding what the Chinese were talking about, largely the result of poor spoken English and frequent resort to Marxist-Leninist jargon. Andy Condron at this stage assumed that 'imperialism' must have something to do with the Royal Family. The enemy's insistence that the camp inmates were all poor peasants who must own a few pigs or chickens and the blanket inability to accept that—as was in fact the case—they were heirs of the industrial revolution who might easily possess radios or motorcycles, made them look foolish. Having to walk down to a freezing, drafty barn in order to be harangued in Chinese

[18] On the questionnaire see NAA, Part 4, AI9/K/BRIT/580, Mne J. E. Goodman; Part 6, AI9/K/BRIT/304, Cpl G. R. Richards.
[19] IWMDS, 13711/1, J. Underwood; see MacDonald, *U.S. Marine Corps Prisoners of War*, 63–6; NAA, Part 3, AI9/K/BRIT/311, Cpl E. J. Curd, 5; Part 5, AI9/K/BRIT/543, Mne P. D. Murphy, 9; Part 6, AI9/K/BRIT/304, Cpl G. R. Richards, 3; NARA, RG 319, entry 85, Phase III summaries, box 1029, John Economy, 1; ibid. George L. Foote, 1.
[20] MacDonald, *U.S. Marine Corps Prisoners of War*, 63–4; NAA, Part 5, AI9/K/BRIT/543, Mne P. D. Murphy, 5. US Army prisoners might also cause trouble for the Chinese: see e.g. <http://www.koreanwar-educator.org> (accessed 13 November 1010), J. DeLong, 7.

by the commandant and then listen to the translation for an hour or more was no one's idea of a stimulating intellectual experience, and it did not help that guards kicked or shoved men who showed signs of inattention. According to Condron 'nobody took an interest' and the lectures 'were a complete flop'.[21]

In terms of getting the prisoners to *act* as if they were becoming true believers, however, the Chinese at Camp 10 were fairly successful. It became clear that at least some of the captives would be allowed to write individual or communal letters home and make radio broadcast recordings indicating that they were being treated well; a big incentive to both American and British prisoners, despite the communist insistence on the odd propaganda phrase, given that loved ones would otherwise have no way of knowing their fate.[22] More attractive still to most prisoners was the Chinese claim that if they did well at their lessons and became suitably 'progressive' they would at the end of the course of study be taken to the front and released back to UN lines.[23] By 'progressive' the camp authorities meant in this instance a willingness to contribute propaganda articles denouncing the war to a camp newspaper, *New Life*, which appeared in January 1951; setting up a camp peace committee to produce a peace declaration and signing the Stockholm Peace Appeal produced by the World Peace Council in February; and showing suitable enthusiasm for the cause in final exams in March.[24]

There seemed little harm in parroting what the Chinese wanted to hear in the way of denouncing the war in the crudely produced *New Life*, and as many as thirty UN prisoners did so.[25] To those unaware of its propaganda purpose, the Stockholm Peace Appeal could seem equally innocuous. As a Royal Marine corporal later explained, 'it seemed a pretty harmless document' that could serve to let relatives know he and the other signatories were alive.[26] The camp peace appeal was more problematic once it became clear that the wording of the camp petition, dated 11 February 1951, would be up to the Chinese rather than the prisoners themselves. Released to the outside world via a Chinese news agency a month later,

---

[21] Condron in the *Daily Express*, 15 October 1962, 7; IWMDS 9693/6, A. Condron; see Cunningham, *No Mercy, No Leniency*, 50; Hayhurst, *Green Berets in Korea*, 220–1.

[22] MacDonald, *U.S. Marine Corps Prisoners of War*, 64–5; see e.g. NAA, Part 3, AI9/K/BRIT/311, Cpl E. J. Curd, 5; Part 5, AI9/K/BRIT/543, Mne P. D. Murphy, 11; see also Dave Brady, *One of the Chosin Few* (London, 2003), 126–7. For many months the communists would not provide the UN with a list of the prisoners they held.

[23] See e.g. NAA, Part 3, AI9/K/BRIT/934, Cpl F. Bradle, 4.

[24] MacDonald, *U.S. Marine Corps Prisoners of War*, 68–71; see NAA, Part 6, AI9/K/BRIT/304, Cpl G. R. Richards, 3; J. Chapman in Knox, *The Korean War*, 342–3. The Stockholm Peace Appeal, issued in March 1950, called for an absolute ban on nuclear weapons, and was produced by the World Peace Council, in principle a non-aligned organization but heavily supported by the communist bloc. See TNA, FO 371/83333; LHASC, CP/CENT/EC02/01, CPGB Executive Committee minutes, 9 June 1951, 1.

[25] MacDonald, *U.S. Marine Corps Prisoners of War*, 68; see e.g. Raymond B. Lech, *Broken Soldiers* (Urbana, Il., 2000), 295–6. What *New Life* looked like can be gleaned from the facsimile of the 17 and 22 January 1951 editions in Department of the Army, *U.S. Prisoners of War*, 231–5.

[26] NAA, Part 3, AI9/K/BRIT/934, Cpl F. Beadle, 4. According to another RM prisoner who also signed, Maj. McLaughlin had consented to this in order to get names out. Part 3, AI9/K/BRIT/61, Mne B. Martin, 3.

this document is worth quoting in full in order to convey the thrust of subsequent petitions in other camps and the dictation of politically correct form and content by non-native speakers:

> To the United Nations. We, the undersigned all being members of the United States, British, or puppet South Korean armed forces, are victims of the Korean war. We have personally experienced the horrors and devastation visited upon these people by this conflict. We have witnessed the agony in the eyes of bewildered civilians who have been made homeless. We have seen the useless slaughter of old men, women and children when towns have been bombed. We have seen babies crying at the breast of a mother who had breathed her last. All this and more we have seen and the reason for all this misery and unhappiness is the manipulation of the United Nations voting and violations of the United Nations Charter by the Anglo-American bloc. The peoples of Asia have heard and can still hear, the thunder of guns and the soul chilling shriek of bombs falling. Soon the entire world will resound to these terrifying sounds and entire nations will be bombed to complete ruin unless a stop is brought to this war soon. We have learned the hard, bitter truth and we believe that the only solution to this threat of another world war to be the following documents and policies which we unanimously advocate and support.
>
> 1. The manifesto the peoples of the world adopted by the second World Peace Congress in Warsaw.
> 2. Immediate cessation of the Korean war by the adoption of China's Foreign Minister Chou En-lai's three point peace proposals to the United Nations.[27]

The document mentioned in the first article listed above contains the only solution to the problem of lasting world peace and will attain this glorious goal. The policy and proposals mentioned in article 2 present the only answer to true peace for the peoples of Asia, especially the 475 million long suffering people of China who have struggled for peace for over 100 long, bitter war torn years in support of the 600 million peace loving peoples of the world who have affixed their signatures to the Stockholm peace appeal. We demand the unconditional prohibition of atomic weapons as a means of mass destruction and the institution of strict international control to enforce this. We demand that the government which first uses the atomic bomb against any other state be branded as a war criminal. We also strongly protest the recent United Nations decision proclaiming the Peoples Republic of China as the aggressor in Korea. Through personal contact and experience with the Chinese People's volunteers we have become convinced of their sincerity of purpose and have come to know them as true representatives of a peace loving people. We add this, our efforts of all the people of the world for the attainment of world lasting peace.[28]

---

[27] This was a reference to points made when rejecting the UN ceasefire proposals of January 1951, on which see Shen Zhuhua and Yafeng Xia, 'Mao Zedong's Erroneous Decision During the Korean War: China's Rejection of the UN Ceasefire Resolution in Early 1951', *Asian Perspective*, 35 (2011), 187–209.

[28] TNA, FO 371/92843, FK 1551/6, Peking Legation to Foreign Office, 15 March 1951. On later petitions and group statements see e.g. ibid. FK 1551/22, Peking Legation to Foreign Office, 5 July 1951; *Daily Worker*, 31 January 1951, 3.

The members of the camp peace committee, having already started down the collaborationist path, were intimidated into signing on behalf of the camp as a whole.[29]

Looking back it also seems likely that the Chinese efforts at changing men's minds were not entirely ineffectual. Though he had little good to say about the compulsory classes, Marine Andy Condron read some of the communist literature provided by the Chinese, including an article by the British communist Palme Dutt in the journal *Labour Monthly* that resonated. 'This made him think,' another Royal Marine observed, 'and he used to remain behind after lectures and read all the literature available.' The seeds that would eventually produce the most dedicated and effective of the British collaborators had been planted at Kangyee. Furthermore, as an analyst working for AI9, the Ministry of Defence branch responsible for British prisoners of war in Korea, later remarked, among the various groups of British prisoners taken during the conflict the Royal Marines captured in November 1950 contained the highest proportion of individuals who would actively collaborate with their captors.[30]

Furthermore, though the Chinese do not appear to have fostered animosity between national contingents at this stage, their cause was helped by the development of a negative attitude among the British towards the Americans. The small group of Royal Marines seems to have got on well with the three-dozen US Marines held in Camp 10. There was, however, a certain degree of contempt for the several hundred US Army prisoners, many of whom appeared to adopt a dog-eat-dog attitude rather than close ranks in order to survive. 'The American soldiers seemed to see the way out of the experience as individuals', Condron later reflected. 'If one stole a bit of food, he would scuffle into the corner and eat it alone. The British and American Marines took it in groups. We stuck together.' He would not be the only Royal Marine whose growing distaste for American soldiers would make it easier to accept the communist line about the war.[31]

At the start of March 1951 the inhabitants of Camp 10 were informed that groups of prisoners were to be released across the front line to carry peace pamphlets and spread the word to their fellow dupes. Everyone was placed aboard southbound trains destined for Anju and morale soared. It eventually became clear, however, that either plans had changed or that the Chinese never had any intention of sending back large numbers of men. In the end less than two-dozen Americans and one Briton were chosen for release in May 1951 while the dispirited remainder were already marching back northward from Somindong. A final irony was that Marine Ruby Nicholls, seeing the Americans being released into no-man's

---

[29] Ministry of Defence, *Treatment of British Prisoners of War in Korea* (London, 1955), 11.

[30] NAA, Part 7, AI9/K/BRIT/310, J. Underwood, p. 2; see Cunningham, *No Mercy, No Leniency*, 48.

[31] Condron in Max Hastings, *The Korean War* (London, 1987), 333; see e.g. IWMDS, 9693/5, A. Condron; 9859/4, G. Richards. It is notable that the broadcast to his family made by Condron was considered far more anti-American than those made by other Royal Marines at this time. See Brady, *One of the Chosin Few*, 127. On the American reactions to Chinese efforts at Kangyee see Lech, *Broken Soldiers*, 82–4.

land and not realizing that he was due to be sent back across a different sector facing the Commonwealth Division, tried to dash away and catch up with the Americans only to be shot dead by his guards.[32]

In retrospect it seemed to analysts as if Camp 10, which was never used again, had hosted a pilot programme.[33] It was certainly true that the Chinese had identified a number of potential collaborators, and that they were preparing in early 1951 to initiate similar programmes while they gained control over some of the larger POW camps along the Yalu River. Conditions at Kangyee had been poor. But as graduates were soon to discover, they could be a lot worse.

[32] Cunningham, *No Mercy, No Leniency*, 53; see Department of the Army, *U.S. Prisoners of War*, 216–17; Hayhurst, *Green Berets in Korea*, 360–1; MacDonald, *U.S. Marine Corps Prisoners of War*, 75; Lech, *Broken Soldiers*, 86.

[33] Department of the Army, *U.S. Prisoners of War*, 84; Cunningham, *No Mercy, No Leniency*, 48; Lech, *Broken Soldiers*, 81.

3

The Ulsters at Pyoktong

I produced a small card which we had all been given on our arrival in Korea. This required that, in the event of capture, we were to be accorded humane treatment, as laid down in the Geneva Convention and by the Red Cross... Then, for the first time, he [a Chinese field interrogator] looked as if he might lose his temper; he looked quite angry. He tore the card in half and threw it into his wastepaper basket, and when he spoke it did my morale no good at all. He said, 'You people are the limit. You have a government that doesn't even recognize China. According to the British Government [Communist] China doesn't exist. Why the hell should we respect your Conventions?'

Trooper Ted Beckerley[1]

The remaining Royal Marines from Kangyee were sent back northward; and on 17 March 1951, when they entered what was to become known as Camp 5 at Pyoktong along the Yalu River, they soon discovered that they were not the only uniformed British captives in enemy hands. Apart from two of their corps who had for unknown reasons not been sent to Camp 10, there were about sixty soldiers who had arrived eleven days earlier, the majority from the Royal Ulster Rifles, who had been taken prisoner by the Chinese at the start of the New Year.[2]

This second and larger batch of British POWs was the result of an engagement that had taken place at the beginning of 1951. By the end of 1950 the Chinese People's Volunteers had pushed UN forces back across the 38th Parallel and were poised to resume the offensive and recapture Seoul. Among the formations opposing them was 29th Brigade. When the two sides clashed on 3 January to the north of the capital, the forward infantry battalions, the Royal Ulster Rifles (RUR) and the Royal Northumberland Fusiliers (RNF), suffered losses but mostly held their ground. Elsewhere along the front the Chinese had greater success against the South Koreans, and by the late afternoon a general withdrawal of UN forces south of the Han River was ordered. Acting as rearguard, 29th Brigade would have to disengage and move rearward while in contact with the enemy. The RNF withdrawal was a success; the RUR retreat that night less so, in part because the Ulsters were

---

[1] IWMDD, E. Beckerley, 8–9.
[2] Of the two Royal Marines already in residence one, Cpl C. R. B. Hill, soon died of his wounds. IWMDS, 10250/2, E. Curd. On the main party of Royal Marines arriving in Camp 5 on 17 March 1951 see NAA, Part 3, AI9/K/BRIT/934, Cpl F. Bradle, 5. On the sixty Ulsters and various others arriving on 6 March 1951 see Cyril Cunningham, *No Mercy, No Leniency: Communist Mistreatment of British Prisoners of War in Korea* (Barnsley, 2000), 28, 58.

furthest forward, in part because the necessary orders arrived later then they should have, and in part because once the withdrawal began the whole scene was lit up for the enemy to see by a succession of flares dropped by an American aircraft. The line of retreat was down a road in a valley with hills on either side which the Chinese soon dominated, and the rearmost sections in particular soon found themselves in trouble. The Chinese, in huge numbers, were pouring down automatic fire, killing men, disabling vehicles, and setting up roadblocks. Even the presence of a handful of Cromwell tanks did not deter them, these vehicles being successfully disabled with pole charges despite enormous casualties. The scene was chaotic amidst hand-to-hand fighting in the dark, and though the Ulsters eventually managed to fight their way out of what they called 'Happy Valley' to safety, they left behind roughly 20 per cent of their number, of whom 106 officers and men had been made prisoners of war.[3]

Those who fell into enemy hands that night were, like the two dozen Royal Marine commandos five weeks earlier, baffled by the behaviour of their erstwhile enemies. As men were captured and parties were gathered together in huts a few miles behind the lines, the few English-speaking Chinese reassured them that no personal items would be taken, and that they were among friends who would treat them well. 'These manifestations of friendship', remembered Rifleman E. F. Spencer, 'took the form of hand shaking and back slapping by those who could not speak English', irrespective of rank. As he correctly surmised, this apparently spontaneous amicability was the result of specific orders;[4] and at least some of the captives instinctively guessed that the enemy was not to be trusted. When a Chinese officer announced to one newly captured group that despite their role as killers of the peace-loving people of Korea they would be treated 'as students of the truth', Lance Corporal William Massey spoke his mind: 'Listen mister: you go f[uck] yourself.'[5]

Whatever their ulterior motives, the Chinese People's Volunteers (CPV) did make some effort to live up to their promises in the days after the battle. There seems to have been only limited stealing of personal items, and CPV officers did their best to prevent local North Korean troops from carrying out their standard practice of killing the wounded and generally mistreating captives. At one point, when Rifleman W. H. Liggett was being questioned by a Chinese officer about the contents of a US field ration pack and Liggett was accidentally struck by a North Korean, the latter 'was at once driven out of the hut by the Chinese officer'.[6]

---

[3] In addition to the 106 officers and men from the RUR, there were twenty-eight prisoners taken by the Chinese from the 8th Royal Irish Hussars along with a dozen men from the Royal Artillery and three others. Peter Gaston, *Korea 1950–1953: Prisoners of War* (Eastbourne, 1976), 4–8, 22–3, 25, 28. On the events of 3–4 January 1951 see Andrew Salmon, *To the Last Round* (London, 2009), ch. 4.

[4] NAA, Part 6, AI9/K/BRIT/3, Rfn E. F. Spencer, 1; see Part 3, AI9/K/BRIT/89, L/Cpl A. W. Buxton, 1; ibid. AI9/K/BRIT/107, Gnr L. Leak, 1.

[5] Max Hastings, *The Korean War* (London, 1987), 330–1.

[6] NAA, Part 5, AI9/K/BRIT/291, Rfn W. H. Liggett, 1; see IWMDD, R. W. McGuire, 4; IWMDS, 19047/4, F. Brodie; NAA, Part 6, AI9/K/BRIT/3, Rfn E. F. Spencer, 1; IWMDS, 10982/4, E. Beckerley; 22347/4, E. Bruford-Davies; IWMDD, E. Beckerley, 14–15. Some Chinese, especially if they were not being watched, did steal items. See e.g. NAA, Part 3, AI9/K/BRIT/287, Tpr S. Carr, 1; Part 6, AI9/K/BRIT/69, Maj. M. D. G. C. Ryan, 1.

While the prisoners were being organized for the journey north a certain amount of individual interrogation took place. Some of those with technical knowledge, such as the troopers from the 8th King's Royal Irish Hussars, were quizzed and got the impression that the Chinese knew the answers already.[7] More generally, prisoners started to be questioned about their civilian jobs, families, and political opinions. The aim, not recognized by the men themselves, was to start drawing up profiles in order to discern who was a potential proletarian friend and who was a likely class enemy.[8]

As parties were gathered together, the Chinese told them glowingly that they would soon be heading north to a place where they would see the light.[9] Once a few hundred UN prisoners had been brought together, the first stage of the march north began. On average about 15 miles over twenty-four hours were covered, the columns only moving at night and lying up in Korean villages during the day for fear of American air attack.[10]

The guards, though warning that anyone trying to escape would be shot and constantly intent on chivvying men along—if need be with a prod from a bayonet or rifle butt—seemed to be eating the same rations as their captives and did not generally behave badly 'provided you kept in line', as Rifleman John Shaw put it. They were even known to pass over tobacco and cigarette paper on occasion.[11]

North Korean troops, when they acted as escorts in the latter stages of the march, often appeared to have lived up to their poor reputation as captors. 'They were very, very unpleasant individuals,' Ted Beckerley remembered, 'striking out with their rifles at the slightest excuse.'[12] Rifleman Edward English recalled a particular sergeant prone to butt laggards with his rifle; Lieutenant Robin Bruford-Davies commented that, unlike the Chinese, the North Koreans were prone to loot prisoners; and they seem to have encouraged—or at the very least not prevented—North Korean villagers beating their charges with sticks when columns passed. In short, as one gunner put it, 'they were anything but friendly'.[13]

---

[7] See e.g. IWMDD, E. Beckerley, 8; NAA, Part 6, AI9/K/BRIT/90, Tpr P. F. Rowley, 3.

[8] See e.g. NAA, Part 3, AI9/K/BRIT/95, Rfn R. Cartlidge, 2.

[9] See e.g. IWMDS, 10749/4, R. Erricker.

[10] Estimates of the average nightly distances covered varied from 5 miles (NAA, Part 3, AI9/K/BRIT/322, Rfn J. Bergin, 2), to 10 miles (IWMDS, 22347/5, E. Bruford-Davies), to 15 miles (NAA, Part 4, AI9/K/BRIT/497, Rfn E. English, 1), or 16 miles (Part 3, AI9/K/BRIT/287, Tpr S. Carr, 2), to anywhere between 12 and 20 miles (Part 6, AI9/K/BRIT/69, Maj. M. D. G. C. Ryan, 2). On having to take cover from roving US aircraft even at night see e.g. NAM 1989-05-163-1, R. Bruford-Davies; IWMDS, 20299/2, J. Shaw.

[11] IWMDS, 20299/2, J. Shaw. On passing along tobacco and cigarette paper see IWMDS, 22347/5, E. Bruford-Davies. On the guards eating the same food as the prisoners see e.g. ibid.; NAA, Part 6, AI9/K/BRIT/3, Rfn E. F. Spencer. On warning that escapees would be shot see IWMDD, R. McGuire, 5. On chivvying men along see IWMDS, 10749/4, R. Erricker; NAM 1989-05-163-1, R. Bruford-Davies.

[12] IWMDD, E. Beckerley, 14; IWMDS, 10982/5, E. Beckerley.

[13] NAA, Part 4, AI9/K/BRIT/317, Gnr E. Digan; see IWMDS, 22347/5, E. Bruford-Davies; NAA, Part 4, AI9/K/BRIT/497, Rfn E. English. On being beaten by North Korean civilians see e.g. IWMDS, 19047/4, F. Brodie; see also ibid. 20299/2, J. Shaw. North Korean troops also appear to have executed the non-walking wounded among the survivors of the RUR's support company. See NAA, Part 4, AI9/K/BRIT/14–18 Part II, Pte A. E. Hunt et al., 4. There were, however, those who thought the North Korean guards were not too bad: see Part 5, AI9/K/BRIT/291, Rfn W. H. Liggett, 2; ibid. AI9/K/BRIT/290, Rfn F. Moxham, 2; IWMDS, 10749/3, R. Erricker.

Guards, in any event, were not as challenging to prisoners as the physical environment they faced on the march. The terrain was a constant difficulty, as a captured reservist explained in his memoirs: 'Oh those Korean hills: so steep, and so high. And when you got to the top of one you saw another range in front of you, even higher than the one you had just climbed. There just always seemed to be another hill to climb, a bit higher than previous one.'[14] Weather conditions moreover were, as Shaw put it, 'grim, atrocious'. The temperature was well below freezing, especially at night; it was often snowing; there were fierce winds from the north; and captives usually only had the uniforms they were captured in for warmth. Not surprisingly there were cases of frostbite. 'It was ruddy cold, I'll tell you', Rifleman Frank Brodie commented feelingly in an interview several decades later.[15]

Sapping energy further was the quantity and quality of the food provided. Usually there were only two meals a day, served out at each end of the night's march, mostly consisting of small amounts of grain—often of a type usually reserved for birds and livestock at home—or soup made from local root vegetables.[16] Hunger was constant, added to which were the miseries of lice, diarrhoea, and dysentery brought about through having to drink melted snow that came from fields fertilized with human manure, a lack of bowls or utensils, and the complete absence of washing facilities. 'We were absolutely filthy and I'm sure stank to high heaven', recalled Bob Erricker. 'We were all infested with lice,' he also noted, 'some sooner than others.'[17]

Matters were not helped by conditions at the main staging posts in the vicinity of Pyongyang that the columns arrived at after about a month on the march. The transit camps at a disused army ground and a former gold mining encampment near Suan were known to the British as the Bean Camp and Bean Pie Camp (alternately known as the Mine or Mining Camp) respectively because of the diet of Soya bean cake provided there for several weeks before the trek northward resumed. Both places were overcrowded, lacked sanitary facilities, and the former was, according to Gunner G. H. May, 'filthy in the extreme'.[18]

There had been no provision for the seriously sick and wounded up to this point except a bullock cart or two to ride in, and it was in the transit camps that men began to suffer seriously from the effects of what they had gone through and would continue to endure in the way of malnourishment and illness despite the best efforts of Major Joe Ryan, the senior captured officer present at Suan, to get the camp

[14] IWMDD, E. Beckerley, 11.

[15] IWMDS, 19047/4, F. Brodie; 20299/2, J. Shaw; see also e.g. Cpl W. Massey diary entries in Cunningham, *No Mercy, No Leniency*, 21–2. On frostbite see e.g. IWMDD, R. McGuire, 5; E. Beckerley, 13. The captured troopers, who had winter tank suits, were better off than the infantry, many of whom only had battle dress designed for the climate of Western Europe. See ibid. 11.

[16] See NAA, Part 6, AI9/K/BRIT/69, Maj. M. D. G. C. Ryan, 2; Part 3, AI9/K/BRIT/287, Tpr S. Carr, 2; Part 5, AI9/K/BRIT/107, Gnr L. Leak, 2; Part 6, AI9/K/BRIT/3, Rfn E. F. Spencer, 2; IWMDS, 22347/5, E. Bruford-Davies.

[17] IWMDS, 10749/4, R. Erricker. The sick, wounded, and older prisoners not surprisingly found the march particularly arduous. IWMDS, 20299/2, J. Shaw.

[18] NAA, Part 3, AI9/K/BRIT/135, Gnr E. H. May, 1; Part 6, AI9/K/BRIT/3, Rfn E. F. Spencer, 2; see IWMDS, 10749/4, R. Erricker.

authorities to isolate the infectious in a 'sick room' and provide a little fuel to heat it. 'The food was sufficient in quantity', Rifleman Spencer stated, 'but extremely unpalatable and some PW were unable to eat enough to maintain their strength.'[19] It was in the Bean Pie Camp that the first recorded death occurred, Lieutenant D. F. P. C. Probyn of the 8th Hussars succumbing to pneumonia and pleurisy.[20]

It was while in these transit camps that the majority of the prisoners were interviewed about their political affiliations and many were issued with an autobiographical form to fill in. Since this questionnaire went beyond name, rank, and number, some were cautious about putting down anything more except facetious answers. Others, though, could see no obvious harm in giving truthful answers as to their age, politics, educational and family background, or civilian job, if not the details of their military occupation. This helped the Chinese identify potential sympathizers—albeit not always correctly—and gave the North Koreans the opportunity to siphon off numbers of men for the propaganda efforts detailed in the next chapter.[21]

Despite their travails the Ulsters were holding up fairly well under the circumstances. According to one rifleman, 'British morale was good' even in the latter stages of the march, one American indicating in his memoirs that, like his compatriots, the British would occasionally sing to keep up their spirits.[22] Major Ryan earned the admiration of fellow prisoners for his efforts to improve conditions. According to Captain M. P. Stott, who interviewed returning prisoners in 1953, the major, though denied any formal authority by the guards, 'commanded the column, saw that everybody received his fair share of any rations which were issued, read burial services over the dead—who were many—supervised the care of the sick and wounded, and continually fought with the escort for better food and conditions.'[23]

The same cohesiveness did not seem to hold true for some of the Americans with whom the British were billeted in the transit camps. Everyone suffered from malnutrition and disease, but the death rate among GIs was at least 25 per cent. Some could not stomach what they were fed, while others simply lost the will to live. There was very little discipline, the Chinese doing their best to undermine the authority of officers and NCOs (whose rank was said to no longer count), and an inability or refusal to cooperate for the common good. It did not help that among the American prisoners in the Bean Camp was one particularly nasty character, a

---

[19] NAA, Part 6, AI9/K/BRIT/3, Rfn E. F. Spencer, 2; see ibid. AI9/K/BRIT/69, Maj. M. D. G. C. Ryan, 2.

[20] IWMDD, E. Beckerley, 12–13; NAA, Part 4, AI9/K/BRIT/497, Rfn E. English; ibid., AI9/K/BRIT/498, Tpr M. Gwadera, 2.

[21] Cunningham, *No Mercy, No Leniency*, 23–4; see e.g. NAA, Part 6, AI9/K/BRIT/3, Rfn E. F. Spencer, 6. An example of the kind of autobiographical form the Chinese presented can be found at Part 4, AI9/K/BRIT/498, Tpr M. Gwadera, App. A. The Chinese checked the addresses given in the forms by issuing letter cards for prisoners to write to their families with. None were delivered. Cunningham, *No Mercy, No Leniency*, 24.

[22] NAA, Part 4, AI9/K/BRIT/497, Rfn E. English, 2. On singing see Lloyd W. Pate as told to B. J. Cutler, *Reactionary!* (New York, 1956), 50.

[23] NAA, Part 6, AI9/K/BRIT/69, Maj. M. D. G. C. Ryan, 3; see also TNA, WO 373/119, citation for Maj. M. D. G. C. Ryan, f. 183.

private soldier who refused to listen to officers, stole food and personal items from the wounded, beat others up, and seems to have been directly responsible for at least one death. An official US Army report later noted that the captured American doctors all thought that 'in many instances the lack of discipline and the failure to assist each other introduced conditions which increased the death toll, particularly among the sick and wounded'.[24]

The march north from the Pyongyang area to the Yalu, which lasted from the middle of February through to the first week of March 1951, was tough. Though after a couple of weeks the guards considered it safe to move in the daylight hours and allow the lighting of fires, the weather was still miserable and both rations and shelter remained inadequate. Not surprisingly, survival took precedence over thoughts of escape. 'We decided it was best to carry on', Bob Erricker recalled: 'At least we were still alive.' Diseases such as pneumonia and dysentery, though, continued to take a toll in terms of fatalities. 'The march is only supposed to last a few more days', Massey, who was now ill, wrote in his secret diary on 23 February, adding: 'Hope I make it.' Despite the fact that he would be trudging on for another thirteen days, he did indeed survive: but many did not, the overall death rate among UN prisoners in the column reaching 20 per cent.[25]

The Chinese continually promised that things were infinitely better in the permanent camps established along the Yalu River, a hope that desperate men could cling to as they staggered northward. Living conditions on arrival at the requisitioned section of the village of Pyoktong, on a peninsular jutting into the Yalu River, therefore likely came as a deeply unpleasant shock to both the Ulsters and the Royal Marines.[26]

At this stage the camp at Pyoktong was run by North Koreans who did not seem to care whether prisoners lived or died.[27] The traditional Korean two-room, wooden-floored huts with mud-and-lathe walls and tiled roofs that served as living quarters were dilapidated, and between ten and twelve men were crowded into each 10-foot-square room cheek by jowl at night.[28] There was no running water,

[24] Department of the Army, *U.S. Prisoners of War in the Korean Operation* (Fort Meade, Md., 1954), 60. On the discipline problems among US troops at the Bean Camp see Lech, *Broken Soldiers* (Urbana, Il., 2000), 50–6. On problems with the food see also e.g. C. Young in Louis Baldovi (ed.), *A Foxhole View* (Honolulu, 2002), 146; D. Elliott in Harry Spiller (ed.), *American POWs in Korea* (Jefferson, NC, 1998), 8.

[25] Cunningham, *No Mercy, No Leniency*, 27; IWMDS, 10749/4, R. Erricker.

[26] Cunningham, *No Mercy, No Leniency*, 59–60; see e.g. IWMDS, 13711/2, J Underwood. On Chinese promises and the shock of the reality of Camp 5 see also e.g. Clarence Adams, *An American Dream*, ed. Della Adams and Lewis H. Carlson (Amherst, Mass., 2007), 46; Ralph D. Moyer in Robert C. Doyle, *Voices from Captivity* (Lawrence, Kan., 1994), 167.

[27] See e.g. IWMDS, 9859/4, G. Richards; NAA, Part 4, AI9/K/BRIT/96, Rfn F. Harper, 2; A. Edwards, <http://www.koreanwar-educator.org/memoirs/edwards_archie/index.htm> (accessed 13 November 2010), 5. Even the Chinese would later blame the North Koreans for the appalling conditions in Camp 5 in the winter of 1950–1. NAA, Part 3, AI9/K/BRIT/106, Rfn B. C. Canavan; Part 5, AI9/K/BRIT/291, Rfn W. H. Liggett, 2.

[28] On the huts and crowding see IWMDS, 19047/4, F. Brodie; 10250/3, E. Curd; 22347/4, E. Bruford-Davies; E. Beckerley, 16–17; NAA, Part 3, AI9/K/BRIT/293, Rfn K. Clarke, 2; Part 6, AI9/K/BRIT/3, Rfn E. F. Spencer, 4.

the latrines overflowed, and there were piles of faeces everywhere. Hygiene, according to the Ulsters' medical officer, was 'absolutely appalling'; indeed 'nonexistent'. The whole place was 'extremely filthy', as one disgusted rifleman put it.[29] If anything the food situation on arrival at Pyoktong was even worse than on the march, in the transit camps, or at Kangyee, daily rations consisting of between 300 and 400 grams of often poorly cooked and nauseating maize, sorghum, or millet.[30] And for the wounded and growing number of sick men there was virtually no medicine to be had in the so-called camp hospital.[31] 'Conditions in the camp were appalling, absolutely appalling', remembered John Underwood, one of the Royal Marines. 'I don't know how to describe it', John Shaw of the Ulsters reflected, adding: 'grim place to be'.[32]

Most shocking of all was the state of the camp population, most of whom were Americans captured many months earlier. After lengthy captivity boots had worn away to nothing and clothing had taken on the aspect of rags. Everyone, it seemed, had dysentery, and on starvation rations plenty of GIs were too weak to make their way to the latrine and slowly died in their own excrement. Lack of vitamins was causing men to suffer from diseases such as beriberi and pellagra. Some soldiers, especially teenagers, simply gave up and refused to eat what little unappetizing food there was.[33] Morale and discipline had collapsed, and though some men did their best to look after their buddies—indeed the heroic Catholic chaplain Father Emil Kapaun performed countless selfless deeds of succor for all and sundry before himself succumbing to the combined effects of hunger and disease about six weeks after the British arrived[34]—others stole food from the dying or, in one notorious case, helped them on their way by throwing them into the snow.[35] 'The Americans were dying like nobody's business', remembered Edward Curd, who had been in Pyoktong since the beginning of the year. 'Sometimes I counted thirty-six every day, day after day, thirty, thirty-six people being carried, dragged away to be buried.'[36]

[29] NAA, Part 3, AI9/BRIT/293, Rfn K. Clarke, 2; Part 4, AI9/K/BRIT/980, Capt. A. M. Ferrie, 2; see ibid. AI9/K/BRIT/96, Rfn F. Harper, 2; Part 6, AI9/K/BRIT/548, Rfn H. Smith, 2; IWMDS, 9859/4, G. Richards.

[30] On the ration scale by February 1951 see William Lindsay White, *The Captives of Korea* (New York, 1957), 85. On the general inadequacy and sheer nastiness of the food in the spring of 1951 at Camp 5 see e.g. IWMDD, E. Beckerley, 18; NAA, Part 3, AI9/K/BRIT/934, Cpl F. Bradle, 5; ibid. AI9/K/BRIT/95, Rfn R. Cartlidge, 4.

[31] NAA, Part 4, AI9/K/BRIT/980, Capt. A. M. Ferrie, 2; Dr Sidney Esensten, 'Memories of Life as a POW 35 Years Later', Part II, *The Greybeards*, 11(6) (1997), 9; see e.g. IWMDD, E. Beckerley, 20.

[32] IWMDS, 20299/2, J. Shaw; 13711/2, J. Underwood.

[33] See e.g. Adams, *An American Dream*, 46–7; Esensten, 'Memories of Life as a POW', Part II, 6–9; Pate in Cutler, *Reactionary!*, 53–5; Arden Allen Rowley, *Korea-POW* (Mesa, Ariz., 2003), 50–5; L. Donovan in Donald Knox, *The Korean War: Uncertain Victory* (San Diego, 1988), 338–9; White, *The Captives of Korea*, 86; James Thompson, *True Colors* (Port Washington, NY, 1989), 23 ff.

[34] See William L. Maher, *A Shepherd in Combat Boots* (Shippensburg, Pa., 1997), chs. 10–11.

[35] Lech, *Broken Soldiers*, 74–5; Philip D. Chinnery, *Korean Atrocity!* (Annapolis, Md., 2000), 112; White, *The Captives of Korea*, 87–8.

[36] IWMDS, 10250/2, E. Curd.

While some of the new arrivals in March recognized that the condition of their allies was due in considerable part to having been held by the enemy for longer and often under worse conditions than they had endured themselves,[37] negative comparisons were often drawn with the Turkish and British contingents. The Turks were universally respected by the British, as none among the roughly 200 men captured in November 1950 and sent to Pyoktong would die, and their discipline remained solid. 'Nothing could get the Turks down', Curd noted admiringly. 'They seemed to be able to withstand the early hardships better than anyone else', Bob Erricker observed. 'They were *really* hard men', thought Ted Beckerley.[38] The British also tended to think that, if not quite as tough as the Turks, they themselves dealt better with the bad conditions in Camp 5 than the GIs. The experience of serious rationing in the 1940s, it was thought, made it easier for reservists and others to adapt to the privations of POW life—especially with respect to food—than was the case for soft American teenagers used to an infinitely higher standard of living both in the United States and while on occupation duty in Japan and often unable to cope.[39] Thus, while the British made an effort to clean themselves up and improve their quarters while getting a little daily exercise, the Americans, so it seemed, just lay around and complained.[40] It was also believed that the British always looked out for one another in a way not always true for the Americans. When individuals became seriously ill, for instance, their mates did their best to make sure they kept eating.[41] Thus while hundreds of Americans died from a combination of starvation, disease, and despair through the spring of 1951 only a handful of British prisoners succumbed.[42] The perceived inadequacies of the GIs combined with a failure to understand that their behaviour was largely the result of starvation and disease on a scale the British had not truly experienced led to widespread contempt. 'It was dreadful to see people behave in that way', commented a junior NCO from the Royal Marines. 'The more you mixed with them the more you despised them', a lance corporal in the Ulsters bluntly opined.[43] This anti-Americanism would play into the hands of the Chinese, who adhered to 'the

[37] Ibid. 22347/5, E. Bruford-Davies; NAA, Part 4, AI9/K/BRIT/96, Rfn F. Harper, 2; see also Part 6, AI9/K/AUST/490 et al., Special Annex, 11 August 1951. Some of those at Pyoktong had survived transit camps such as 'Death Valley' that were, if anything, worse than those the British had passed through. See Department of the Army, *U.S. Prisoners of War*, 92–3; see also e.g. NARA, RG 319, entry 85, Phase III summaries, box 1027, John A. Clayton.

[38] IWMDS, 10982/5, E. Beckerley (see also reel 6); 10749/6, R. Erricker; 10250/2, E. Curd; see ibid. 09972/3, J. Arnall; 13711/2, J. Underwood.

[39] See e.g. IWMDS, 10982/6, E. Beckerley; NAM 1989-05-161-1, R. Bruford-Davies; IWMDS, 9693/5, A. Condron; 20299/2, J. Shaw; NAA, Part 4, AI9/K/498, Tpr M. Gwadera, 9; Part 6, AI9/K/BRIT/3, Rfn E. F. Spencer, 4.

[40] See e.g. IWMDD, E. Beckerley, 19–20; IWMDS, 09972/3, J. Arnall; NAA, Part 4, AI9/K/BRIT/96, Rfn F. Harper, 2; Part 5, AI9/K/BRIT/291, Rfn W. H. Liggett, 2; Part 6, AI9/K/BRIT/548, Rfn H. Smith, 2.

[41] See e.g. IWMDS, 19047/4, F. Brodie; 10250/2, E. Curd; 10749/4, E. Erricker; 13711/2, J. Underwood.

[42] NAA, Part 3, AI9/K/BRIT/106, Rfn B. C. Canavan, 1; Part 6, AI9/K/BRIT/548, Rfn H. Smith, 2; IWMDS, 10982/5, E. Beckerley. On causes of death among the Americans see e.g. NARA, RG 319, entry 85, Phase III summaries, box 1029, Marvin E. Dorsay; box 1027, William F. Chassereau.

[43] NAA, Part 4, AI9/K/BRIT/338, L/Cpl R. Evans, 2; IWMDS 9859/4, G. Richards.

principle of "divide and conquer"', as one GI put it, when they began to apply the Lenient Policy.[44]

Even before the start of April, when the North Koreans departed and the Chinese assumed full control of Camp 5, political representatives of the latter had been trying to educate prisoners. On arrival the British were formed into a separate company with the dozen or so men in each hut considered a squad. For each squad a monitor was appointed. The function of the monitor, it emerged, was to supervise discussion, based on assigned talking points, arising from periodic lectures by two Chinese political officers. The lectures, delivered in very bad English in the open air, went on for hours and dealt with current affairs from the communist standpoint. The captive audience was supposed to lap all this up and after discussion return the politically correct responses. At first there were objections, especially from amongst the squad made up of British officers led and monitored by Major Ryan, with men jumping to their feet and challenging the lecturers' facts and interpretations. The Chinese, however, singled out both the troublemakers and their squad-mates for cross-examination and further discussion, which meant missed meals. For men on the verge of starvation this was a serious matter, and it was eventually accepted by many that if parroting back what the Chinese wanted was the price of eating, then agreement with the CPV interpretation of, say, which government Formosa belonged to or who started the Korean War, then the price would have to be paid.[45]

Full-scale indoctrination, however, did not commence until the spring of 1951 when the 3,000-odd prisoners at Pyoktong, hitherto inhabitants of the North Korean-run Camp 3, became students in what the Chinese now dubbed Camp 5. Everyone was made to listen to lengthy explanations of the new, enlightened order the enemy would henceforth insist on based around the Lenient Policy of treating UN captives as promising students rather than war criminals. Each of the five prisoner companies, each consisting of hundreds of men broken into forty squads of up to fifteen men each, would elect a committee to oversee matters such as sanitation, messing, mail, sports, entertainment, and library resources. Members of these company committees would in turn elect from their number a Daily Life

[44] NARA, RG 319, entry 85, Phase III summaries, box 1029, David T. Ellenberger; see also box 1032, Clarence D. Johnson. On anti-Americanism see Cunningham, *No Mercy, No Leniency*, 59; NAA, Part 4, AI9/K/BRIT/498, Tpr M. Gwadera, 9; Part 6, comment by Capt. R. L. Brignall on AI9/K/BRIT/100, Tpr R. S. Parker, 2. While some American POWs agreed that the British were better than the Americans at coping (see Department of the Army, *U.S. Prisoners of War*, 60; White, *The Captives of Korea*, 84–5), others in Camp 5 thought that the British, along with other minorities, were better treated than themselves by the Chinese (see e.g. NARA, RG319, Phase III summaries, box 1025, William M. Allen, Walter D. Ashpole; box 1029, Howard E. Estell, Maurice E. Field, James W. Fulk; box 1027, Billy E. Clark; box 1030, Louis B. Garrett; box 1032, Robert T. Hesselink; box 1034, John A. Molitor; box 1035, Clifford L. Petney, John P. Pingree).

[45] Cunningham, *No Mercy, No Leniency*, 60–2; see e.g. IWMDD, R. W. McGuire, 5–6; IWMDS, 09972/3, J. Arnall; 10250/2, E. Curd. Conversely, at least one officer had the impression that those who adhered to the party line received better medical treatment as an incentive to others. NARA, RG 38, entry 1015 (1), box 27, Phase II Questionnaire, John N. McGlauchlin, question 16 response. According to one prisoner these early lectures were also about the reasons for the Second World War, as well as Leninism and Stalinism. See NAA, Part 4, AI9/K/BRIT/299, L/Cpl T. Flanaghan, 2.

Committee for the entire camp which would coordinate activities and liaise with the Chinese authorities. At the base of the organizational pyramid, chosen squad leaders would make sure that individual squad members obeyed camp regulations. Each day would now be given over to study, with lectures in the morning followed by group discussions in the afternoon in what the Americans came to label Pyoktong University (a phrase which was soon shortened to the simpler and more evocative acronym 'P.U.').[46]

Some of these innovations were at first cautiously welcomed by the British, at least those which validated their ongoing efforts to improve sanitation and hygiene. Indeed the Chinese, always willing to exploit potential areas of dispute between the UN contingents, gave the British the impression that they were the ones the camp authorities 'relied upon to get the camp in order', and reputedly 'pointed out to the Americans that they could thank the British for improved conditions'.[47] Such positive signs, though, were somewhat undermined from the Chinese perspective when it emerged that efforts at improving conditions extended to British soldiers quietly disassembling unoccupied huts as a source of firewood.[48]

At first it looked as if the selection and election of squad leaders and Daily Life Committee members would be, as promised, in the hands of the prisoners themselves. Ballot boxes and paper were provided, and votes counted by the men 'rigorously and carefully', as one popular candidate in the British company put it.[49] The Chinese, however, retained the right to ratify appointments, and it soon became evident to many that only those they favoured—that is to say, individuals who did not challenge their views and showed signs of political sympathy—would be allowed to run for or remain in office. Interference was most blatant among the UN officers confined in a separate compound, all but one of whose choices were rejected; but by the time elections and reshufflings had come to a halt in the summer it was evident that the committee structure was in the hands of a group of prisoners who if nothing else shared a 'progressive' attitude towards the Chinese.[50]

Efforts to convert prisoners to the communist cause through the compulsory instruction programme, meanwhile, met with little apparent success. The daily morning lectures in an old theatre atop a hill, on subjects such as the nature of capitalism, imperialism, and socialism, were tedious and usually went above the heads of the majority of the audience. Passionate efforts by Comrade Lim, the political officer most often facing the British contingent, to get the message across

---

[46] Cunningham, *No Mercy, No Leniency*, 62–3. On the deliberately disrespectful acronym P.U. see e.g. John W. Thornton, Jr, *Believed to Be Alive* (Middlebury, Vt., 1981), 168. On the makeup of the companies, which varied over time, see Department of the Army, *U.S. Prisoners of War*, 114–16; see also Richard M. Bassett with Lewis H. Carlson, *And the Wind Blew Cold* (Kent, O., 2002), 45–6.

[47] NAA, Part 6, AI9/K/BRIT/548, Rfn H. Smith, 2; Part 5, AI9/K/BRIT/291, Rfn W. H. Liggett, 2; see IWMDS, 9693/5, A. Condron; 16853/3, G. Hobson.

[48] Cunningham, *No Mercy, No Leniency*, 64; IWMDS, 10250/2, E. Curd. Those caught stealing or otherwise breaking regulations might also be flung into one of the numerous pits dotted around the outside of the camp for days or weeks, freezing in winter and boiling in summer. See e.g. IWMDD, R. W. McGuire, 7.

[49] IWMDS, 9693/5, A. Condron.

[50] Cunningham, *No Mercy, No Leniency*, 65–7.

more often than not backfired. An RUR lance corporal recalled how Lim harangued them almost every day, 'his speech being punctuated with vigorous gestures, such as jumping up and down and beating the air with his fists, accompanied by shouting'. Little wonder that the high-cheek-boned Lim quickly acquired 'The Screaming Skull' as a nickname.[51] Neither the lectures nor the discussions were popular, leading to attempts at sabotage by some and a willingness to catch up on sleep or play cards from others.[52] 'We were trying to tell the POWs that capitalism was due to collapse and that socialism was bound to win', a Chinese instructor later recalled, 'but after a couple of months we found that such a theory was untenable, was unacceptable, to most POWs.' Hence at the end of 1951 compulsory classes were quietly dropped.[53]

Yet treating prisoners as students was not an entirely futile exercise, especially once the Chinese began to understand that their initial efforts were sometimes having the opposite effect to the one intended. Though they were perfectly capable of employing physical coercion—in one notorious instance a US Army officer, after publicly saying that communist claims were not worth the paper they were written on, was deemed to have insulted the people's papermaking industry and was taken away and beaten so badly that he died from internal injuries two weeks later[54]—the Chinese liked to believe that the truth of their worldview would be obvious once it was explained. Hence it was belatedly recognized that, for instance, threatening Rifleman J. R. Bartlett with death for not agreeing with the party line was probably counterproductive.[55]

A less confrontational approach to interaction, such as that pursued by Comrade Chang—who had reputedly visited Liverpool at some point while serving as a naval petty officer and was known as 'The Admiral' or 'Boy Blue'—generated a certain amount of trust. 'We didn't dislike him at all', Edward Curd later, remarked; 'quite a nice chap', was the verdict of George Richards, who added that 'some of them were very nice people'.[56] Even the fanatical Lim provoked laughter on one occasion when, after he was stung on the finger in mid-diatribe, exclaimed 'Ah!

[51] NAA, Part 5, AI9/K/BRIT/98, L/Cpl W. Massey, 3; see Part 7, AI9/K/BRIT/286, L/Cpl A. Wynn, 2; see also Cunningham, *No Mercy, No Leniency*, 64–5. On the subjects covered see e.g. NAA, Part 4, AI9/K/BRIT/498, Tpr M. Gwadera, 5. On the material going over men's heads see e.g. Part 3, AI9/K/BRIT/125, Rfn R. Gore, 4; ibid. AI9/K/BRIT/124, Rfn R. W. McGuire, 4; Capt. R. B. Trant comment in Part 4, AI9/K/BRIT/96, Rfn F. Harper, 3.

[52] On the unpopularity and lack of attention paid to lectures see e.g. NAA, Part 3, AI9/K/BRIT/93, Pte D. Ackroyd, 1; ibid. AI9/K/BRIT/95, Rfn R. Cartlidge, 3; Part 4, AI9/K/BRIT/497, Rfn E. English, 2. On sabotage efforts see e.g. Cunningham, *No Mercy, No Leniency*, 64; IWMDS, 20299/2, J. Shaw; Fred Hayhurst, *Green Berets in Korea* (Cambridge, 2001), 378.

[53] Wu Henian in *They Chose China* (National Film Board of Canada, 2005). On the dropping of compulsory classes in December 1951 see Cunningham, *No Mercy, No Leniency*, 74. Prisoners were, however, still made to watch Chinese and Soviet propaganda films on occasion. See IWMDS, 10749/7, R. Erricker; NAA, Part 4, AI9/K/BRIT/299, L/Cpl T. Flanaghan, 1; ibid. AI9/K/BRIT/85, Pte J. Heslop, 2.

[54] See NARA, RG 319, entry 85, Phase III summaries, box 1032, Charles F. Howard, Robert P. Howell; box 1034, Robert E. Nehrling; NAA, Part 6, AI9/K/BRIT/69, Maj. M. D. G. C. Ryan, 15.

[55] NAA, Part 4, AI9/K/BRIT/338, L/Cpl R. Evans, 2.

[56] IWMDS, 9859/5, G. Richards; 10250/3, E. Curd; see NAA, Part 4, AI9/K/BRIT/497, Rfn E. English, 2; ibid. AI9/K/BRIT/299, L/Cpl T. Flanaghan, 2; Part 6, AI9/K/BRIT/90, Tpr P. F. Rowley, 5.

You see that now, a capitalist bee!' To at least one prisoner he therefore became 'quite a decent chap...he wasn't too bad at all'.[57]

More important overall was a shift after a few months away from political theory and toward issues where prisoner agreement could be used to good effect in the international propaganda war. 'Prime Minister Zhou [Enlai] told us,' remembered Cheng Shaokun, a former camp officer, '"Not too much lecturing, not too much political education. Concentrate on the principle of opposing the war, for peace."'[58]

Even in terms of straight politics, among the disgruntled reservists there were a handful of men who already had links to the CPGB, and others who were already left-wing in outlook and thus susceptible to accepting the Chinese view of the struggle between capitalism and communism.[59] In his post-release interrogation, Gunner Jack Arnall, for instance, already a socialist before going to Korea, commented that 'the Communists were right in what they preached', and in an interview decades later was still arguing that 'a lot of the things they told us were right'.[60] There were political neophytes, moreover, who rather liked being treated as thinking individuals rather than just rank-and-file bodies. 'When the Chinese were putting all these idea forward,' reflected former marine John Underwood, 'if you're in any way intelligent you're seeking answers for certain things, aren't you?' Fellow marine Andy Condron, he observed, 'listened quite intently' to lectures, even though Condron himself later claimed these were rather 'ham-fisted efforts' at conversion.[61] The Chinese hope that such men could be turned into 'progressives' was reflected in their rise to key positions in the camp hierarchy, collectively known to some of their more jaundiced fellow prisoners as the Big Wheel.[62] Their choices were vindicated after compulsory indoctrination had ended through the formation of a flourishing set of voluntary study groups. As one AI9 officer put it, 'a handful of progressive prisoners' had 'persuaded their chums to undertake voluntary study'; and, since there was no coercion involved and the discussion leaders were British rather than Chinese, over a quarter of the British population at Pyoktong chose to participate.[63]

In cultivating both the core group of 'progressives' and other less committed but nevertheless open-minded men, the Chinese were greatly aided by their control of what prisoners could read. A reading room of sorts was set up in the latter part of

---

[57] IWMDS, 10749/5, R. Erricker; see Hastings, *The Korean War*, 344.

[58] Cheng Shaokun in *They Chose China* (National Film Board of Canada, 2005); see also Wu Henian, ibid.

[59] Cunningham, *No Mercy, No Leniency*, 65. On those with existing party connections see NAA, Part 3, AI9/K/BRIT/294, Rfn J. C. Burton, 2; Part 4, AI9/K/BRIT/314, Rfn S. Higginson; Part 5, AI9/K/BRIT/736, Cpl H. Manning, 2.

[60] IWMDS, 09972/4, J. Arnall; NAA, Part 3, AI9/K/BRIT/86, Gnr J. Arnall, 2; see also e.g. L/Cpl F. Quibell in *Korea: The Unknown War* (Thames Television, 1988).

[61] SLV, MS 10254, Wilfred G. Burchett Papers, box 4.9, Condron to Whom It May Concern, 3 February 1969; IWMDS, 13711/9859/5, G. Richards; 13711/2, J. Underwood; see e.g. NAA, Part 3, AI9/K/BRIT/293, Rfn K. Clarke, 3.

[62] Cunningham, *No Mercy, No Leniency*, 66.

[63] Ibid. 126. On the origins of these voluntary study groups see NAA, Part 3, AI9/K/BRIT/316, Tpr E. G. Beckerley, 2. On the way in which compulsory indoctrination could produce a voluntary interest in communism see e.g. ibid. AI9/K/BRIT/105, Rfn L. G. Tanner.

1951 which, along with a limited number of carefully vetted novels, contained volumes by Marx and other communist luminaries, polemical tracts by fellow travellers such as D. N. Pritt, and out-of-date copies of English-language party newspapers such as the *Daily Worker* and *Shanghai News*. Once compulsory classes ended prisoners tended to look for something to occupy themselves, and reading—'the sheer joy of having the opportunity to read the printed word', as one enthusiast put it[64]—became one way of passing the time.[65] Condron later claimed that he came to accept communist ideas 'not because I was told to accept them but simply through reading'. The books initially provided were 'a bit heavy on the Marxist classics, and not exactly what I would have chosen to read', but in the absence of alternatives and with a growing sense of understanding Condron read *Das Kapital* 'at least twice, maybe more' and went on to devour various works by Mao and others. While he admitted that 'the majority of people took no interest at all' in the heavy communist tomes, another prisoner recalled that perusing the pages of old copies the London *Daily Worker*—the organ of the CPGB—was 'very popular' as it was 'a link with home'.[66]

There were also those who had little real interest in what the Chinese were saying during the compulsory education phase but through sheer repetition got the message. As Rifleman W. H. Liggett admitted, 'through being forced to listen hours on end' to the Chinese view of things, he did 'absorb much of the teaching'.[67] It was also much easier for the majority to go along with the enemy line, at least on the surface, than to openly disagree. 'In [squad] discussions, if there were any contrary opinions, the discussion [supervised by an English-speaking Chinese instructor] went on until all had fallen into line and sometimes until ten o'clock at night', an RUR lance corporal explained. This meant missed meals for men on the verge of starvation: 'In the end you were forced to concede.'[68]

The same was often true for the ongoing personal interrogations aimed at assessing a prisoner's class background and general malleability.[69] Though questions such as how much livestock individuals possessed—'How many pigs have you? How many cows have you?'—continued to undermine the credibility of the enemy's grasp of life in contemporary industrial Britain,[70] the Chinese wore men down through sheer repetition and pressure until they got what they wanted. 'They used to make you write an autobiography', Edward Curd recalled. 'It started off one page; that was good enough [for you], one page; and then it wouldn't satisfy them, so then they'd keep you apart [from the others] and make you write another, and

[64] A. Condron in the *Daily Express*, 15 October 1962, 7.
[65] See e.g. IWMDS, 09972/4, J. Arnall. On the reading room see NAA, Part 3, AI9/K/BRIT/293, Rfn K. Clarke, 3.
[66] IWMDS, 10749/6, R. Erricker; 9693/7, A. Condron; see ibid. 9859/5, G. Richards; NAA, Part 6, Tpr P. F. Rowley et al., AI9/K/BRIT/90 et al., 7.
[67] NAA, Part 5, AI9/K/BRIT/291, Rfn W. H. Liggett, 2; see IWMDS, 10982/6, E. Beckerley; NAA, Part 3, AI9/K/BRIT/316, Tpr E. G. Beckerley; Part 6, AI9/K/BRIT/120, Rfn H. W. Payne, 3; Part 3, AI9/K/BRIT/L/Cpl A. Gill, 4.
[68] NAA, Part 4, AI9/K/BRIT/338, L/Cpl R. Evans, 2.
[69] See NAA, Part 4, AI9/K/BRIT/498, Tpr M. Gwadera, 5–6.
[70] IWMDS, 9859/5, G. Richards; see e.g. ibid. 13711/2, J. Underwood.

then you got two pages, three pages, four pages, and it [still] wasn't good enough for them.'[71] There seemed little harm in mouthing back what the Chinese seemed to want to hear, and overt resistance was in any event not well received, as the outcome of a sit-in against so many quizzing sessions indicated.

Tired of men being hauled off for interrogation, the British contingent decided one day to refuse to appear for the morning and evening roll calls in protest. 'The next morning they told us we had to come out [of our huts],' remembered George Richards, 'otherwise we wouldn't get any food. And the next morning the gong sounded for morning roll call, still nobody moved. So in the end they said if we didn't come out they would have to bring the army in and make us come out— some people would get shot, and this sort of thing.' At first it was thought the Chinese were bluffing, but when machine-guns were set up and bullets were fired in the air 'we sort of gave in', as Andy Condron sheepishly put it.[72]

This was symptomatic of the ongoing efforts of the Chinese to prevent any prisoners from serving as autonomous authority figures. It was true that the representative whom they had allowed to rise to the top of the camp committee structure, Marine Andrew Condron, was able to achieve over time a certain degree of improvement in living conditions through negotiation. Even a rifleman who had little time for communism argued that Condron 'did a lot of work in the interests of PWs' welfare' and was 'well-liked by the other PWs'.[73] Yet when all is said and done Condron only served at the behest of the Chinese; and as the abortive strike over interrogations illustrated, they would not tolerate anything that even hinted at subversion of their efforts to shape words and actions. If this was true of their carefully groomed British representative, it was even more the case in relation to anyone or anything that might likely serve as a countervailing influence on the rank and file.

Thus, for instance, no religious activities were permitted at first;[74] and when the senior British NCO, Sergeant Jim Taylor of the 8th Hussars, failed to salute a Chinese officer one day in April 1951, he was instantly taken away and made an example of by being placed in a hole in the ground for several stifling days and then made to make a public confession of his crime in order to deter similarly obstruc-

---

[71] Ibid. 10250/2, E. Curd. On having to write autobiographies over and over again and being subjected to a certain amount of physical pressure for giving the wrong answers or, conversely, receiving small rewards in the form of tobacco for the right ones see e.g. NAA, Part 3, AI9/K/BRIT/833, Rfn P. May, 2. Multiple autobiographies and interrogations about the contents also helped the Chinese spot lies through discrepancies. Cunningham, *No Mercy, No Leniency*, 23–4; see e.g. IWMDS, 9859/5, G. Richards.

[72] IWMDS, 9693/5, A. Condron; 9859/5, G. Richards. A similar protest in 1952 yielded no better result. NAA, Part 6, AI9/K/BRIT/90, Tpr P. F. Rowley et al., 6; IWMDD, J. Shaw diary, 13–20 April 1952.

[73] NAA, Part 4, AI9/K/BRIT/497, Rfn E. English, 3. This was the view of men with often widely differing views of communism: compare IWMDS, 09972/4, J. Arnall; 10250/3, E. Curd; 10749/8, R. Erricker; 9859/5, G. Richards; NAA, Part 3, AI9/K/BRIT/606, Gnr J. C. Dabbs, with Part 5, AI9/K/BRIT/828, Mne R. Ogle, 3; ibid. AI9/K/BRIT/98, L/Cpl W. Massey, 2. See also Cunningham, *No Mercy, No Leniency*, 66; Hayhurst, *Green Berets in Korea*, 406–7. On Condron's own view of his negotiating skills with the Chinese see IWMDS, 9693/5, A. Condron.

[74] See NAA, Part 3, AI9/K/BRIT/131, Rfn R. Dodd, 3. Once the armistice talks began, supervised religious services were allowed. Ibid., AI9/K/BRIT/297, Tpr R. Dooley, 2; Part 5, AI9/K/BRIT/98, L/Cpl W. Massey, 4 (see also the *Catholic Herald*, 14 August 1953, 1).

tive behaviour.[75] Several months later he, along with Sergeant N. E. Balfour of the Ulster Rifles and thirteen others identified as 'reactionaries'—men such as Corporal Fred Beadle, the senior Royal Marine, who was notorious for arguing back during compulsory lectures—along with a larger number of similarly recalcitrant Americans were transferred to a new camp at Changson (Camp 3, Branch 1) approximately 30 miles away.[76] From the start the Chinese had separated the officers from the British other ranks at Camp 5. But, led by Major Joe Ryan, through their presence and demeanour during lectures and other communal events the officers were still, in the words of Lieutenant Robin Bruford-Davies of the Ulsters, 'stiffening the backbone of the soldiers to resist all the way along the line'.[77] So six months after their arrival at Pyoktong they were sent away to their own camp at Pinchonni (Camp 2, Branch 1). In the summer of the following year the remaining senior NCOs—who had a few months earlier refused to attend a parade in protest at the peace campaign and forced the Chinese to temporarily back down[78]—were also transferred to a separate camp at Kuuptong (Camp 4).[79] This made it easier for the Chinese to get the remaining prisoners to cooperate: according to Edward Curd disrupting the chain of command, thereby breaking 'your system of army life', and producing 'a breakdown of the British system of order'.[80] It doubtless also did not help that one of the riflemen who went on to collaborate with the enemy told the others that Ryan, before leaving Pyoktong, had left instructions for the Ulsters to keep out of the struggle and play along with the Chinese.[81]

Providing 'proof' that prisoners were being well treated was one Chinese goal, but this soon became intertwined with efforts to make POWs part of an orchestrated 'peace' campaign designed to put pressure on the United States and its allies in Korea, especially once armistice talks got underway in the summer of 1951. A year later prisoners were also enlisted in the campaign to prove to the world that the Americans were dropping germ bombs on Korea. Along the Yalu the party line for the captives after compulsory classes stopped was contained in the camp newspaper, *Toward Truth & Peace*,[82] while propaganda for the outside world took the form of individual letters, vetted articles for the communist press, radio broadcasts,

---

[75] See Cunningham, *No Mercy, No Leniency*, 64; IWMDS, 10749/5, R. Erricker.

[76] NAA, Part 3, AI9/K/BRIT/934, Cpl F. Beadle, 5; see ibid. AI9/K/BRIT/293, Rfn K. Clarke, 3; Hayhurst, *Green Berets in Korea*, 378.

[77] NAM 1989-05-161-1, R. Bruford-Davies. On Ryan's leadership see TNA, WO 373/119, citation for Maj. M. D. G. C. Ryan, ff. 183–4.

[78] See IWMDD, J. Shaw diary, 16–23 March 1952.

[79] Cunningham, *No Mercy, No Leniency*, 60, 72–3. Subsequent to the departure of the British officers and virtually unknown to the rest of the camp population, at least two other British officers, both from the Royal Navy and suspected of possessing specialist knowledge, was brought to Pyoktong and kept in isolation for extended periods except for prolonged and harsh interrogation sessions. See Dennis Lankford, *I Defy! The Story of Lieutenant Dennis Lankford* (London, 1954), 40 ff.; NAA, Part 5, AI9/K/ BRIT/1013, Lt RNVR D. A. Lankford, 11–12; ibid. AI9/K/BRIT/1020, Lt RN D. G. Mather, 6; Mather in John R. P. Landsdown, *With the Carriers in Korea* (Southside, 1997), 388–90.

[80] IWMDS, 10250/3, E. Curd.

[81] NAA, Part 3, AI9/K/BRIT/89, L/Cpl A. W. Buxton, 2.

[82] Ibid. AI9/K/BRIT/320, Tpr R. A. Cocks, 6; see Department of the Army, *U.S. Prisoners of War*, 227–9.

and scripted petitions and events. There were also carefully staged photographs and films, plus camp visits by a select group of fellow-travellers from the West. Meanwhile at home the CPGB sought to utilize relatives—understandably anxious about their menfolk given the communist refusal to allow in representatives of the International Red Cross—in the cause of 'peace'.[83]

In the spring of 1951 the Chinese had let it be known that prisoners would be allowed to write home. There was, however, a quid pro quo involved: correspondents would have to support their captors' propaganda goals. They would have to give as their return address the number of the camp, care of the 'Committee of Chinese Congress Defenders of World Peace, Peking, China', and, once they became available, use Chinese letter cards stamped with a dove of peace. More importantly, prisoners would have to include positive statements about their treatment and their desire for peace if a missive was to get through and a letter from home received. One or two men refused; but most took the view that, as Bob Erricker put it, 'it didn't matter if you put in a bit of bullshit about how well they were looking after you.'[84] As for true believers such as Andy Condron—remembered as early as the autumn of 1951 by the departing senior US Marine officer as someone who 'appeared to be thoroughly indoctrinated in communism'[85]—they had no hesitation at all in singing the praises of their captors and damning the capitalists at length for starting and continuing the war. In a letter penned in early March 1952, for example, Condron urged his parents to write to their MP to press for a quick end to the armistice talks while confidently stating several weeks later that 'I can honestly say that the treatment I have received has been absolutely first class.'[86] He, along with a handful of others in the inner circle, could easily also be induced to sign petitions and write propaganda articles for communist publications.[87]

On the receiving end, the relatives of POWs were contacted by the *Daily Worker* and urged to send letters via the 'All-China Committee for World Peace' in Beijing, the CPGB capitalizing on the fact that, in the absence the channels usually established by the International Red Cross, the Communist Party controlled the only means of communication.[88] Relatives were sent free copies of the *Daily Worker* along with anti-war leaflets and visited by representatives of communist-front organizations such as the National Assembly of Women and urged to attend a

---

[83] Cunningham, *No Mercy, No Leniency*, 133.

[84] IWMDS, 10749/7, R. Erricker; see e.g. IWMDD, J. Shaw diary, 15–22 June 1952; NAA, Part 3, AI9/K/BRIT/95 et al., Rfn R. Cartlidge et al., 4; Part 5, AI9/K/BRIT/308, Rfn F. Moore, 3; ibid. AI9/K/BRIT/828, Mne R. Ogle, 3; see also Part 3, AI9/K/BRIT/93, Pte D. Ackroyd, 2; *Daily Worker*, 6 March 1951, 1.

[85] NARA, RG 38, entry 1015 (a), Case files of US POWs during the Korean War, box 27, Phase II Questionnaire, John N. McGlauchlin, question 46a response (see also question 4 response).

[86] TNA, ADM 1/24997, Condron to Parents, 15 May 1953; ibid. 3 March 1952; see also *Daily Worker*, 27 July 1953, 1.

[87] See NAA, Part 3, AI9/K/BRIT/95, Rfn R. Cartlidge et al., 4; *Shanghai News*, 3 July 1951; *Daily Worker*, 21 December 1951, 1; *Labour Monthly*, 35 (1953), 324–7.

[88] NAM 1989-05-163-1, R. Bruford-Davies, reading letter from editor of *Daily Worker* to his father. The Postmaster-General and War Office decided to go along with this, allowing outgoing letters to be sent to Beijing and later through Panmunjom. See TNA, WO32/16163, Encl. 15A, Strachey to Lindgren, 24 April 1951; *Daily Worker*, 15 March 1951, 1; 30 March 1951, 1.

march on the House of Commons on 25 June 1952 demanding that the government 'Bring Back our Lads from Korea'.[89] The effectiveness of all this was highly
questionable given the continuous slide in the popularity of the CPGB during the
Korean War—the National Assembly of Women march only attracted a hundred
supporters[90]—but prisoners themselves were on occasion warned that their relatives might be in danger if they did not cooperate.[91]

More occasionally prisoners were also given the opportunity to make brief
recordings to be broadcast by radio from Beijing. The main incentive to agree to
state 'that the Chinese were looking after us and they were a peace-loving people',
as Edward Curd put it, was to get one's name out and let the family and others
know one was still alive.[92] It was recognized that this meant participating in an
enemy campaign for hearts and minds, but on balance many men decided that the
positive outweighed the negative and, as a visiting communist newspaperman
commented, with 'few exceptions' they were willing to support Chinese calls for a
ceasefire 'on the radio and off it'.[93] As Lance Corporal Bob Guess of the Royal
Norfolk Regiment, one of the comparatively few British prisoners taken in the latter part of the war (he was captured in the spring of 1952 and sent to Camp 5),
later explained in an interview:

> Just before Christmas the Chinese approached me and said that they were going to
> make wire recordings and broadcast messages from prisoners, and would I consider
> making a message to my folks at home. I sort of had misgivings about this. I didn't
> want to be part of any propaganda scheme, which was obviously what it was. But in
> [*sic*] the same token, I know that my parents and my loved ones, they didn't know I
> was alive. I'd written letters. But I never got any back so I assumed that the letters were
> never sent by the Chinese . . . Anyway, I'd mulled this over in my mind, about making
> this, shall we say, propaganda message, and I thought 'Well, what the hell, if there are
> any repercussions then I will excuse myself at a later date.'[94]

An AI9 officer considered such an attitude symptomatic of a 'lack of determination
to stand out against the enemy'.[95]

These, however, were individual efforts. What the Chinese were most interested
in were collective endeavours designed to suggest that the captives as a group agreed
with their positions. In the run-up to the start of the armistice negotiations in the

[89] Cunningham, *No Mercy, No Leniency*, 133.
[90] Keith Laybourn, *Marxism in Britain* (London, 2006), 33.
[91] Cunningham, *No Mercy, No Leniency*, 134. On the slide in the popularity of the CPGB see
Henry Pelling, *The British Communist Party* (London, 1958), 162–3.
[92] IWMDS, 10250/3, E. Curd (see also NAA, Part 3, AI9/K/BRIT/315, Cpl E. J. Curd); see e.g.
IWMDS, 10749/7, R. Erricker; 13711/2, J. Underwood; NAA, Part 4, Rfn F. Harper, 3.
[93] Alan Winnington, *Breakfast with Mao* (London, 1986), 163.
[94] IWMDS, 24610/10, B. Guess; see also e.g. NAA, Part 3, AI9/K/BRIT/311, Mne T. R. Darby,
5; ibid., AI9/K/BRIT/297, Tpr R. Dooley, 3. See *Daily Worker*, 16 April 1951, 1; *Shanghai News*, 26
April 1951, 1; 27 April 1951, 1; 29 April 1951, 1; 3 May 1951, 3; 4 May 1951, 1; 5 May 1951, 1; 6
May 1951, 1; 8 May 1951, 3; 15 May 1951, 3; 17 May 1951, 1; 18 November 1951, 2; 20 November
1951, 3; 21 November 1951, 2; 1 December 1951, 2; 4 December 1951, 3; 7 December 1951, 2; 9
December 1951, 2; 11 December 1951, 3; 18 December 1951, 3; 28 December 1952, 2.
[95] NAA, Part, 4, AI9/K/BRIT/96, Rfn F. Harper, 3.

summer of 1951 the camp authorities held carefully choreographed elections for peace committees from the squad level on up, those elected at one stage voting on the candidates for the next, right up to the camp level: though needless to say only politically acceptable candidates were allowed to stand for office.[96] In the British company the man chosen was a reservist, Rifleman E. F. Spencer, who was told by an instructor that he had been voted in unanimously by a show of hands despite the fact that many men had not voted at all. The company representatives were told to organize a peace petition, which Spencer did with assistance from two other suspected progressives, Marine John Underwood and Lance Corporal Alland McKell of the Royal Electrical and Mechanical Engineers. The rest of the company was then urged to sign. With the Chinese watching, no less than 70 per cent agreed to do so. The draft document, however, was quickly superseded by a camp-level peace petition addressed to the forthcoming World Peace Council meeting in Vienna that 93 per cent of the prisoners agreed to sign.[97]

This turned out to be only the first of a series of petitions—to the Minister of Defence, Lord Alexander, for instance, or to the Trades Union Congress[98]—that many of the British inmates of Camp 5 put their names to over the next two years. Given the propaganda purpose of these documents the motives of the signers are worth investigating.

The progressives, of course, thought it was simply the right thing to do. As Trooper A. E. Surridge, another reservist and a member of the daily life committee later explained to his AI9 interrogator, peace was obviously in every country's interest, not least Britain's.[99] Many ordinary soldiers, meanwhile, rather naively agreed and saw no harm in such documents because, in the words of another progressive, there was nothing in the petitions 'that was considered by the general census of the PWs to be disloyal'.[100] As one soldier observed, he 'signed petitions because he hoped that by signing, peace would be brought about more quickly'.[101] Others knew, if only instinctively, that signing meant working for the enemy, but nevertheless succumbed to pressure from peers or hoped that there would be no consequences once the war was over.[102] To be fair, when the Chinese wanted full compliance they made no bones about the negative consequences of refusal. Rifleman B. C. Canavan, for instance, at one point demurred when presented with yet another peace appeal, to which Comrade Lim responded by branding him a

[96] Cunningham, *No Mercy, No Leniency*, 69–70; see NAA, Part 1, Interrogation Report on British Ex-P.W. Released in Korea, Batch 2 (Supplementary), 28 June 1953, 3; Part 6, AI9/K/BRIT/69, Maj. M. D. G. C. Ryan, 10.

[97] NAA, Part 6, AI9/K/BRIT/3, Rfn E. F. Spencer, 8; see also Part 3, AI9/K/BRIT/311, Mne T. R. Darby, 5.

[98] See NAA, Part 5, AI9/K/BRIT/291, Rfn W. H. Liggett, 3; *Daily Worker*, 17 April 1952, 1; 13 June 1952, 1; *Shanghai News*, 5 January 1952, 1, 4.

[99] NAA , Part 6, AI9/K/BRIT/5, Tpr A. E. Surridge, 2; see also e.g. Part 3, AI9/K/BRIT/294, Rfn J. C. Burton, 1.

[100] Ibid. Part 7, AI9/K/BRIT/305, Fus. W. Whiting, 3.

[101] Ibid. Part 4, AI9/K/BRIT/85, Pte J. Heslop, 2; see e.g. ibid. AI9/K/BRIT/312, Rfn R. Green, 3; ibid. AI9/K/BRIT/300, Tpr C. H. Holland, 3; Part 5, AI9/K/BRIT/318, Pte K. Millward, 3.

[102] See e.g. IWMDS, 10250/2, E. Curd. On peer pressure see e.g. NAA, Part 5, AI9/K/BRIT/291, Rfn W. H. Liggett, 3.

warmonger—if he did not want peace then he must 'want war, which is a crime'—and threatened unspecified 'punishment' if he did not give in.[103] On another occasion the entire camp population was paraded and ordered to sign the Stockholm Peace Appeal on pain of a cut in rations.[104]

The other subject the Chinese authorities were very keen for prisoners to comment on was germ warfare. As a means of explaining the typhus and other disease epidemics that had spread among troops and civilians through the first winter of the war and putting pressure on the UN, the communists in 1952 began a propaganda campaign designed to convince the world that the United States was dropping germ bombs over North Korea.[105] To back up this claim a supposedly impartial but in fact carefully selected international panel of scientists along with a few Western communist or fellow-traveller newspapermen were allowed to inspect pieces of physical evidence and publish reports confirming its truth. Meanwhile seventy-eight shot-down Americans were continuously harassed and tortured until thirty-eight of them 'confessed' to their role in this dastardly affair.[106]

To judge by the great effort made to convince the rest of the prisoner population through photographs, pamphlets, and filmed interviews with, or supervised talks in person by, pilots repeating their confessions, the Chinese hoped that large numbers would sign a petition protesting the use of this inhumane and indiscriminate method of waging war.[107] In the case of the British the camp authorities could also hope to play on their already evident anti-Americanism in order to both obtain signatures and increase disharmony between national contingents. Most of the progressives, naturally enough, tended to take everything at face value, and indeed two of them went on to read out a pamphlet on the subject to their fellow prisoners.[108] Some of the latter refused to sign anything either because they were uninterested—which was apparently quite common[109]—or due to a natural suspicion that the Chinese could not be trusted.[110] Others, though, were not entirely sure that it

[103] NAA, Part 3, AI9/K/BRIT/106, Rfn B. C. Canavan, 2.

[104] Ibid. Part 3, AI9/K/BRIT/131 et al., Rfn R. Dodd et al., 3.

[105] Milton Leitenburg, 'False Allegations of U.S. Biological Weapons Use during the Korean War' in Anne L. Clunan, Peter R. Lavoy, and Susan B. Martin (eds), _Terrorism, War or Disease?_ (Stanford, 2008), ch. 6; Albert E. Cowdry, '"Germ Warfare" and Public Health in the Korean Conflict', _Journal of the History of Medicine and Allied Sciences_, 39 (1984), 153–72. On the propaganda associated with this campaign see e.g. LHASC, CP/CENT/PEA/02/08.

[106] On the extraction of confessions from American aircrew see Lech, _Broken Soldiers_, 162 ff.; Department of the Army, _U.S. Prisoners of War_, ch. 8; see also e.g. Walker 'Bud' Mahurin, _Honest John_ (London, 1962), 203 ff.; Roland W. Parks in Robert E. Davis _Ex-POWs of Alabama_ (Montgomery, Al., 1984), 455–8; NARA, RG 38, entry 1015 (a), Case files of POWs—Korean War, box 7, Phase II Questionnaire question 17 response, Roy H. Bley; box 38, Frank H. Schwable file.

[107] On the petition see Adams, _An American Dream_, 58.

[108] Two of the Royal Marines, Andy Condron and George Richards, were said to have lectured on the subject of germ warfare: see NAA, Part 5, AI9/K/BRIT/8, Rfn J. N. McNally, 5. On other progressives believing germ warfare claims see e.g. IWMDS, 9693/9, A. Condron; NAA, Part 3, AI9/K/BRIT/86, Gnr J. Arnall, 3–4; ibid. AI9/K/BRIT/293, Rfn K. Clarke, 3; Part 5, AI9/K/BRIT/290, Rfn F. Moxam, 2; Part 6, AI9/K/BRIT/304, Cpl G. R. Richards, 4.

[109] See ibid. Part 3, AI9/K/BRIT/93, Pte D. Ackroyd, 2.

[110] See e.g. ibid. AI9/K/BRIT/95 et al., Rfn R. Cartlidge et al., 4; IWMDS, 10749/7, R. Erricker.

was all a hoax, while there were those who signed on simply because it was made clear that a good meal awaited those willing to agree.[111]

At the end of 1951 the armistice talks at Panmunjom turned to the question of prisoners of war and official lists were exchanged. In contrast to the figure of over 65,000 captives reported over the radio and in news releases the official communist list contained fewer than 12,000 names, leading to renewed fears on the UN side about how captives had been and were still being treated.[112] It was therefore necessary, given the ongoing refusal to allow in the International Red Cross, for the Chinese to try and convince the world that all was well in the POW camps.

Conditions in Camp 5 had in fact already begun gradually to get better in the wake of the Chinese takeover from the North Koreans and the truce talks starting, and continued to do so in the following months and years.[113] Sanitation was improved not only through instituting proper latrine arrangements but also, in 1952, by the issue of toothbrushes, razors, and soap; the building of a bathhouse and—eventually—bunks; and major efforts to get rid of pests such as flies, lice, and bedbugs.[114] Medical arrangements that year, though still very primitive by Western standards, also showed signs of improvement, including compulsory disease inoculations—the camp authorities really did believe that the Americans were engaging in germ warfare—and the arrival of an X-ray machine.[115] In addition the increasingly ragged uniforms of the prisoners, supplemented only under the North Koreans by a blanket and greatcoat, were replaced in the summer of 1951 with blue cotton uniforms, complete with underwear, worker cap, and rubber-soled black canvas shoes.[116] For the next two winters cotton quilted and padded uniforms were passed out along with padded canvas-and-rubber boots, padded gloves, coats, a cap with earflaps, and a padded cotton bed-quilt.[117]

Religious services were allowed during the second Christmas of the war and, in the wake of the abandonment of compulsory education, the question of recreation began to be addressed. The prisoners were allowed to make a sports ground on

[111] On agreeing to sign in order to get a good meal see IWMDS, 10250/3, E. Curd. On uncertainty about the germ warfare claims see e.g. NAA, Part 3, AI9/K/BRIT/89, L/Cpl A. Buxton, 3; ibid. AI9/K/BRIT/95 et al., Rfn R. Cartlidge et al., 4; Part 4, AI9/K/BRIT/85, Pte J. Heslop, 2.

[112] See Walter G. Hermes, *United States Army in the Korean War: Truce Tent and Fighting Front* (Washington, DC, 1966), 141–2.

[113] See IWMDD, E. Beckerley, 35; IWMDS, 13711/2, J. Underwood; NAA, Part 3, AI9/K/BRIT/86, Gnr J. Arnall, 3; ibid. AI9/K/BRIT/95 et al., Rfn R. Cartlidge et al., 3.

[114] Sidney Esensten, 'Memories of Life as a POW 35 Years Later', Part III, *The Greybeards*, 12(1) (1998), 37. On anti-pest efforts see IWMDD, J. Shaw diary, 30 March–6 April 1952; IWMDS, 10250/4, E. Curd; 10749/5–6, R. Erricker; NAA, Part 3, AI9/K/BRIT/285, Pte M. J. Ambrose, 2. On the bathhouse, razors, soap, and bunks see IWMDS, 10749/5–6, R. Erricker; IWMDD, J. Shaw diary, 8–15 June 1952. On toothbrushes see NAA, Part 3, AI9/K/BRIT/293, Rfn K. Clarke, 2.

[115] On the X-ray machine see NAA, Part 5, AI9/K/BRIT/98, L/Cpl W. Massey, 3; IWMDS, 24610/10, B. Guess. On the inoculations see NAA, Part 3, Pte M. J. Ambrose, 2; ibid. AI9/K/BRIT/89, L/Cpl A. W. Buxton, 3; ibid. AI9/K/BRIT/95 et al., Rfn R. Cartlidge et al., 4. On the extremely limited medical support of the first months see e.g. IWMDS, 10749/4, R. Erricker.

[116] IWMDS, 10749/5, R. Erricker. New issues were made the following summer. See IWMDD, J. Shaw diary, 20–27 April 1952. On the Korean issue see NAA, Part 3, AI9/K/BRIT/293, Rfn K. Clarke, 2.

[117] IWMDD, E. Beckerley, 30–1.

which the British could play football.[118] Boxing gloves, skipping ropes, and various other exercise implements were also provided, and during the summer prisoners could swim in the river.[119] They were also on occasion allowed to put on theatrical performances and do Dick-Barton-type radio plays over the camp public address system, though scripts had to first pass a rigorous censorship.[120]

For relaxation beyond reading, decks of cards and chess sets were manufactured and dancing to musical accompaniment allowed.[121] A limited amount of tobacco could be obtained from the Chinese. In addition, the Turks and the Hispanic US Army prisoners discovered marijuana plants growing wild on the mountainsides when out on wood-foraging expeditions, and at least some of the British took up the habit of smoking the dried leaves. This was frowned on by some of the camp staff, but others apparently turned a blind eye. 'They used to call it the giggling weed,' an 8th Hussars trooper recalled of those who indulged, 'because there was a lot of laughter and silly nonsense.'[122]

The Chinese themselves in 1952 also brought in touring drama groups which put on plays, as well as dance and music performances that 'were strongly laced with the party line'.[123] Particularly memorable at the end of the year was a lengthy revolutionary opera entitled *The White Haired Girl*, which dealt with the horrors endured by the daughter of a peasant at the hands of a rapacious landowner. It was a sign of how comparatively docile the inmates of Camp 5 had become that, despite the alien tonal scale, there were those who watched *The White Haired Girl* not once but twice. 'It was something one didn't know about', Bob Erricker later explained. 'So off you went to see it.'[124]

Most important of all, the rations slowly improved. Sorghum, millet, and soy beans were still staples, and vitamin deficiencies continued to produce problems such as night blindness.[125] But edible greens (along with winter firewood) were collected from the surrounding mountainsides, and eventually a few scrawny pigs arrived, thus allowing for a very limited distribution of pork. There was also a small sugar and tea ration and the occasional chicken, egg, or onion, plus a more common rice issue or flour which could be made into dumplings. Condron, according to various sources, was responsible for obtaining potatoes—which the Chinese considered cattle feed—for the British company instead of rice. In combination with better sanitation, improved and more varied rations helped to drive down the

---

[118] IWMDS, 10250/3, E. Curd; see e.g. IWMDD, J. Shaw diary, 23–30 March 1952; IWMDS, 10749/6, R. Erricker. On the Chinese allowing Christmas 1951 to be celebrated as a religious event see Lankford, *I Defy!*, 37–8.

[119] IWMDD, J. Shaw diary, 27 April–4 May, 11–18 May 1952.

[120] IWMDS, 9859/5, G. Richards; E. Beckerley, 35 ff.; NAA, Part 7, AI9/K/BRIT/305, Fus. W. Whiting, 3. The consequences of evading censorship were evident when, after a Christmas celebration skit in 1952 in which an American made an impromptu joke about germ warfare, the author was arrested. Part 3, AI9/K/CDN/25, Gnr O. J. Jenkins, 3.

[121] See IWMDD, J. Shaw diary, 13–20 July, 3–10 August, 7–14 September, 21–28 December 1952.

[122] IWMDS, 10749/6, R. Erricker; see ibid. 09972/4, J. Arnall.

[123] NAA, Part 7, AI9/K/BRIT/305, Fus. W. Whiting, 3.

[124] IWMDS, 10749/7, R. Erricker.

[125] See IWMDS, 10250/2, E. Curd; 09972/3, J. Arnall.

death rate among UN prisoners significantly.[126] By the last two summers there were three meals a day instead of two, and holidays were celebrated with extra food and even a little local alcohol. 'The change in our food was truly remarkable', as Ted Beckerley put it, though hunger always remained.[127]

With arguments heating up over the winter of 1951–2 at Panmunjom over the treatment of POWs it was necessary for the Chinese not only to sharply reduce the death rate by improving conditions but also provide credible evidence that all was well along the Yalu. Letters, broadcasts and petitions might be dismissed as having been made under captor pressure. Staged propaganda films had been made and photos taken already to show how well UN wounded were being cared for, but these had the disadvantage in the non-communist world of having been made by the captors themselves.[128]

One means of getting round this credibility problem was to take up a suggestion by the Associated Press (AP) conveyed by the fellow-traveller journalist Wilfred Burchett and Alan Winnington of the *Daily Worker* at the truce talks to allow through a camera for Frank Noel, an American AP photo-journalist held at Pyoktong, to take photographs confirming communist claims of good treatment of prisoners.[129] Needless to say, Noel was only ever allowed to send out pictures and text that upheld the party line that the captives were entirely happy with how they were being looked after. Rifleman J. J. Buckley, who somehow seems to have gained access to a camera and taken pictures of the mass grave outside the camp known as boot hill, was betrayed and accused of being an enemy agent, after which he was so badly beaten that he lost the power of speech.[130]

Another approach was to have a few communists and fellow-travellers from the West pay visits to and lecture at the camps in 1952 under carefully controlled conditions and then allow them to take photographs and write about how well the Chinese were treating their UN captives. As it happened three of the four sympathizers who made the trek to North Korea via China were British. Fellow-traveller Monica Felton made several trips as a representative of the National Assembly of

---

[126] On the decline in the death rate see Jeffrey Grey, 'Other Fronts: Resistance, Collaboration and Survival Among United Nations Prisoners During the Korean War' in Peter Dennis and Jeffrey Grey (eds), *The Korean War* (Canberra, 2000), 145.

[127] IWMDD, E. Beckerley, 34; see IWMDS, 9859/5, G. Richards; 24610/10, B. Guess; 10250/2–3, E. Curd; 10749/5–6, R. Erricker; NAA, Part 4, AI9/K/BRIT/292, Rfn W. Heaney, 2; Part 6, AI9/K/BRIT/545, Fus. W. Reed, 4; Part 3, AI9/K/BRIT/285, Pte M. J. Ambrose, 2. On Condron's role as go-between see IWMDS, 09972/4, J. Arnall; E. Curd 10250/3–4; 10749/5, R. Erricker. On hunger see e.g. ibid. 19047/4, F. Brodie.

[128] On staged photos see NAM 1989-05-163-1, R. Bruford-Davies; see also e.g. *Daily Worker*, 23 November 1951, 2; 18 December 1951, 2; 19 December 1951, 1; 17 April 1952, 1; *Shanghai News*, 9 January 1952, 3. On staged films showing good medical treatment see NAA, Part 3, AI9/K/BRIT/322 et al., Rfn J. Bergin et al., 3. At one point a group of men were used as extras in a film showing a Chinese attack on some bunkers (Part 3, AI9/K/CDN/25, Gnr O. J. Jenkins, 6).

[129] See Tibor Méray, *On Burchett*, tr. Mátyás Sárközi (Kallista, Vic., 2008), 70; Edward Hunter, *Brainwashing* (New York, 1956), 129.

[130] Cunningham, *No Mercy, No Leniency*, 72. On Buckley taking pictures of the graves see NAA, Part 3, AI9/K/BRIT/531 et al., Cpl H. Aitken et al., 7. On Noel's pictures see Robert J. Dvorchak, *Battle for Korea* (Cambridge, Mass., 2003), 127; W. Funchess in Spiller, *American POWs in Korea*, 57; see also e.g. *Daily Worker*, 4 March 1952, 3, 1 October 1952, 3; *Shanghai News*, 15 June 1952, 2, 4.

Women, CPGB activist Jack Gaster went as part of a communist-sponsored International Association of Democratic Lawyers group investigating germ warfare claims, and party member Alan Winnington travelled as correspondent of the *Daily Worker*. The fourth visitor was Wilfred Burchett, an Australian fellow-traveller correspondent then working for the left-wing French newspaper *Ce Soir*. Burchett, like Winnington, had been travelling in China before arriving in Korea from the north to cover the armistice talks. Interaction between these visitors and the inmates of Camp 5 generally took the form of lectures followed by more intimate discussions, often over special meals, with groups of progressives or individuals; which, along with staged outdoor scenes of contented men relaxing and at play, could be photographed.[131]

The response among the prisoners to such events was mixed. Patriots were, as Gunner G. H. May put it, 'disgusted' that people like Felton and Winnington were collaborating with the enemy.[132] Monica Felton did not meet with a particularly positive reception among the British contingent as a whole. 'When she walked through the British compound', an American prisoner observed, 'the British prisoners yelled so many things the Chinese had to march her quickly though.'[133] With the progressives she was more popular—'agreeable', Ted Beckerley remembered, 'she was from home, she brought news from home'.[134] For those considered reactionaries by the Chinese at Pyoktong it was galling some months afterward to read in the communist press how Felton 'had visited the prison camps and seen how well we were being treated'.[135] Gaster also left a largely negative impression by saying, as Rifleman John Shaw put it, 'how wonderfully the Chinese were treating [us] and all that sort of crap'.[136] Corporal T. B. McHaffey argued that his visit 'did more harm than good as far as Communism is concerned', as Gaster 'proved himself to be unreliable' in the information he passed on to prisoners and seemed to be intent on lowering their morale.[137]

As for Alan Winnington, a sympathetic observer recalled decades later in an interview how, when the journalist first came to talk to the assembled British and American prisoners in the theatre about world affairs, he:

> got on the stage, and he says, 'I'm Alan Winnington of the London *Daily Worker*.' Well there was such a howl went up, 'blackguard' and 'traitor', and God knows what

[131] NAA, Part 3, AI9/K/BRIT/531 et al., Cpl H. Aitken et al., 7; ibid. AI9/K/BRIT/93, Pte D. Ackroyd, 2; Part 4, AI9/K/BRIT/85, Pte J. Heslop, 2; Part 5, AI9/K/BRIT/290, Rfn F. Moxham, 2; IWMDS, 10749/7, R. Erricker; NARA, RG 319, entry 85, Phase III summaries, box 1032, Booker T. Johnson, 2; box 1034, Edwin R. Meyers, 2; see *Daily Worker*, 12 August 1952, 1; 13 August 1952, 3; 15 August 1952, 3; 19 August 1952, 3; 20 August 1952, 3.
[132] NAA, Part 3, AI9/K/BRIT/135, Gnr G. H. May, 2. Others, not interested in politics, were simply bored by their speeches: see e.g. ibid. AI9/K/BRIT/97, Pte D. Kennedy, 2.
[133] Bassett and Carlson, *And the Wind Blew Cold*, 66; see IWMDS, 09972/4, J. Arnall; 10749/7, R. Erricker; NAA, Part 6, AI9/K/BRIT/137, Cpl P. J. Roots, 3.
[134] IWMDS, 10982/6, E. Beckerley. On Felton's version of this visit to Camp 5 see *Daily Worker*, 2 October 1952, 2.
[135] Pate in Cutler, *Reactionary!*, 65; see e.g. *Daily Worker*, 2 October 1952, 2.
[136] IWMDS, 20299/3, J. Shaw.
[137] NAA, Part 3, AI9/K/BRIT/31 et al., Rfn R. Dodd et al., 4.

they were shouting and staring at him. And he let 'em all calm down, and spoke to them men for about an hour and a half. And whatever he said on that platform, no-one could disagree with him. Because everyone in that hall had known and experienced those things [working-class exploitation] at home or in the war [of 1939–45]…And they cheered him off that stage when he'd finished.[138]

'Most of the British-POWs in the early nineteen-fifties were depression children raised in radical, Labour and trade union traditions', Winnington argued in his memoirs. 'Class politics was normal and many of them knew Communists personally.'[139]

It was certainly true that Winnington won over some prisoners, including an otherwise politically unaffected lance corporal in the Ulsters who believed that a complaint he made to the journalist about not receiving letters directly led to the regular arrival of mail from his loved ones in 1953.[140] But it is worth noting that the working-class Scot, Marine Andy Condron, despite—or perhaps because of—being the leading progressive at Camp 5, had distinctly mixed feelings about this representative of the CPGB:

The first time he came to the camp I didn't like him much. I hadn't spoken to him, I didn't like what I saw. He struck me as being a very arrogant person. He was much better dressed, certainly, than we were—he had a Chinese uniform on and a fur hat and what not [this was early in the year[141]]. When I first spoke to him my initial impressions of him being arrogant and so on were increased.…Winnington had this kind of air of being a very superior Englishman, which I didn't like.

Condron did concede, however, that complaints to Winnington about mail delivery and recreational needs seemed to produce results.[142]

Winnington would soon collaborate with Wilfred Burchett on a pair of pamphlets condemning UN treatment of communist prisoners,[143] but Burchett, the down-to-earth Australian newspaperman, was more to Condron's taste and that of other progressives ('we liked Burchett very much' commented Ted Beckerley[144]), though for the more reactionary types such as John Shaw 'we just knew [what he was saying] was a load of rubbish'.[145] Burchett too produced pro-Chinese propaganda that eventually made its way back to the camps themselves. 'Every article I saw heaped praise on the Chinese and North Koreans for the excellent treatment of POWs under their control', one bitter American who had spent many months at Camp 5 wrote. 'Sometimes the articles were accompanied by photos showing

[138] IWMDS, 09972/4, J. Arnall.

[139] Winnington, *Breakfast with Mao*, 162.

[140] NAA, Part 5, AI9/K/BRIT/98, L/Cpl W. Massey, 2; see IWMDS, 10982/6, E. Beckerley.

[141] NAA, Part 3, AI9/K/CDN/25, Gnr O. J. Jenkins.

[142] IWMDS, 9693/7, A. Condron. Winnington also struck others as rather a cold fish. See Méray, *On Burchett*, 21.

[143] Alan Winnington and Wilfred Burchett, *Plain Perfidy* (London, 1954); Wilfred Burchett and Alan Winnington, *Koje Unscreened* (London, 1953).

[144] IWMDS, 10982/6, E. Beckerley; see ibid. 9693/7, A. Condron; SLV, MS 10254, Wilfred G. Burchett Papers, box 4.9, Condron to Whom It May Concern, 3 February 1969; see also Méray, *On Burchett*, 21.

[145] IWMDS, 20299/3, J. Shaw.

POWs engaged in sports, in excellent living quarters, or eating a hearty meal. It was all a bunch of crap.'[146]

The largest single effort to show the outside world that all was well, with which many prisoners at Pyoktong cooperated with enthusiasm, involved staging a POW inter-camp 'Olympic Games' held over two weeks in the autumn of 1952: 'that went down very well', according to Bob Erricker, who noted that it gave prisoners from various places a chance to mingle and swap stories.[147] It also gave the Chinese the opportunity to take large numbers of still photographs and moving images that gave a totally false impression of vigorous good health in the Yalu camps that could be exploited in English-language propaganda publications such as *'United Nations' POW's in Korea* put out by the Chinese People's Committee for World Peace the following year.[148] It is a measure of how potent the film footage was that over fifty years later it was being used in a Canadian-financed documentary to demonstrate how well the UN prisoner population was being treated: 'When I came across this film archive,' Chinese filmmaker Shui-Bo Wang noted without a trace of irony, 'I could not believe my eyes.'[149]

It is important to note that even after most of the overt troublemakers were removed few of the inhabitants of Pyoktong saw themselves as slavish tools of the Chinese. Even among the progressives there was tendency to look down on the ordinary peasant guards and the more owlish instructors. 'There was always the feeling that we were in some way superior to them', Condron later reflected, and ragging—talking only in broad regional dialects that the Chinese could not make out, pretending not to understand orders issued in pidgin English or teaching guards the wrong words for things[150]—went on 'all the time'.[151] The story of how the question 'What is the highest form of class struggle?' from an instructor had brought forth the answer 'Travelling first class with a third class ticket' became part of Camp 5 folklore.[152] This sort of thing, though, was hardly a threat to the Chinese agenda.

The degree of control exercised by the Chinese at Camp 5 was reflected in the intertwined issues of escape and informing. Getting out of Pyoktong was easy—there was only a strand or two of barbed wire separating the camp from the rest of the village—but thereafter apparently insuperable problems presented themselves. Immediately to the north lay communist China, while to the south, once the front stabilized in the summer of 1951, the nearest UN troops were around 200 miles

---

[146] William H. Funchess, *Korea POW* (Clemson, SC, 1997), 116. On the tenor of Burchett's supremely rosy version of life for UN prisoners see Wilfred G. Burchett, *This Monstrous War* (Melbourne, 1953), 300–2; *Shanghai News*, 20 May 1952, 3; 23 May 1952, 3.

[147] IWMDS, 10749/6, R. Erricker.

[148] *'United Nations' POW's in Korea* (Beijing, 1953), 73–81; see also e.g. *Daily Worker*, 23 April 1953, 3. On the communists using the camp Olympics as a propaganda exercise see e.g. NAM 1989-05-163-1, R. Bruford-Davies.

[149] *They Chose China* (National Film Board of Canada, 2005). To judge by the response on the NFB website, viewers also accepted these images as accurate representations of camp conditions. <http://www.nfb.ca/film/they_chose_china> (accessed 7 December 2010).

[150] See e.g. IWMDS, 10250/3, E. Curd; Winnington, *Breakfast with Mao*, 160.

[151] IWMDS, 9693/6, A. Condron.

[152] Winnington, *Breakfast with Mao*, 161–2.

away as the crow flies. Potential escapers might think instead of aiming for the Yellow Sea, 75-odd miles to the west, in the hope of stealing a boat or constructing a raft from which they might be picked by roving friendly warships. Either way this meant an arduous journey on foot across very rugged terrain while trying at all times to avoid being spotted by the locals, as Caucasian features were a dead giveaway. 'I think most of us—well all of us in our camp—we pretty well accepted that we were prisoners of war', one semi-progressive commented, 'and that we were going to have to stay there.'[153] Even someone in other ways a reactionary had to admit that 'we didn't bother escaping'.[154]

In fact there were a few escape attempts from Pyoktong, but only a handful of men got out and nobody remained at large for very long before being brought back, sometimes showing signs of having been beaten, to publicly 'confess' in front of the assembled prisoners how wrong they had been to misbehave in such a way.[155] Even more problematic than the challenges beyond the confines of the camp and the likelihood of punishment if caught for those few who were not deterred were the severe difficulties in preparing for a break within the camp itself. There is evidence to suggest that the Chinese persuaded dozens of British prisoners to become secret informers on their fellows either through physical coercion, blackmail (threatening to let the other side know just how much they had revealed in interrogation or about documents that they signed which had not yet been released but were potentially quite compromising), or promises of better treatment.[156] Thus on those comparatively rare occasions when two or three men decided that they would try and defy the odds and make a break during the summer months they were consistently betrayed. As Captain G. L. N. Langworthy wrote after interviewing a group of eight RUR repatriates from Camp 5, 'every time anyone planned to make an escape and started to collect food, someone in the camp always informed the Chinese'.[157] It was perhaps telling that another AI9 interrogating officer, Captain R. B. Trant, noted that while there were many complaints about 'squealers' among men returning from Pyoktong, the inmates 'do not appear to have over excited themselves in their efforts to pin point them'.[158]

As AI9 eventually calculated, 92 per cent of the British at Pyoktong had participated in enemy propaganda activities to a greater or lesser degree by March 1953.[159] When progress towards an armistice allowed for an exchange of sick and wounded

[153] IWMDS, 10982/6, E. Beckerley; see e.g. ibid. 09972/3, J. Arnall; 10250/3, E. Curd.

[154] Ibid. 20299/2, J. Shaw; see e.g. ibid. 19047/4, F. Brodie.

[155] See ibid. 19047/4, F. Brodie.

[156] On blackmail see NAA, Part 3, AI9/K/BRIT/320, Tpr R. A. Cocks, 6. On the suspected numbers of informants among the British see e.g. ibid. AI9/K/BRIT/531 et al., Cpl H. Aitken et al., 6. On physical coercion see Cunningham, *No Mercy, No Leniency*, 150. On cooperative prisoners receiving small treats such as tobacco see e.g. NAA, Part 3, AI9/K/BRIT/135, Gnr G. H. May, 2.

[157] Ibid. AI9/K/BRIT/95 et al., Rfn R. Cartlidge et al., 6; see ibid. AI9/K/BRIT/89, L/Cpl A. W. Buxton, 3; ibid. AI9/K/BRIT/131 et al., Rfn R. Dodd et al., 6 *re* Cpl T. B. McHaffey; Part 4, AI9/K/BRIT/497, Rfn E. English, 3; ibid. AI9/K/BRIT/96, Rfn F. Harper, 2; Part 5, AI9/K/BRIT/291, Rfn W. H. Liggett, 3.

[158] Ibid. Part 4, AI9/K/BRIT/96, Rfn F. Harper, 2.

[159] Cunningham *No Mercy, No Leniency*, 74.

the following month and the Chinese took the opportunity to include as many progressives as they could to convince the world that they were treating UN prisoners well, almost a third of the Britons came from Pyoktong—and all of them were judged by British Intelligence to be security risks.[160] Four months after that, while everyone else went home after the armistice was signed (the announcement of which generated the shouts and cheers in some quarters that the camp authorities expected[161]), Andy Condron chose to stay with the communists.[162] It was therefore not surprising that a Top Secret report submitted by AI9 dubbed Pyoktong 'the most progressive camp throughout the whole war'.[163]

This, though, was only true in reference to the places run by the Chinese. Even after they had ceded control of the Yalu camps to their allies, the North Koreans still controlled various facilities in the region of Pyongyang in which often brutal efforts were made not only to extract military information but also force American and British captives to become propaganda tools. If there was a location where POW collaboration was most concentrated, it was Camp 12—the so-called Peace Fighters' School.

---

[160] NAA, Part 1, App A to AI9(a)/S/150/87, 8 May 1953; ibid. App A to AI9(a)/S/150/87, 12 May 1953.

[161] Derek Kinne, *The Wooden Boxes* (London, 1955), 184; though see IWMDS, 20299/3, J. Shaw.

[162] On Condron see S. P. MacKenzie, 'The Individualist Collaborator: Andy Condron in Korea and China, 1950–62', *War & Society*, 30 (2011), 147–65.

[163] TNA, WO 208/4012, Report on the success of Communist indoctrination among British PW in North Korea, with particular reference to after effects on their return to the UK, 23 October 1953, 4. Some of the returning Americans also remembered some of the British in Camp 5 being notably pro-communist: see NARA, RG 38, entry 1015 (a), box 32, Phase II Questionnaire, question 46a, William R. Petit; box 40, Willie C. Stewart.

4

Peace Fighters and Others in Pyongyang

There's no way we're surviving this place [Camp 9].
Rifleman George Hobson[1]

I know that the Peace Fight [in Camp 12] was wrong but I was unable to get away...

Sergeant Fred Andrews[2]

I must confess I was terrified [at the imminent prospect of torture].
Captain Tony Farrar-Hockley[3]

In the first half of 1951 the Chinese progressively assumed control from their allies of the camps along the Yalu. This did not mean, however, that the North Korean authorities relinquished all interest in captured UN personnel. For many months the Political Bureau of the North Korean People's Army sought to maintain control of POW propaganda, and throughout the war military intelligence officials and representatives of the state security police harshly interrogated those prisoners who fell into their hands. The North Koreans, moreover, did not always pass over captives to their allies if they were not already in the main camps, and made sure that their greatest prize, Major General William F. Dean, taken prisoner in the first months of the war while leading the US 24th Infantry Division, was never handed over to the Chinese.[4]

As early as July 1950 the political bureau had put pressure on individual prisoners to sign petitions and make broadcasts condemning the war, which a number of US Army personnel agreed to in the hope of letting their families know they were alive or because they were threatened with torture or death.[5] It was only at the start

---

[1] IWMDS, 16853/3, G. Hobson.

[2] NAA, Part 3, AI9/K/BRIT/845, Sgt F. Andrews, 2; see <http://www.koreanwar-educator.org/memoirs/jaunal_jack/index.htm> (accessed 11 January 2011).

[3] IWMDS, 30102/2, A. Farrar-Hockley.

[4] See William F. Dean as told to William L. Worden, *General Dean's Story* (New York, 1954). On the North Korean organizations involved with POW matters see Cyril Cunningham, *No Mercy, No Leniency: Communist Mistreatment of British Prisoners of War in Korea* (Barnsley, 2000), 10–11. On the groups of British prisoners not being used for propaganda or interrogation purposes but rather for slave labour, see ibid. 22.

[5] See Department of the Army, *U.S. Prisoners of War in the Korean Operation* (Fort Meade, Md., 1954), 512; Department of the Army, *Communist Interrogation, Indoctrination, and Exploitation of Prisoners of War* (Washington, DC, 1956), 19. Even General Dean, who otherwise resisted all North Korean efforts to get him to broadcast and sign petitions, agreed to write a letter to the commander of the 8th Army urging him to stop the USAF from attacking non-military targets. Dean in Worden, *General Dean's Story*, 130–1.

of the following year, however, that a concerted effort was made to create a specific cadre of prisoners whose task would be to produce anti-UN propaganda. At the end of January 1951, the second-in-command of the bureau, Colonel Kim Dong Suk, gathered up a diverse group of twenty tired and weak Americans from Pyoktong whom he thought could be influenced and took them to Pyongyang, where they became the nucleus of the so-called Peace Fighters' School, otherwise known as Camp 12. Moved around the capital until ensconced in a battered school building on the north bank of the Taedong River, this party would soon be joined by groups of captives from other locations, until by the summer the camp population numbered just under eighty officers and men. Those selected endured a harsh regime in which communist indoctrination was mixed with demands—usually accepted to at least some degree through the efforts of the elected leader, Lieutenant Colonel Harry Fleming, to keep everyone alive—for signed petitions and broadcast recordings backed up by far-from-idle threats to cut already meagre rations or consign recalcitrant captives to the nearby Kandong Caves.[6]

Camp 9, the official designation of the prisoner facility at Kandong, consisted of a few huts and nine deep, dark, and dank tunnels dug deep into a hillside. There was massive overcrowding, no light, almost no heat, no sanitation or proper medical treatment, and UN prisoners often received less than their daily ration of two bowls of cracked corn or millet due to the fact that South Korean captives were in charge of distribution and kept more than their fair share. Not surprisingly prisoners incarcerated in this infamous place for any length of time, whether permanently (in the case of South Koreans) or while theoretically in transit (in the case of UN captives) did not survive long. A group of fourteen newly captured GIs were deliberately starved to death there in order to encourage Fleming to accept the demands of Colonel Kim at Camp 12, and in all several hundred American and other UN prisoners, along with an unknown number of Koreans, died in the caves.[7]

Soon after Colonel Kim had brought the first twenty American 'peace fighters' to Pyongyang he visited the transit camps outside the capital in search of British recruits in order to give his school a more international flavour. His invitation to join the other peace fighters having been spurned by the two groups of men he spoke to, Kim simply selected sixteen British captives—one officer, five sergeants, and ten other ranks—whom he wished to work on and sent them under guard to Pyongyang. The officer, Lieutenant A. H. C. 'Spud' Gibbon of the Royal Artillery, had told Kim to his face what he could do with his offer, so presumably was included either because there was no other British officer available or in the expectation that he could be broken. The colonel had more opportunity to pick and choose among the remaining captives in the transit camps, and, as a result of consulting the personal intelligence already gathered by the Chinese, was able to

    [6] Raymond B. Lech, *Broken Soldiers* (Urbana, Il., 2000), ch. 5.
    [7] Lech, *Broken Soldiers*, 124–5; Cunningham, *No Mercy, No Leniency*, 29–30. On the overcrowding and limited rations see e.g. NAA, Part 3, AI9/K/BRIT/320, Tpr R. A. Cocks, 3; Part 7, AI9/K/BRIT/289, Cpl J. H. Taylor, 2.

include two card-carrying members of the CPGB, two members of the Young Communist League, and a pair of fellow-travellers.[8]

On arrival in the capital, they were assembled in a barrack hut together with ten further Americans and asked by Kim to join the fight for peace, the colonel promising better living standards and early release and reminding them of the poor conditions from which they had been rescued. Kim then made the mistake of asking Spud Gibbon what he thought. The artillery lieutenant stoutly replied: 'I am an English officer and couldn't do a thing like that.' Before being hustled away he warned the other British prisoners not to agree or engage in any propaganda activities.[9]

Some of them were then sent directly to Camp 12,[10] while others remained over the next couple of days to be interviewed by Michael Shapiro, a British communist from China writing for the London *Daily Worker* and the *Shanghai News* who was looking for quotable comments about the devastation caused by the American bombing of Pyongyang. Gibbon apparently called Shapiro a traitor to his face, Sergeant Laurence Kavanagh of the Ulsters threatened to wring his neck, and even Trooper Ronald Cocks of the 8th Hussars, himself a member of the CPGB, later claimed to have thought the journalist a disgrace to the Party. The negative response did not deter Shapiro from fabricating a completely false story about his encounter for the *Shanghai News*,[11] but nevertheless provided more evidence for Colonel Kim that a degree of coercion would be needed in order to get at least some of these men to volunteer to be peace fighters. This was necessary in part because some of those sent directly to Camp 12 were proving less cooperative than hoped.[12]

On 21 February the group that had met Shapiro was consigned to the Kandong Caves in order to demonstrate the alternative to cooperation. Gibbon started complaining about the inadequate food, and for his pains he and another troublemaker, Sergeant Frank Nugent of the Ulsters, were removed for interrogation. After a few weeks Kim returned and again invited prisoners to join the peace fighters. This time he had two takers, Cocks and a rifleman ill with beriberi.[13] The former, having thrown in his lot with the peace fighters—there is evidence to suggest that his conversation with Shapiro had been less confrontational than Cocks later claimed[14]—accompanied Kim on further trips to the caves in an effort to persuade others to join him. In the middle of April a further six British stragglers from the January fight found themselves in Camp 9, along with Sergeant W. P. O'Hara of the Ulsters who, after being sent to Camp 12, had refused to record messages for broadcast. After four days they were visited by Kim

---

[8] Cunningham, *No Mercy, No Leniency*, 26.

[9] Ibid. 30; NAA, Part 5, AI9/K/BRIT/999, Sgt W. P. O'Hara, 2.

[10] NAA, Part 5, AI9/K/BRIT/999, Sgt W. P. O'Hara, 2; see also Part 3, AI9/K/BRIT/845, Sgt F. Andrews; Part 4, AI9/K/BRIT/844, Rfn J. Hibbert; Part 6, AI9/K/BRIT/307, Rfn J. Stevenson.

[11] Cunningham, *No Mercy, No Leniency*, 31–2; NAA, Part 3, AI9/K/BRIT/320, Tpr R. A. Cocks, 2. On the encounter between Kavanagh and Shapiro see also TNA, WO 373/119, f. 323.

[12] See e.g. NAA, Part 5, AI9/K/BRIT/999, Sgt W. P. O'Hara.

[13] NAA, Part 3, AI9/K/BRIT/320, Tpr. R. A. Cocks, 5; Part 4, AI9/K/BRIT/288, Rfn. J. Horrobin, 2.

[14] See Cunningham, *No Mercy, No Leniency*, 31–2. Cocks himself admitted that when Kim approached him in Camp 9 about changing his mind, the colonel delivering a letter of persuasion penned by Shapiro. NAA, Part 3, AI9/K/BRIT/320, Tpr. R. A. Cocks, 5.

and Cocks, who explained that conditions in Camp 12 were much better. Corporal A. E. Campbell of the 8th Hussars had been wounded and suspected that he would not survive long in the caves, and so immediately agreed to go. RAMC Corporal J. H. Taylor along with Corporal P. F. Williams and Rifleman F. Moore from the Ulsters all initially refused, but soon changed their minds. Before they left Sergeant O'Hara warned them not to sign anything at Camp 12.[15]

In the end Kim with help from Cocks managed to persuade ten of the British captives in his hands to cooperate, which was understandable in view of the fact that few of the remainder survived the war.[16] The same softening-up approach was taken a couple of months later after the largest single batch of British prisoners fell into communist hands (see chapter five). In May 1951 a party of sixteen or so fit and not-so-fit captives, having been handed over by the Chinese to the North Korean police during the march northward toward the Yalu, were sent to the Kandong Caves where, as Rifleman George Hobson explained after his eventual release, conditions 'were below a level necessary to sustain life'.[17] After a period of starvation rations and practically no medical attention in overcrowded, dark, and dank conditions the men were visited by Colonel Kim, who invited them to join the peace fighters in Camp 12 where living conditions and medical provision were much better. The only British officer in the caves at this point was Second Lieutenant Terry Waters, who, like everyone else, could see that the group's chances of survival were diminishing by the day and therefore ordered those whom Kim would accept to go and join the peace fighters. He himself, though suffering from a largely unattended head wound that would soon prove fatal in the appalling conditions in the caves, refused to accompany Kim. 'I don't think I can go Sgt. Hoper', the senior NCO present remembered him saying, 'I believe I know the reason for this camp [12], but it is better for the men to go than to remain in this death hole.' Only those able to walk were allowed out.[18] Waters was posthumously awarded the George Cross.[19]

Living conditions in Camp 12 were indeed a considerable step up from Camp 9. Haircuts and clean clothing were provided, along with soap, a towel, and a toothbrush, and there were three meals a day.[20] There was no fence, no guards

[15] NAA, Part 5, AI9/K/BRIT/308, Rfn F. Moore, 2; ibid. AI9/K/BRIT/999, Sgt W. P. O'Hara, 5; see also Part 7, AI9/K/BRIT/289, Cpl J. H. Taylor, 2. A few wounded men, it should be noted, also passed through Camp 9 around this time, some apparently for only a day or so (see Part 3, AI9/K/BRIT/811, 816, Bdr L. Bristow and Gnr R. Thompson, 2), others for far longer (see ibid. AI9/K/BRIT/554, Rfn R. S. Clifford, 1–2).

[16] Cunningham, *No Mercy, No Leniency*, 32.

[17] NAA, Part 1, AI9(a)/S/150/7, Interrogation Report on British Ex-P.W. Released in Korea, Batch 1 (supplementary), 2.

[18] Ibid. Part 4, AI9/K/BRIT/1001, Sgt P. J. Hoper, 3–4; see ibid. AI9/K/BRIT/823, Fus. K. Fowler, 2; ibid. AI9/K/BRIT/9, Rfn G. L. Hobson, 2; Part 7, AI9/K/BRIT/895, Pte A. G. W. Tremblett, 2; IWMDS, 16853/3, G. Hobson.

[19] Cunningham, *No Mercy, No Leniency*, 33; see Michael Ashcroft, *George Cross Heroes* (London, 2010), 247–9.

[20] See IWMDS, 16853/3, G. Hobson; NAA, Part 3, AI9/K/BRIT/287, Tpr S. Carr, 2; Part 4, AI9/K/BRIT/489, 4; ibid. AI9/K/BRIT/87, Fus. W. Ellis; Part 5, AI9/K/BRIT/999, Sgt W. P. O'Hara, 3; Part 7, AI9/K/BRIT/289, Cpl J. H. Taylor, 2.

beyond the camp staff, and the peace fighters could move around whichever local-
ity in the Pyongyang area they were in up to and including the final camp location
established in the spring of 1951.[21] There was of course a price that had to be paid
for this comparative largesse and freedom, as was quickly made clear by the North
Korean authorities.

In order to help the peace fighters understand the communist ideology and
terminology behind the kind of propaganda they would be required to produce for
foreign consumption, the peace fighters were required, under threat of being sent
to the caves, to attend two hours of compulsory lectures and discussions led by the
senior American officers based on a variety of communist works.[22] Most men
played along with this indoctrination on the principle that it did no harm to say
one thing and think another.[23] Nevertheless, and quite apart from those already
inclined towards Marxism-Leninism, the classes did influence some men and
induced the full-scale political conversion of at least one British soldier. A corporal
in the Glosters freely admitted after his eventual release that 'he first became interested [in communism] during the first compulsory lectures at Camp 12', and by
the time the camp closed he was 'keen on the subject'.[24]

One rifleman from the Ulsters along with a US Army Master Sergeant were
eventually sent to teach military and civilian students English at Kim Il-sung University,[25] and early on a group of about twenty, including three British prisoners,
were used as extras in a North Korean documentary film on the liberation of
Pyongyang.[26] The central purpose of the peace fighters in Camp 12 throughout
1951, however, remained to produce English-language propaganda for foreign
consumption. A mixture of questionable rationalizations, sleight of hand, small
rewards for good behaviour, and justified fear among the peace fighters usually
allowed Colonel Kim to get his way in the form of signed peace petitions and surrender appeals, along with letters to the press and radio broadcasts condemning
the war.

Perhaps not surprisingly in view of his party membership Trooper Cocks was the
most enthusiastic of the peace fighters, telling the senior American officer that he was
'in this all the way I tell you, all the way' and arguing that those who merely went
along with the programme were 'insincere' and 'not really behind the people's cause'.[27]

---

[21] See NAA, Part 6, AI9/K/BRIT/3, Rfn E. F. Spencer, 6; Part 4, AI9/K/BRIT/489, Cpl G. Elliott,
4; NARA, RG 319, entry 85, Phase III summaries, box 1025, Dwight E. Coxe, 22–3, 25.
[22] See NAA, Part 3, AI9/BRIT/298, L/Cpl A. E. Campbell, 2; ibid. AI9/K/BRIT/287, Tpr S. Carr,
3; Part 4, AI9/K/BRIT/489, Cpl G. Elliott, 6; ibid. AI9/K/BRIT/9, Rfn G. L. Hobson, 2; Part 6,
AI9/K/BRIT/137, Cpl P. J. Roots, 3.
[23] See NAA, Part 4, AI9/K/BRIT/87, Fus. W. Ellis, 2; ibid. AI9/K/BRIT/1001, Sgt P. J. Hoper, 3;
Part 7, AI9/K/BRIT/151, Cpl P. F. Williams, 2; Lech, *Broken Soldiers*, 120.
[24] NAA, Part 4, AI9/K/BRIT/489, Cpl G. Elliott, 7; see Part 7, AI9/K/BRIT/289, Cpl
J. H. Taylor, 3.
[25] Ibid. Part 4, AI9/K/BRIT/844, Rfn J. Hibbert, 2; see also Part 6, AI9/K/BRIT/3, Rfn
E. F. Spencer, 13.
[26] Ibid. Part 5, AI9/K/BRIT/999, Sgt W. P. O'Hara, 5.
[27] Lech, *Broken Soldiers*, 133; see e.g. NARA, RG 319, entry 85, Phase III summaries, box 1025,
Dwight E. Coxe, 23.

He made recordings for broadcasts, composed pamphlets calling on UN troops to surrender, and eventually was made vice-president of the communist-sponsored Central Peace Committee.[28] Cocks did recognize that what he was doing verged on the treasonous—'This one will really hang me', he was overheard to say laughingly of one surrender leaflet that he had composed[29]—which was a problem given that he wanted to return to the UK when the war was over. But he defended his behaviour then and later by arguing that by collaborating with the North Koreans he was saving the lives of men who otherwise would have died in the Kandong Caves and was able tone down some of the propaganda emanating from Camp 12.[30]

Though he took a leading role, especially among the British inmates of Camp 12, Cocks was far from alone in collaborating with the enemy. Though some men resisted to a greater or lesser degree,[31] almost everyone put their signature to something or recorded scripted messages for broadcast. Many had qualms about what they were doing, but Colonel Kim was adept at outwitting and coercing his charges. When asked to put their signature on documents to which strong objection was taken, for instance, prisoners could be persuaded to sign blank sheets of paper instead, those concerned either not realizing that the signatures would simply be copied onto the document or maintaining that as they had signed a blank paper they could not be held responsible for what was subsequently done with it.[32]

Treats such as peanuts or apples might follow cooperative action, and at various points it was hinted or suggested that cooperation would lead to early release.[33] More significantly, Colonel Kim made it clear that prolonged opposition would lead to a return to the Kandong Caves and likely death by starvation. As one British corporal later explained to an interrogator from military intelligence, 'it was surprising what an empty stomach would do', and the transfer of the stubborn Sergeant O'Hara back to Camp 9 was duly noted.[34]

British collaborators could also take solace from the fact that they were, at least in a manner of speaking, obeying orders. Those in the first batch sometimes managed to convince themselves that Lieutenant Gibbon had admonished them not to

---

[28] Cunningham, *No Mercy, No Leniency*, 35–9. Ronald Cocks also seems to have acted as an interrogator for the enemy on at least one occasion. See NAA, Part 3, AI9/K/BRIT/976, Lt R. Cooke, 2–3.

[29] Cunningham, *No Mercy, No Leniency*, 35–9; see also ibid. 139.

[30] NAA, Part 3, AI9/K/BRIT/320, Tpr R. A. Cocks, 5. Interestingly Cocks was not the only one to argue that he saved lives: see, ibid. AI9/K/BRIT/287, Tpr S. Carr, 3; Part 6, AI9/K/BRIT/3, Rfn E. F. Spencer, 10; Part 1, Interrogation Report on British Ex-P.W. Released in Korea, Batch 1 (Supplementary), 2.

[31] See e.g. ibid. Part 5, AI9/K/BRIT/308, Rfn F. Moore, 2; Part 6, AI9/K/AUST/490–491, Pte R. Parker and Pte D. P. Buck, 4.

[32] See e.g. ibid. Part 3, AI9/K/BRIT/320, Tpr R. A. Cocks, 5; Part 4, AI9/K/BRIT/288, Rfn J. Horrobin, 2; Part 5, AI9/K/BRIT/999, Sgt W. P. O'Hara, 3; Part 6, AI9/K/BRIT/307, Rfn J. Stevenson, 2; Part 7, AI9/K/BRIT/289, Cpl J. H. Taylor, 3.

[33] See ibid. Part 5, AI9/K/BRIT/999, Sgt W. P. O'Hara, 3; Cunningham, *No Mercy, No Leniency*, 40.

[34] NAA, Part 7, AI9/K/BRIT/289, Cpl J. H. Taylor, 3; see Part 4, AI9/K/BRIT/1001, Sgt P. J. Hoper, 3; Part 6, AI9/K/BRIT/3, Rfn. E. F. Spencer, 10; ibid. AI9/K/BRIT/307, Rfn J. Stevenson, 2; Part 1, Interrogation Report on British Ex-P.W. in Korea, Batch 1 (Supplementary), 1, 3.

give away military information rather than refuse to engage in political matters and that when warning against signing anything Sergeant O'Hara had meant actual documents rather than blank sheets of paper.[35] Some weeks later the survivors of the Imjin battle could perhaps argue that in allowing them to get out of the Caves while knowing the purpose of Camp 12, Lieutenant Waters had in effect acknowledged that sheer survival trumped political scruple.[36] More importantly, the only commissioned officer prisoners in Camp 12 were from the United States; and led by the senior man, Lieutenant Colonel Paul Liles, they all counselled a policy of outward cooperation with Colonel Kim and his staff. According to Corporal Taylor, the senior American officer told everyone 'to follow their captor's policy' and reassured them that 'if they were charged on return, he would take full responsibility for their actions'.[37]

Propaganda activity centering on Camp 12 reached its climax in the late spring of 1951 in the run-up to the start of armistice talks at Kaesong in July 1951. Peace committee delegates from the main camps as well as the peace fighters' school convened in Pyongyang; Trooper Cocks was elected vice-president of the central peace committee, and the first heavily choreographed meeting was held under a blaze of media attention from around the communist world at the end of June.[38] The tenor of the proceedings can be gathered from a speech made by Cocks as vice-president of what was dubbed the US-British War Prisoners Organization:

> It was not by accident that we became prisoners of war. We are prisoners because we came to Korea as tools to further the designs of the warmongers and capitalists, who foment wars for their own personal mercenary designs. Nor was it an accident that, after becoming prisoners of war, we as a group, learning the true facts behind the Korean War, became strongly imbued with the desire to form a peace fighter's organization and contribute our energies, small though they may be, in the fight for a peaceful and tranquil world. We therefore desire to band ourselves together to direct our fight as a collective group in the struggle against wars, which retard progress, destroy civilization and, if brazenly continued, will decimate all mankind.[39]

The inhabitants of other camps were kept informed of the work done at Camp 12 through a newspaper, *The Peace Fighters' Chronicle*, set up by Cocks with assistance

---

[35] Ibid. Part 5, AI9/K/BRIT/999, Sgt W. P. O'Hara, 3; Cunningham, *No Mercy, No Leniency*, 30–1.

[36] See NAA, Part 4, AI9/K/BRIT/9, Rfn G. L. Hobson, 2; ibid. AI9/K/BRIT/1001, Sgt P. J. Hoper, 3. George Hobson, who admitted that he had played along with the enemy and written some propaganda (see IWMDS, 16853/3, G. Hobson)—for which he was apparently rewarded by being sent home early in the first exchange of sick and wounded in the spring of 1953 despite being relatively fit (see NAA, Part 1, Appendix A to AI9(a)/S/150/87, 8 May 1953)—when questioned about the move from Camp 9 to Camp 12 either ignored the role of Lt Waters entirely (see ibid. Interrogation Report on British Ex-P.W. Released in Korea, Batch 1 (Supplementary), 2; IWMDS, 16853/3, G. Hobson) or stated that Waters had ordered the men to go to Camp 12 (NAA, Part 4, AI9/K/BRIT/9, Rfn G. L. Hobson, 2).

[37] NAA, Part 7, AI9/K/BRIT/289, Cpl J. H. Taylor, 4; see Part 5, AI9/K/BRIT/308, Rfn F. Moore, 2; Part 6, AI9/K/BRIT/307, Rfn J. Stevenson, 2; IWMDS, 16853/3, G. Hobson.

[38] See NAA, Part 4, AI9/K/BRIT/1001, Sgt P. J. Hoper, 3; Lech, *Broken Soldiers*, 139; NARA, RG 319, entry 85, Phase III summaries, box 1025, Dwight D. Coxe, 24–6.

[39] Cunningham, *No Mercy, No Leniency*, 39.

from Liles.[40] More significantly, in the wake of the first meeting of the US-British War Prisoners Organization, a 300-page report on the event under the title *Our Fight for Peace* was issued for foreign consumption to communist-front organizations such as the International Peace Congress meeting in Vienna.[41]

Despite all this effort, there were doubts in certain circles about the level of commitment among the bulk of the inhabitants of Camp 12. Many remained 'either apathetic to the peace fight', in the words of an enthusiastic British representative from Camp 5, 'or unwilling to give full assistance'.[42] It was reported that, though most could be coerced into ongoing propaganda activity of one sort or another through a mixture of carrot and stick, only half could be induced, often with a certain degree of sleight of hand, to endorse leaflets or read radio scripts calling outright for UN troops to surrender.[43] Indeed, though nothing came of it, certain American officers apparently talked in secret about such grossly 'reactionary' activities as murdering the overenthusiastic Cocks and staging a mass breakout.[44] To supplement the supposedly spontaneous but in fact carefully scripted and rather stiff radio panels designed to broadcast comments on various communist-inspired peace campaigns, the North Korean authorities introduced roundtable discussions of cultural subjects in the summer of 1951, the idea being to foster politically correct viewpoints indirectly in a way that the prisoners would not spot.[45]

Towards the end of the year it looked as if the peace fighters would shortly be going home. The truce talks, after being broken off in August, had resumed in October. Enough progress was made that month for members of the central peace committee to be told that the war would soon be over, a prediction reiterated in a speech to the rest of the peace fighters by a senior North Korean official, reputedly Kim Yong-ju, younger brother of Kim Il-sung.[46] Preparations were made to close Camp 12 and send the inhabitants to the Yalu camps where the Chinese would handle the handover of POWs; but immediately after this transfer occurred in December, the truce talks began to bog down over whether repatriation of POWs should be compulsory or voluntary, a thorny issue that would help extend negotiations for another nineteen or so months.[47] Instead of being freed, the peace fighters found themselves long-term prisoners of the Chinese, who, having worked on their own ideas for POW indoctrination and propaganda had no interest in perpetuating the North Korean setup. The Chinese staff at Camp 5 had little patience

[40] NAA, Part 6, AI9/K/BRIT/3, Rfn E. F. Spencer, 12; Department of the Army, *U.S. Prisoners*, 219.

[41] Cunningham, *No Mercy, No Leniency*, 39–40.

[42] NAA, Part 6, AI9/K/BRIT/3, Rfn E. F. Spencer, 12.

[43] Department of the Army, *U.S. Prisoners*, 521; see also Lech, *Broken Soldiers*, 127–8.

[44] Lech, *Broken Soldiers*, 133, 136–9; though see also NAA, Part 6, AI9/K/BRIT/3, Rfn E. F. Spencer, 15.

[45] NAA, Part 6, AI9/K/BRIT/3, Rfn E. F. Spencer, 12. On the radio panels see Department of the Army, *U.S. Prisoners*, 520–1.

[46] NAA, Part 4, AI9/K/BRIT/489, Cpl G. Elliott, 4; Part 6, AI9/K/BRIT/3, Rfn E. F. Spencer, 13; Part 3, AI9/K/BRIT/320, Tpr R. A. Cocks, 5; Part 5, AI9/K/BRIT/308, Rfn F. Moore, 2; IWMDS, 16853/3, G. Hobson.

[47] On the negotiations see Allan E. Goodman, *Negotiating While Fighting* (Stanford, 1978).

with attempts by the peace fighters to live and work on their own terms.[48] The American officers were quickly sent on to the compound at Pinchon-ni, where they were met with hostility by their peers as having come from 'Traitor's Row'.[49] The rest found that the Chinese had their own groups of progressives and either gratefully or with a certain amount of bitterness 'slipped into the background' like Cocks.[50]

That, however, was not the end of the story as far as British prisoners, the North Koreans, and the Pyongyang area were concerned. The region also contained a military interrogation centre situated in a brickyard surrounded by wire just north-east of the city and an interrogation facility based in a farm building some 3 miles north of the capital. At least fifteen British servicemen would pass through the former and at least four through the latter.[51]

The main military centre, known as 'Pak's Palace' or 'Pak's Death House', was set up in early April 1951 to consolidate North Korean efforts at extracting information from captives thought likely to possess technical or other useful information. In addition, some effort was made to impart the communist view of the war. At first conditions were somewhat better than in the transit camps, with three meals of cabbage soup, rice, and millet provided each day, and the first commander, a colonel, was relatively humane. After a month or so, though, he was replaced by a mercurial major by the name of Pak—hence the nicknames of the place—under whose direction rations were severely cut both in quantity and quality and sick inmates were forced to perform physical labour. As more captives were brought in, the place became very overcrowded and utterly unsanitary. Pak set an example for his staff by bullying, threatening, and occasionally striking or torturing prisoners who displeased him. Three officers from the US Army as well as a USAF lieutenant-colonel died there from malnutrition, dysentery, and physical abuse. According to a US Department of Defense report, it was possibly the worst camp in which American POWs found themselves during the Korean War.[52]

---

[48] See NAA, Part 6, AI9/K/BRIT/3, Rfn E. F. Spencer, 13–14; Cunningham, *No Mercy, No Leniency*, 40–1.

[49] Lech, *Broken Soldiers*, 146–7.

[50] NAA, Part 3, AI9/K/BRIT/3, Tpr R. A. Cocks, 6.

[51] Known to have passed through the army interrogation centre known as Pak's Palace were five Royal Marines (QMS J. Day, Cpl J. W. Peskett, plus Mnes A. Aldridge, P. H. Banfield, and S. D. Hicks); seven British Army officers (Capt. A. H. Farrar-Hockley, Capt. H. J. Pike, Lt G. F. B Temple, and Lt H. C. Cabral, all from the Glosters, as well as Capt. R. F. Washbrook and Lt A. H. G. Gibbon of the Royal Artillery, and Capt. J. H. S. Majury of the Ulsters); Sgt F. Nugent of the RUR; and two pilots from the Fleet Air Arm (Lt R. H. Johnson and Lt D. G. Mather). Farrar-Hockley also endured a stay at security police HQ, as did Gloster privates A. E. Marsh, G. N. Hunter, and M. C. W. J. Penrose.

[52] United States, Department of Defense, *POW* (Washington, DC, 1955), 9; James Angus MacDonald Jr, *The Problems of U.S. Marine Corps Prisoners of War in Korea* (Washington, DC, 1988), 120; see Department of the Army, *U.S. Prisoners*, 155–60; see also e.g. William Lindsay White, *The Captives of Korea* (New York, 1957), 68–9; Lewis H. Carlson, *Remembered Prisoners of a Forgotten War* (New York, 2002), 183; Duane Thorin, 'Pak's Palace', <http://www.usgennet.org/usa/topic/preservation/journals/pegasus/pegasus.html> (accessed 6 January 2011); John W. Thornton, *Believed to Be Alive* (Middlebury, Vt., 1981), 140–60.

It was certainly no picnic for its first two British inmates, Lieutenant Spud Gibbon and Sergeant Frank Nugent, brought from the Kandong Caves after refusing to become peace fighters, in the first weeks of the centre's existence. Nugent, already wounded, was treated so poorly that he died later in the month shortly after being returned to one of the transit camps. Spud Gibbon not only resisted questioning but also helped cover an escape attempt by three other prisoners on 28 April 1951. An American pilot later reported what happened next:

> On 2 May 1951 the Korean camp authorities in the 'Brickyard' removed Lt Gibbon (identified as 304047 Lt A. H. G. Gibbon RA) from his hut in the camp and within sight of the other PW in the camp, including Source [Captain Zach W. Dean, USAF], tied his hands behind him and slung another rope over the limb of a tree. They then fastened one end of the rope to that binding his hands which were behind his back, and pulled him off the ground until his toes were just clear of the ground. A Korean Major Pak, and two Korean soldiers then approached him and undid his trousers, allowing them to fall to the ground. They then brutally twisted and turned his testicles and at the same time beat him in the face and on the body. This treatment which was mainly carried out by Major Pak continued for some time, during which they kept asking him for the plans and route taken by the three escapees. To all these questions Lt Gibbon stated he did not know, and if he had known he would not have told them. This brutal treatment continued until Lt Gibbon fainted. He was then taken down from the tree and water was thrown in his face until he recovered. Lt Gibbon had throughout the treatment suffered considerable pain and continually screamed in agony.
>
> Lt Gibbon then had a rope fastened round his neck which was then twisted tight, and he was then sat up. A pistol was held to his head and he was given 30 seconds to give them the information they required. Lt Gibbon replied that if he knew he would not disclose the information. After 30 seconds they removed the pistol without firing it.
>
> Lt Gibbon then had his hands tied to a board and the Koreans produced some sharpened bamboo shoots which they drove under his finger nails. He again fainted after refusing to give the information they sought. They then returned him to the hut and now considered he did not know of the plans of the escapees. Here he lay for some days during which it was considered that he would die of the treatment he had received.[53]

Gibbon survived and was eventually sent northward, being awarded the George Medal after the war for his exemplary fortitude while at Pak's Palace. 'I have nothing but admiration for the British', an American fellow inmate later commented.[54]

Flyers were of particular interest to the interrogators, and among the first to be questioned was Pilot Third Class R. H. Johnson, arriving at Pyongyang on 18

---

[53] NAA, Part 1, AI9/K/US/1, Part I, Capt. Zach W. Dean, 21–2.

[54] R. Wilkins in Edward Hunter, *Brainwashing* (New York, 1956), 140; see Peter Gaston, *Thirty-Eighth Parallel* (Glasgow, 1976), 82; *Daily Telegraph*, obituary 27 October 2008. On the escape see NAA, Part 3, AI9/K/AUST/37, Flt Lt G. R. Harvey, 5–6. When Gibbon arrived in Camp 5 the truck that delivered him took away Capt. James Majury (RUR) for questioning at Pak's Palace (see Part 6, AI9/K/BRIT/69, Maj. M. D. G. C. Ryan, 3). He would not be the only British servicemen sent from the Yalu to Pyongyang (see Part 3, AI9/K/AUST/37, Flt Lt G. R. Harvey, 4; Cunningham, *No Mercy, No Leniency*, 45).

April eight days after being shot down while piloting a Sea Fury launched from HMS *Theseus*. He was softened up with threats, starvation, and some physical coercion before he was questioned there. Luckily he was able to construct a plausible cover story about his identity that enabled him to claim that he did not know the answers to the questions about force structures, unit strengths, personalities plus air and naval technical information that were being asked. Johnson always managed to remember what he had said, which as he later explained 'was absolutely essential as it [the cover story] had to stand up to endless cross questioning and checking at various times'.[55] After five days of solitary confinement and intensive questioning in the building known as the Pagoda he was released into the Brickyard. For the next three months Johnson was threatened regularly and periodically re-interrogated to no avail. Finally in the summer he was sent northward, eventually settling in the officers' camp at Pinchon-ni.[56]

By the late summer eleven other British servicemen had arrived at Pak's Palace. The first were from the transit camps through which soldiers captured in the Imjin River battle were passing on their way to the Yalu (see chapter 5), officers from North Korean military intelligence selecting a group of half-a-dozen officers, mostly from the Glosters, whom they wished to interrogate. Though the questioning was sometimes rather arbitrary—it was observed that the North Korean intelligence staff here and elsewhere relied a good deal on Soviet advisors for truly relevant questions[57]—the interrogators were nothing if not persistent. Johnson had started with name, rank, and number but had found it impossible to refuse to answer questions in the face of pressure, forcing him to lie plausibly.[58] The captains and lieutenants from the Imjin battle were also forced to think on their feet, never having been briefed on what could or not be discussed but having been warned by their CO that he expected them to behave like officers and gentlemen while prisoners of war.[59]

The experience and reactions of Second Lieutenant Guy Temple of the Glosters are illustrative. In his first session he was pressed to concede that South Korea had started the war and told to draw a map of the London docks. He refused: 'I was then taken outside to a little hole' and had a pistol put to his head. Temple decided that discretion was the better part of valour—the layout of the docks hardly counted as a military secret—and drew a map. Over the following days he was asked to redraw it, the North Koreans always being keen to see if information provided in one session could be validated by replication in another. Why they were 'so stupid' as to ask for something that was freely available in any London newsagent's shop remained a mystery to the young subaltern. Temple was on safer ground when questioned by an interrogator known as the professor, who wanted to know (in a manner typical of the rather unrealistic questions drawn up by the

---

[55] NAA, Part 4, AI9/K/BRIT/1019, R. H. Johnson, 6.   [56] Ibid. 4–7.
[57] Cunningham, *No Mercy, No Leniency*, 43–4.
[58] NAA, Part 4, AI9/K/BRIT/1019, R. H. Johnson, 3, 6.
[59] On Carne's admonition to his officers see Cunningham, *No Mercy, No Leniency*, 76. On having no formal briefing on what not to say if interrogated see IWMDS, 15557/4, G. Temple.

North Koreans) the strength of the Royal Canadian Navy and was happy to accept Temple's extemporized exaggeration. A greater challenge began once a Russian started to pose informed questions about the radio sets of infantry battalions. Because he knew that these radios had been sent from Britain to Russia during the Second World War, Temple decided to give way. 'Probably wrong to have done that', he reflected decades later, 'but we didn't have a lot of guidance in the matter.' When giving correct answers did seem to matter, Temple went on to assert, he and the other British officers 'refused to give them the information'.[60] The health consequences could be grave: two of the three other officers with Temple were dead within a matter of months.[61]

Commissioned officers by virtue of their command functions were of potential intelligence value, but the North Koreans were also interested in NCOs and other ranks believed to possess specialist knowledge. Thus in July Sergeant J. W. Holberton of the 8th Hussars, though he had passed unscathed through the transit camps, was brought back down to Pyongyang from the Yalu in order to be interrogated about the Centurion tank. Despite the fact that the North Koreans possessed the driver's maintenance book and the handbook for the tank itself they grilled him hard. He was returned 'in a very emaciated condition' and in the opinion of at least one observer 'was a broken man'.[62]

In the latter part of September a party of five from 41 Commando Royal Marines was delivered up to the doors of Pak's Palace. These men had been aboard a landing craft that had broken down and been washed ashore in heavy weather north of UN lines near Wonsan the previous month. The NCO in charge, Quartermaster Sergeant James Day, had shortly after capture urged his men 'to be a credit to the Royal Marines'.[63] What this meant in the context of individual interrogations each of the Royal Marines would have to decide on his own. As Corporal John Peskett explained decades later, 'my problem—our problem—was we hadn't been briefed as to what was likely to happen', going on to argue 'if we'd known that it was a huge game of bluff that sometimes got very nasty, we could have prepared ourselves for it'.[64]

Marine P. H. Banfield was asked questions about his family background and about the structure and personnel of his unit. When he thought the major interrogating him knew the answers to the latter and was testing his truthfulness, Banfield gave the correct answers. To all other queries he pleaded ignorance or provided inaccurate information. Suffering from dysentery, he played up his weakness by staging fainting spells while being interrogated which, he thought, led to the

---

[60] IWMDS, 1557/4, G. Temple.

[61] Lt H. C. Cabral and Capt. R. F. Washbrook died on 21 and 27 November 1951 respectively. E. D. Harding, *The Imjin Roll* (Gloucester, 1981), 49, 75. On the circumstances see NAA, Part 4, AI9/K/BRIT/38, Capt. A. Farrar-Hockley, 23–4; Part 5, AI9/K/BRIT/4 Part II, Sgt W. A. Lucas, 1; Part 6, AI9/K/BRIT/850, 851, 2021, Capt. H. J. Pike, Capt. G. D. Lutyens-Humfrey, Lt G. D. Costello, 3.

[62] NAA, AI9/K/BRIT/428, L/Cpl J. W. L. King, 1.

[63] Ibid. Part 6, AI9/K/BRIT/479, Cpl J. W. Peskett, 2.

[64] IWMDS, 14025/4, J. Peskett.

curtailment of questioning after four days.[65] Marine S. D. Hicks was ordered by a sergeant to draw maps of Plymouth, the commando school, and other locations. He drew them badly, and when in his second interrogation was asked to do the maps again—repetition of what was said, written, or drawn being a favourite communist means of checking prisoners' claims—Hicks drew, in considerable detail down to the level of furnishings, a completely different set of drawings. By his third and final session he seems to have convinced his interrogator that he was slightly unhinged, as the sergeant complained that Hicks made him nervous.[66] Corporal Peskett, who had already withstood a beating for refusing to answer questions while en route to Pak's Palace, was no doubt surprised to find that, while he was questioned extensively on military matters, he was not threatened or physically abused.[67] Balancing this was the fact that Marine A. J. Aldrich was allowed to die from dysentery.[68]

As for QMS Day himself, he tried to pass himself off as a mere PT instructor, which despite the absence of rough stuff required a good deal of effort. He was interrogated repeatedly by North Koreans and in one case a couple of Russians about UN activity in the Wonsan area, technical details, and, like the others, his personal history. Keeping his cover story consistent proved tough ('he did at times find great difficulty in concealing the fact that he did know a certain amount about the subjects on which he was being interrogated' his British debriefing officer later noted) but he stuck with it. Like everyone else he found his physical strength eroding on the starvation rations provided by Pak—'it was an effort to do anything' he reflected in a letter to a USMC officer writing about the Marine Corps prisoner experience some years after the war[69]—but his moral strength remained. In mid-October, after a month in Pak's Palace, he and his party were marched to Camp 9 as a prelude to being sent north to the Yalu.[70]

Life in the Brickyard run by military intelligence was bad, but conditions in the farmyard interrogation facility run by the security service were, if anything, considerably worse. The latter competed with the former to question aircrew prisoners and took a particular interest in interrogating UN prisoners who had made escape attempts and been recaptured. Though there is very little information available on the circumstances, it is suggestive that of three privates from the Glosters who were taken there after being recaptured in May 1951, one died the next month while another passed away four months later.[71] Then there was the well-documented case of Captain Anthony Farrar-Hockley, the robust adjutant of the Glosters who had made a total of four bids for freedom before being sent to Pyongyang in October

[65] NAA, Part 3, AI9/K/BRIT/846, Mne P. H. Banfield, 2.

[66] Ibid. Part 4, AI9/K/BRIT/482, Mne S. D. Hicks, 2.

[67] Ibid. Part 6, AI9/K/BRIT/479, Cpl J. W. Peskett, 2.

[68] Ibid. Part 3, AI9/K/BRIT/62, QMS J. Day, 4; MacDonald, *The Problems of U.S. Marine Corps Prisoners of War in Korea*, 120.

[69] Day to MacDonald, 14 April 1960 in MacDonald, *The Problems of U.S. Marine Corps Prisoners of War in Korea*, 120.

[70] NAA, Part 3, AI9/K/BRIT/62, QMS Day, 4.

[71] Pte M. C. W. J. Penrose died on 1 June, Pte G. N. Hunter died on 5 November. Harding, *The Imjin Roll*, 58, 64. Only Pte A. A. Marsh survived. NAA, Part 5, AI9/K/BRIT/894, Pte A. A. Marsh, 1.

1951. Prisoners were housed in the building meant for animals without light, heat, or proper bedding and fed a diminishing ration of boiled millet and very thin soup that eventually produced starvation. Inmates were also forced to do heavy manual labour while constructing an air-raid shelter for the commander as well as performing menial and humiliating tasks such as cleaning out the headquarters building latrine with their bare hands. 'The staff of the interrogation centre were the most unpleasant and unscrupulous captors I had encountered up to that time,' Farrar-Hockley later wrote, 'being either fanatical Communists, sadists, or a combination of both.'[72]

Farrar-Hockley had first been interrogated by a civilian interpreter about politics in the vain hope that he could be turned into a peace fighter. He was then questioned by a North Korean officer known as the Young Major, who clearly hated his captives. Like his counterparts in Pak's Palace and elsewhere when unaided by Soviet advisors, the Young Major was unable to match his questions to the likely level of knowledge of the man being interrogated: 'Give us the organization, means of recruitment and training, method and dispatch, and system of communication of the British Intelligence Services throughout Europe and the Far East.' Farrar-Hockley was so taken aback by the ridiculousness of this question that he smiled. This was a mistake, as he was then beaten about the head. 'After an hour of threats, blows, and a warning to reconsider my attitude the next day,' Farrar-Hockley wrote in his memoir of captivity, 'I was taken back to the barn.'[73]

His attitude, as it happened, including organizing an escape with a pair of pilots that involved digging through the outside wall of the barn. The next night, 9 November 1951, the three men got away. Unhappily, Farrar-Hockley was recaptured the following night and brought to police HQ in Pyongyang for intensive questioning. Accompanied by the Young Major, a guard, and a translator, he was taken to a sealed chamber and told to strip to the waist and kneel down next to a small chair.

> I saw the Young Major's hand come round to strike me on the temple, the first of a series of blows that he and Poker-Face released upon me. Kim joined them when they began to kick; and it was he who covered my face, when the Young Major saw that I was anticipating some of the blows and ducking. Just before the cloth came down over my eyes, I saw to my horror that the Young Major's face had assumed an expression of savage pleasure: he was really enjoying my suffering.
>
> In my innocence, I had thought this maltreatment was to be my either my punishment, or a means of inducing me to give information about Jack and Ron [1Lt Jack E. Henderson USAF and P/O Ron Guthrie, RAAF, the other escapees]. I discovered it was merely the overture. The covering was removed and I was assisted by Kim and Poker-Face into the tiny chair. I almost thanked them for what seemed to be an act of remorse or compassion. It was neither. They now bound my legs to the front of the

[72] Anthony Farrar-Hockley, *The Edge of the Sword* (London, 1954), 172; see ibid. 171, 175; NAA, Part 4, AI9/K/BRIT/38, Capt. A. H. Farrar-Hockley, 16–17; Part 3, AI9/K/AUST/58, F/O R. D. Guthrie, 5; Colin C. King and Ronald D. Guthrie, *Escape from North Korea* (Riverwood, NSW, 2002), 54–8.

[73] Farrar-Hockley, *The Edge of the Sword*, 174–5.

chair, my arms to the two uprights at the back. My wrists, still secured, were tied down with a second piece of rope to the cross-piece between the two back legs. The Young Major kicked me in the chest and the chair fell over, with me, on to its back.

Poker-Face now produced a towel, as the Young Major threw two or three dippers of ice-cold water over my face and neck, drawn from the barrel in the corner. Still I did not understand, thinking, as I lay shivering with the cold, that I was to be chilled to the bone by repeated dousing. But Poker-Face placed the towel over my face and, a second later, more water was thrown over me.[74]

Farrar-Hockley was undergoing a variation of what today would be called water-boarding. As the towel became saturated 'each successive breath provided less and less oxygen for my labouring lungs'.[75] He eventually passed out; but on continuing to refuse to answer questions about the escape was subjected to this treatment four times more over the following six days, as well as being exposed to other tortures. Luckily by this point the others had been recaptured too, which made his silence moot. In very poor shape Farrar-Hockley was then dumped in the Kandong Caves, from where he and others were sent on a nightmarish journey to Pyoktong in which several men died of a combination of disease, exposure, and exhaustion.[76]

This was also the fate of many of the dozens of men from the Ulsters and other units who, through wounds, escape attempts, or simple bad luck got separated from the main columns heading for Pyoktong at some point and were detained for use as expendable slave labour in the capital and elsewhere. Fusilier Derek Kinne, for instance, passing through the railway junction of Suchon with other sick prisoners in May 1951, came across two British soldiers captured back in January and a group of GIs being used this way by the local North Korean police, all of whom had been reduced to 'pitiful skeletons' by this point.[77] Another rifleman, a former decorator, having been lost in the Pyonyang prison system for several months, found himself consigned to a labour gang made up of fifteen unfortunate GIs on a logistical site north of the capital hauling ammunition and supplies for the North Korean army. The food was almost non-existent, there were no washing facilities or replacement clothing, and the North Korean guards were not slow to beat him and others with rifle butts for not working hard enough. He was lucky to survive long enough to be 'discovered' by the Chinese and transferred to Pyoktong in June 1952, which meant that he did not number among the thirty-odd individual British soldiers seen by others being used as slave labourers in the Pyongyang region who thereafter disappeared without trace.[78] It is telling that he commented fourteen months later to an AI9 interrogator that 'life there was far worse than when he was a prisoner of the Japanese'.[79]

---

[74] Farrar-Hockley, *The Edge of the Sword*, 183–5.
[75] Ibid. 185.
[76] Ibid. 181–203; IWMDS, 30102/2, A. Farrar-Hockley; NAA, Part 4, AI9/K/BRIT/38, Capt. A. H. Farrar-Hockley, 17–24.
[77] Derek Kinne, *The Wooden Boxes* (London, 1955), 53.
[78] Cunningham, *No Mercy, No Leniency*, 22.
[79] NAA, Part 4, AI9/K/BRIT/844, Rfn J. Hibbert, 2.

By the time the former decorator arrived in Camp 5, and the men of the British Army contingents captured in January and April of the previous year almost all dead or in the camps along the Yalu run the by the Chinese, the North Korean interrogators based in Pyongyang and elsewhere were chiefly concerned with getting information from downed flyers through the rest of the war. Almost all of these were Americans, but there was one other Fleet Air Arm pilot who fell into their hands. This was Lieutenant D. G. Mather, shot down in a Sea Fury launched from HMS *Glory* in January 1953. He spent seven weeks in the capital being questioned under conditions that were 'extremely bad': the supply of food, medicine, and heat was entirely dependent on how cooperative a particular prisoner was. Mather luckily discovered that as long as some answer was given to a question, however factually inaccurate it might be, the North Korean interrogators seemed satisfied. Like most other officers he ended up in Camp 2.[80]

The behaviour of the British servicemen sent to Pyongyang represented both ends of the spectrum of possible reactions to enemy demands. At one end were those willing to endure torture and face death in order to defy their captors. At the other end were those who not only collaborated but effectively changed sides. In between were men who had to decide how far they could or could not go. In Pak's Palace and the Brickyard, they seem to have made the right choices. In the Kandong Caves, perhaps, and most certainly in Peace Fighters' Camp, servicemen faced with difficult choices often took the path of least resistance and thereby seriously compromised their honour as members of His Majesty's forces. It was probably not coincidental that commissioned and non-commissioned officers performed better than reservist other ranks in this respect, having already shown themselves capable of initiative and independent thought and possessing more of a stake in their unit and service.[81]

Nevertheless the camps in the Pyongyang area were not in the same league as Pyoktong either in size or scope. The former were either staging posts or specialist establishments where choices were unusually stark while the latter—excepting certain interrogation and disciplinary facilities—was much bigger and meant to house and indoctrinate well over a thousand men for the duration rather than a few dozen for a limited time. In order to understand what did and did not happen in Camp 5 at Pyoktong, it is instructive to examine developments in the second main camp along the Yalu in which large numbers of British prisoners were held, Camp 1 at Chongson.

---

[80] Ibid. Part 5, AI9/K/BRIT/1020, Lt D. G. Mather.

[81] Resisting officers such as e.g. Farrar-Hockley, Gibbon, and Temple, not to speak of senior NCOs like O'Hara and Day, were all regulars; while the likes of Cocks, Horrobin, and Spencer were all reservists. To be fair, once their own leaders were removed, those sent to Camp 12 naturally took their lead, at least to some degree, from the American officers, who as we have seen pursued are more flexible line than their British counterparts.

5

The Glosters at Chongson

Any P.O.W. can hold any different political opinion or view on any subject. In fact, we welcome such differences with the Chinese Peoples Volunteers, as long as they do not stubbornly regard such views [as] correct and those of the instructors incorrect. Should he maintain such an attitude, he or they will be punished.

Commandant,
Camp 1,
19 July 1951[1]

One morning towards the end of April 1951 an excited Comrade Lim made an announcement to the assembled prisoners in Camp 5 at Pyoktong. 'The Chinese People's Volunteers have destroyed a British regiment. Your Gloucester Regiment has been wiped out! Those who are not killed are our prisoners.' The audience responded with assorted catcalls ('Bollocks! Rubbish! Bullshit!'), but in fact the information Lim had conveyed was not an exercise in communist propaganda. Though immediate efforts were made to bring it up to operational strength again, it was indeed the case that less than 10 per cent of the first battalion of 'the Glosters' had escaped death or captivity at the Battle of the Imjin River.[2]

The only thing Lim got wrong was the implication that most of the battalion had died in action. Under orders from higher authority not to retreat, the Glosters, under the command of Lieutenant Colonel J. P. 'Fred' Carne, found themselves surrounded on a hilltop position from which they could not be extracted. They were caught up in the last great Chinese offensive effort to win the war, and were in action almost continuously from before midnight on 22 April through the early morning of 25 April. The Glosters generated very large numbers of enemy casualties in sixty-odd hours of almost non-stop combat for the loss of around sixty killed in action. But by 10 a.m. on the 25th they had nearly run out of ammunition, and with the last hope of rescue by friendly forces extinguished the CO gave the order for those still fit enough to form into small parties and try and infiltrate their way back to UN lines. Only one group managed to do so, the rest—just over 600 in all[3]—falling into enemy hands.[4] Comrade Lim also left out the fact that an

---

[1] K. V. Godwin in *The Back Badge*, 4(15) (1953), 231; see also Anthony Farrar-Hockley, *The British Part in the Korean War*, 2 vols. (London, 1995), II, 267.

[2] IWMDD, E. Beckerley, 27–8; see E. D. Harding, *The Imjin Roll* (Gloucester, 1981), 36.

[3] This figure included Royal Artillery personnel and others attached to the battalion. Harding, *The Imjin Roll*; Peter Gaston, *Korea 1950–1953: Prisoners of War* (Eastbourne, 1976), 8–20, 22–5, 27–8.

[4] Andrew Salmon, *To the Last Round* (London, 2009), chs. 6–9.

additional 140-odd prisoners had been taken from adjoining units in 29th Brigade during the Imjin battle, principally from the luckless Ulsters and, to a lesser extent, the Northumberlands, in the course of a poorly coordinated fighting withdrawal a few hours after the Glosters had dispersed.[5]

Whether feeling a sense of shame at having to surrender or secret delight at having survived the battle as they put their hands up singly or in small groups, these dazed and exhausted men were now face-to-face with the enemy soldiers whom they had been trying to kill only a short time before. 'I stood up and an amazing sight met my eyes', Private David Green related. 'A horde of armed, leather belted men in sand-coloured uniforms were hugging and shaking hands with our blokes who, like me, were in a state of shock.'[6] Indeed, most of the Chinese People's Volunteers remained true to their orders and to the great surprise of their erstwhile foes grinned, shook hands, passed out safe-conduct passes and cigarettes and repeated the English phrase 'good fight' that they had been made to memorize.[7]

At least one or two Chinese soldiers, to be sure, found it understandably difficult to forget that these foreigners had been killing their friends minutes or even moments earlier. Despite getting bogged down in a paddy field a sergeant in the 8th Hussars had continued to fire the coaxial machine-gun of the Centurion tank he commanded until the ammunition ran out. Only then did he open the turret hatch and put his hands up, at which point he was soundly bashed about the face with weapon butts by the surrounding Chinese.[8] Private Sam Mercer, apparently failing to respond fast enough to the orders of a Chinese as he hobbled away from the regimental aid post, was shot through the knee and might have then been shot dead if the soldier in question had not wandered off.[9] The leadership cadres, though, did their best to adhere to the first stage of the Lenient Policy. Thus, after a Chinese soldier tried to scare newly captured Private Ronald Norley by firing a sub-machinegun under his armpit, a Chinese officer immediately slapped the offender in the face.[10] When a party of Chinese soldiers initially came across the Gloster regimental aid post and starting firing, their

---

[5] Ibid. ch. 10; Gaston, *Korea 1950–1953*, 3–8, 20–3, 26, 28.

[6] David Green, *Captured at the Imjin River* (Barnsley, 2003), 104. On feelings of shame see e.g. Lofty Large, *One Man's War in Korea* (London, 1988), 71; IWMDS, 21729/4, F. Cottam; Farrar-Hockley in *Forgotten Heroes* (BBC, 2001). On being glad to be alive see e.g. R. F. Matthews as told to Francis S. Jones, *No Rice for Rebels* (London, 1956), 21. Many, after days of constant stress with very little food, water, or sleep, were simply dazed and numb. See e.g. Anthony Farrar-Hockley, *The Edge of the Sword* (London, 1954), 77–8; IWMDS, 17468/2, D. Kaye.

[7] See e.g. Matthews in Francis S. Jones, *No Rice for Rebels*, 20; Henry O'Kane, *O'Kane's Korea* (Kenilworth, 1988), 65; IWMDD, F. Carter, 33; IWMDS, 12783/3, A. Eagles; 15557/2, G. Temple; 19664/2, V. Whitamore.

[8] IWMDS, 19664/2, V. Whitamore. The sergeant was sufficiently concussed to intuit efforts to administer first aid to those with groin injuries as attempts to cut the testicles off prisoners.

[9] NAM 1989-05-1-1, S. Mercer; IWMDS, 12605/5, S. Mercer. See also e.g. TNA, WO 208/2314, KWC 639; George Cooper, *Fight, Dig and Live* (Barnsely, 2011), 45.

[10] IWMDS, 15338/4, B. Murphy.

commander ran up and ordered them to cease fire—shooting dead the one man who failed to heed the order.[11]

It was nevertheless worrying that here and elsewhere on the battlefield the Chinese refused to allow any prisoners, even doctors and medical attendants, to stay with the stretcher cases rather than be marched away. In some cases, as feared, the enemy seems to have engaged in what may have been seen in some instances as mercy killings and in others as revenge for fallen comrades.[12] Sam Mercer, who was with stretcher cases at the aid post after Dr Bob Hickey his staff had been sent away, recalled how the Chinese 'were obviously sorting us out into those who could move and those who couldn't. They were dispatching those who couldn't, quite simply. One of our sergeants, Sergeant [K. D.] Eames, was quite badly wounded, and couldn't move... so they simply shot him.'[13]

This was not known to most of the Glosters who had been escorted away, and when the Chinese asked for volunteers to drive captured British vehicles in order to transport the non-walking wounded to the rear they had a number of takers. When it turned out that they were moving supplies rather than wounded men, the volunteer drivers sabotaged those vehicles still in working order.[14]

For everyone else the next order of business was usually a personal search. The Chinese seem to have been under orders not to loot prisoners, and while many did not—'most of the PW who were searched were allowed to retain their personal possessions including matches, cigarettes and watches', admitted Tony Farrar-Hockley, the Glosters' adjutant who soon made himself no friend of his captors[15]— at least a few CPV soldiers could not resist temptation and stole rings, watches, cameras, and whatever else took their fancy. 'They weren't inclined to argue about it', Fusilier William Alexander remembered, 'if you tried to hang on to it, you got the butt end of a rifle in your face'.[16] It was perhaps some compensation for those Glosters who lost valuables to witness one hapless Chinese soldier rummage through some kit, find a tin, open it, and consume the sweet-tasting contents

[11] Farrar-Hockley, *The Edge of the Sword*, 76.

[12] On cases of seriously wounded being killed see e.g. TNA, WO 208/4005, KWC 865; IWMDS, 18439/2, A. Tyas; 12605/5, S. Mercer; NAA, Part 3, AI9/K/BRIT/955, Lt S. W. Cooper, 3; see also Derek Kinne, *The Wooden Boxes* (London, 1955), 30–1. On not being allowed to stay with or return for the Gloster stretcher cases see IWMDS, 16061/2, Dr R. Hickey; 16618/3, C. Papworth; 19871/1, W. Westwood; NAA, Part 3, AI9/K/BRIT/979, Sgt S. J. Brisland, 1; Part 4, AI9/K/BRIT/958, 2/Lt D. J. English, 1.

[13] NAM 1989-05-1-1, S. Mercer. He also remembered in a different interview another British stretcher case being killed as well. IWMDS, 12605/5, S Mercer.

[14] Large, *One Man's War in Korea*, 75; NAA, Part 7, AI9/K/BRIT/454, Pte H. Wheeler, 1; see also Part 3, AI9/K/BRIT/893, L/Cpl J. R. Hyland, 7; Farrar-Hockley, *The Edge of the Sword*, 78.

[15] NAA, Part 4, AI9/K/BRIT/38, Capt. A. H. Farrar-Hockley, 3; see e.g. Part 3, AI9/K/BRIT/869, WOII G. E. Askew, 1; Part 4 AI9/K/BRIT/858, L/Cpl S. J. Hardacre, 2; Part 6, AI9/K/BRIT/469, Pte M. Pendle, 1; IWMDS, 19871/1, W. Westwood.

[16] IWMDS, 16850/3, W. Gibson. On the looting of personal items (which might occur further back as well as at the front) see e.g. K. Walters in *The Back Badge*, 4(15) (1953), 229; *Daily Express*, 28 February 1955, 2; Large, *One Man's War in Korea*, 74; IWMDS, 18439/2, A. Tyas; 19664/2, V. Whitamore; NAA, Part 3, AI9/K/BRIT/165 et al., Gnr D. Boulton et al., 2; Part 5, AI9/K/BRIT/4, Sgt W. A. Lucas, 1; Part 6, AI9/K/BRIT/977, Lt A. Peal, 2; ibid. AI9/K/BRIT/342, Pte H. C. Remnant, 2. Sometimes only certain prized items were taken: see e.g. IWMDS, 16337/1, J. Grosvenor; NAA, Part 3, AI9/K/BRIT/92, Pte D. R. Butcher, 2.

without realizing that this was in fact cooking fuel. Within five minutes, as Bob Hickey predicated, he was being violently sick: 'all the soldiers thought this was great fun'.[17]

Over the next several days the Chinese concentrated most of their captives in and around the hamlet of Choksong just south of the Imjin, sometimes unable to feed them while arrangements were sorted out and only able at this point to ask for name, rank, and number and further interrogate a few officers, NCOs, and others in haphazard fashion.[18] The prisoners were then made to ford the Imjin River at night—Farrar-Hockley taking the opportunity and slip under the water and make the first of many bids for freedom, the rest 'too dazed and tired to think of escape', as a Gloster corporal put it[19]—and assembled in a pair of villages about 10 miles north of the river prior to the start of the march to the Yalu.[20]

Some of the wounded men received medical attention from the CPV in this initial period of captivity, but this was often of a decidedly rudimentary nature. There was little or no care, dressings were changed infrequently, and operations carried out without anesthetic by inexperienced personnel: in the case of one sergeant from the Glosters, for instance, whose arm became infected due to the shrapnel embedded in it, with a pair of rusty nail scissors and tweezers.[21] Matters were not helped by the way in which, as a wounded Lieutenant Tony Perrins of the Northumberlands remembered, the Chinese 'did not like our own doctors looking after us'.[22] When the march north began many of the walking cases still carried shrapnel and bullets in their bodies.[23]

Two columns set out on foot in the first stage of the long, roundabout trek northward, prisoners walking between 10 and 20 miles per night with short breaks every hour or so while resting up under cover by day.[24] Thanks to the advance of the UN front line in the spring prior to the opening of the enemy offensive in which they had been taken, the Glosters and their compatriots started off about 30 miles closer to their ultimate destination than had the Ulsters taken almost four

[17] IWMDS, 16061/1, R. Hickey.

[18] On questions at this stage see S. J. Davies, *In Spite of Dungeons* (London, 1954), 31–3; O'Kane, *O'Kane's Korea*, 15; IWMDS, 16850/5, W. Gibson; 17929/4, D. Sharp (see also TNA, WO 373/119, ff. 246–9); NAA, Part 3, AI9/K/BRIT/42, Lt J. M. C. Nicholls, 2; Part 4, AI9/K/BRIT/391, Dmr A. Eagles, 1; ibid. AI9/K/BRIT/4, Sgt W. A. Lucas, 3; Part 5, AI9/K/BRIT/736, Cpl H. Manning, 1; ibid. AI9/K/BRIT/882, Sgt D. McAnulty, 2; ibid. AI9/K/BRIT/65, Capt. W. B. D. Morris, 1; Part 6, AI9/BRIT/847, W.O. II J. H. Riddlington, 2; ibid. AI9/K/BRIT/456, Tpr S. Sears, 1; ibid. AI9/K/BRIT/156, L/Cpl H. C. Sharpling, 2; Part 7, AI9/K/BRIT/449, Cpl S. H. Truan, 1. On the rations problem see e.g. Part 6, AI9/BRIT/850 et al., Capt. H. J. Pike et al., 2; ibid. AI9/K/BRIT/847, W.O. II J. H. Riddllington, 2; Part 7, AI9/K/BRIT/159, Pte N. Ward, 1.

[19] Walters in *The Back Badge*, 229; see also e.g. O'Kane, *O'Kane's Korea*, 69; IWMDS, 18262/5, F. Carter. On Farrar-Hockley's first escape attempt see Farrar-Hockley, *The Edge of the Sword*, 79 ff.

[20] See e.g. NAA, Part 3, AI9/K/BRIT/407 et al., Fus. J. Aitken et al., 6.

[21] Ibid. Part 6, AI9/K/BRIT/2, Sgt S. Robinson, 2; Part 3, AI9/K/BRIT/954, Lt T. Conneeley, 2; see e.g. Part 4, AI9/K/BRIT/489, Cpl G. Elliott, 2.

[22] IWMDS, 19387/5, A. Perrins.

[23] NAA, Part 4, AI9/K/BRIT/14–18, Pte A. E. Hunt and Cpl L. Manley, 2.

[24] On distances see Green, *Captured at the Imjin River*, 111; IWMDD, F. Carter, 39; IWMDS, 19664/2, V. Whitamore; 30075/4, J. Wiseman; NAA, Part 4, AI9/K/BRIT/421, Cpl D. W. Hansford, 2; Part 5, AI9/K/BRIT/4, Sgt W. A. Lucas, 2.

months earlier. Much more importantly, the weather had vastly improved. 'It was a good job the winter was over and the days were warm', Private Frank Carter reflected in his memoirs, '—in fact sometimes it was quite pleasant.'[25]

This did not mean, however, that the march northward in the spring of 1951 was anything but a severe test of endurance. Lesser paths and tracks were taken instead of major roads much of the time in order to avoid the attentions of roving American aircraft whose task was to strike at anything seen on known supply routes if dusk, dawn, or flares revealed a presence. Nonetheless on a number of occasions the prisoners were bombed and strafed—luckily without anyone being killed or seriously wounded—while the guard escort lost their way amid the meandering byways, thereby adding stress ('I for one was always glad to hear the engines die away in the distance', Carter remembered) and the time spent tramping in single file from one village to another.[26] Therefore while the distance from the Imjin to Camp 1, the final destination, was less than 200 miles as the crow flies, the columns ended up walking perhaps double this distance.[27]

Men soon began to become seriously fatigued. 'Many of us often fell asleep during the five minute breaks', wrote Private 'Lofty' Large decades later. 'I remember falling asleep on a pile of loose rocks, in pouring rain.' Sam Davies, Chaplain to the Glosters, among others, fully endorsed such memories. 'I recall vividly the terrible physical and mental weariness of the marches', he wrote not long after he was repatriated.[28]

The food provided by the Chinese were both unappetizing and, more importantly, inadequate. Meals were provided only before and after each night's march, usually consisting of millet or the standard Chinese field ration of powdered sorghum which had to be boiled and then eaten out of whatever was available—everything from cigarette tins and berets to handkerchiefs and hands. To the British palate both 'bird seed' and 'bug dust' tasted 'pretty nauseous', as Lieutenant Peter Whitamore of the Ulsters recalled.[29] More importantly the vitamin content was limited and there was not very much of it: roughly 680 grams of dry meal per man per day.[30]

[25] IWMDD, F. Carter, 39; see also Green, *Captured at the Imjin River*, 114.

[26] IWMDD, F. Carter, 39. On air strikes and near misses see Davies, *In Spite of Dungeons*, 36; Green, *Captured at the Imjin River*, 110, 111; IWMDS, 21729/4, F. Cottam; 16850/5–6, W. Gibson; 17468/2, D. Kaye; 12664/2, P. Weller; 30075/4, J. Wiseman. On the escort getting lost see O'Kane, *O'Kane's Korea*, 70; IWMDS, 18262/1, F. Carter; 21729/4, F. Cottam; 17468/2, D. Kaye; 15338/5, B. Murphy.

[27] Frank Cottam estimated that he had walked 500 miles. IWMDS, 21729/4, F. Cottam. Another soldier produced a more conservative estimate of 300 miles. Ibid. 30075/4, J. Wiseman.

[28] Davies, *In Spite of Dungeons*, 35; Large, *One Man's War in Korea*, 82; see also e.g. IWMDD, F. Carter, 39; IWMDS, 19664/2–3, V. Whitamore.

[29] IWMDS, 19664/3, V. Whitamore; see also e.g. ibid. 12783/4, A. Eagles; 18544/1, C. Sharpling. On the powdered meal being labeled 'bug dust' see ibid. 16759/1, D. Patchett; 15557/2, G. Temple; 19871/1, W. Westwood. On millet as 'bird seed' see e.g. ibid. 21729/5, F. Cottam. On the problem of what to eat out of see ibid., 15338/5, B. Murphy; 19871/1, W. Westwood; Davies, *In Spite of Dungeons*, 35; Green, *Captured at the Imjin River*, 109.

[30] See Matthews in Francis S. Jones, *No Rice for Rebels*, 28. It can be assumed that the 50lb bags he mentions were meant to feed a squad until the Pyongyang area was reached in approximately ten days' time.

Ironically, just as their own food consumption was undergoing a drastic shift the prisoners found that they themselves were being fed upon. Unable to properly wash or shave and resting either in the open or in often filthy huts, men quickly found their clothing became infested with parasites. As RAMC Corporal Cyril Papworth explained, 'you would find that you were scratching and find that you were lousy'. Seams could be checked for eggs to break between finger and thumb-nail, but as there was no opportunity to boil uniforms or keep clean, it proved impossible to get rid of lice once they appeared during the march.[31]

The inability to wash was eclipsed, though, by the problem of clean drinking water. In a land where paddy fields were fertilized with human manure, soldiers knew the importance of boiling water to kill bacteria, and the Chinese did their best to encourage the practice at halts.[32] In many cases, however, men were so thirsty on the march that they drank directly from streams or, even worse, from paddy fields. The result in most cases was diarrhoea or full-blown dysentery, the effects of which were both highly debilitating and very humiliating, especially when guards grew impatient with those who of necessity had to stop to relieve themselves. Corporal Bill Westwood, for instance, 'was not allowed to complete his business, but was forced at the end of a burp [submachine] gun to double after the remainder of the party', while Private J. W. Wood was on one occasion kicked in the face for falling out without permission.[33]

Not all the Chinese guards were so dislikable, the nasty ones often balanced out by those with a sense of common humanity. David Green remembered one who was 'a miserable bastard' and another who was 'a cheerful, friendly fellow' who slipped men cigarettes. In short there were good Chinese and bad Chinese. As Fusilier Derek Kinne reflected in his memoirs: 'Sometimes we were lucky; the guard would change and a kind man would be in charge of us; sometimes a man who evidently hated us; and often one who neglected us due to complete indiffer-ence.'[34] In some cases guards protected prisoners from the attentions of angry civil-ians as they moved on occasion through towns and villages; in other cases they let them be spat at or bombarded with stones.[35] In any event most were a good deal better than the North Koreans with whom some of the Imjin battle stretcher cases in May came in contact during their separate journey northward by cart, motor

---

[31] IWMDS, 16618/4, C. Papworth; see e.g. Matthews in Francis S. Jones, *No Rice for Rebels*, 29; IWMDS, 16337/1, Grosvenor; NAA, Part 3, AI9/K/BRIT/955, Lt S. W. Cooper, 2; ibid. AI9/K/BRIT/92, Pte D. R. Butcher, 2.

[32] See IWMDD, F. Carter, 39.

[33] NAA, Part 7, AI9/K/BRIT/157, Cpl W. K. Westwood, 5; see Part 6, AI9/K/BRIT/403 et al., Cpl E. G. Rogers et al., 3; see also ibid. AI9/K/BRIT/961, WO II F. G. Strong, 3; Large, *One Man's War in Korea*, 86. On dysentery see also e.g. Green, *Captured at the Imjin River*, 110; O'Kane, *O'Kane's Korea*, 73; IWMDD, F. Carter, 39; IWMDS, 17468/2, D. Kaye; 15338/5, B. Murphy; On drinking contaminated water see e.g. IWMDS, 16850/5, W. Gibson; 15539/3, R. Norley; 16618/4, C. Papworth.

[34] Kinne, *The Wooden Boxes*, 47; Green, *Captured at the Imjin River*, 110–11. On good and bad Chinese on the march see also e.g. Davies, *In Spite of Dungeons*, 43–4.

[35] On Chinese guards protecting prisoners from angry Korean civilians see e.g. IWMDS, 15475/3, S. Davies. On Chinese guards allowing civilians to spit or attack them see e.g. ibid. 17468/2, D. Kaye; L. Jones in Donald Knox, *The Korean War: Uncertain Victory* (San Diego, 1988), 335.

vehicle, and train. As Sam Mercer put it, while the Chinese 'were no angels'—he had, after all, been shot in the leg after surrendering by one of them—the North Koreans 'were ten thousand times worse.'[36]

In the main columns the attitude of the guards was of particular importance to the walking wounded. 'The Chinese made it very plain [that] anyone who fell to the side would be shot', Rifleman Bill Gibson remembered.[37] RAMC personnel were sometimes allowed to help those in difficulty, and there might be bullock carts at certain stages for the worst off, but doctors and NCOs could do relatively little in the absence of sufficient medical supplies.[38] Lofty Large, who was moving on foot despite having been hit twice by bullets and broken some ribs, later stated that when he compared himself to some of the others 'my couple of nice clean holes seemed nothing compared to their wounds'.

> One [man] had a lot of shrapnel in the top of his head. I can hear his screams now as his friends held him down and tried to bring him some relief, by pulling the worst pieces out with a pair of ordinary pliers. No anesthetic of course. Another young lad would give subdued screams and moans for the first two miles every night, until the stiffness went from his wounded leg. He had a large bullet hole through his thigh. Others had smashed hands, smashed wrists, gaping wounds were quite common. Several had bullets in their chests and shoulders.[39]

When a man collapsed and fell by the wayside a guard would be detached to stay with the unfortunate individual. Some former captives remember hearing shots once the column had moved on. Others recalled that, though the detached guard might try to bully or even beat the laggard into getting to his feet again, there was no shooting and stragglers simply caught up with the column at the next halt or were placed on a bullock cart.[40]

The seriously sick and wounded experienced some relief after about ten days on the move around a school building north of Pyongyang on the Taedong River near Munha-ri known as Halfway House. Here the columns rested for several days and those considered by the Chinese too ill to continue were allowed to remain for a time when the march resumed and given some rudimentary medical attention. 'I think we needed that rest,' Private Bill Clark, who had shrapnel in one foot, later reflected, 'as we were all not just physically but mentally drained.'[41]

---

[36] IWMDS, 12605/5, S. Mercer; see also e.g. ibid. 16853/2, G. Hobson.

[37] IWMDS, 16850/5, W. Gibson; see also e.g. ibid. 17283/4. The Chinese did indeed kill some prisoners on the march. See e.g. TNA, WO 208/4005, KWC 754, 1282.

[38] See IWMDS, 16061/2, Dr B. Hickey; 16759/1, Dr D. Patchett; Matthews in Francis S. Jones, *No Rice for Rebels*, 22.

[39] Large, *One Man's War in Korea*, 80–1.

[40] On laggards being allowed to catch up again see NAA, Part 5, AI9/K/BRIT/4, Sgt W. A. Lucas, 2. On being placed aboard a bullock cart see Part 6, AI9/K/BRIT/456, Tpr S. Sears, 1. On hearing shots see IWMDS, 17283/4, A. Eagles; 18544/2, C. Sharpling.

[41] IWMDS, 18459/2, W. Clark; see Davies, *In Spite of Dungeons*, 38 ff.; ibid. 16618/4, C. Papworth; NAA, Part 3, AI9/K/BRIT/42, Lt J. M. C. Nicholls, 2; ibid. AI9/K/BRIT/70 et al., Capt. T. R. Littlewood et al., 2; ibid. AI9/K/BRIT/907 et al., Fus. J. Aitken et al., 7; ibid. AI9/K/BRIT/1000, Sgt S. F. Baxter, 1; Part 4, AI9/K/BRIT/958, 2/Lt D. J. English, 3; ibid. AI9/K/BRIT/878, Sgt J. R. Hunter, 1.

Allowing their captives to take a break, though, was not the only objective for the Chinese at this point. The halt provided the opportunity to ask questions, enforce discipline, and generate propaganda for foreign consumption.

Selective but often intensive interrogations took place of officers and NCOs diverted from Halfway House after arrival on military and political matters. Those who refused to cooperate were threatened and in some cases subjected to punishments favoured by the Chinese such as being flung into holes in the ground for lengthy periods or being strung up by the wrists with their arms tied behind them.[42]

Indeed, while up to this point the need to keep the column moving had limited the extent to which misbehaviour could be dealt with, at Halfway House the Chinese made it clear that non-compliance with their wishes could be and would be severely punished. Three men—perhaps only coincidentally an officer, a sergeant, and a private—were strung up for hours after heatedly arguing with guards and, in at least two cases, forced to make publicly admission of the error of their ways. These confessions were baffling and distasteful to Western sensibilities, but there was no gainsaying that the men concerned had been made an example of to discourage disorderly conduct.[43]

There were also some potential propaganda points to be scored. Filthy and unshaven though they were, the survivors of the Imjin battle were gathered in one place a column at a time, and the opportunity was taken to take pictures—one of which was eventually published in *Picture Post*.[44] Prisoners were also given the opportunity to write a letter home on rather flimsy paper, the Chinese correctly guessing that at least some captives would be desperate to let their loved ones know they were alive and that only positive depictions of their treatment would pass muster and actually be posted. 'Some refused to write', wrote Lofty Large, 'saying it was obviously some sort of Commie trick.' He and others, though, thought and acted as anticipated:

> I sat for a long time looking at that piece of paper, weighing up the pro's and con's. If I wrote and told the truth it would be very unlikely to get out of North Korea. Also, if by some miracle, the letter did get home [with a truthful account of conditions] what good would it do? My family would be worried sick, to say the least. I wrote a letter saying I had been slightly wounded and taken prisoner. I was being well treated and not to worry!

This letter and others did indeed arrive in the UK several months later.[45]

The Chinese also started issuing questionnaires. 'This form required us to complete details of number, rank, name, date of birth, unit, function of unit,

---

[42] NAA, Part 3, AI9/K/BRIT/79, Bdr D. J. Fitzgerald, 2; IWMDS, 17929/4, D. Sharp (see also TNA, WO 373/119, f. 248); Farrar-Hockley, *The Edge of the Sword*, 120–1; see also Large, *One Man's War in Korea*, 116; Davies, *In Spite of Dungeons*, 40; NAA, Part 3, AI9/K/BRIT/64, Rev S. J. Davies, 2; Part 5, AI9/K/BRIT/882, Sgt D. McAnulty, 2; ibid. AI9/K/BRIT/977, Lt A. Peal, 2.

[43] See Kinne, *The Wooden Boxes*, 55; Farrar-Hockley, *The Edge of the Sword*, 118–19.

[44] Davies, *In Spite of Dungeons*, 38; Farrar-Hockley, *The Edge of the Sword*, 118; NAA, Part 7, AI9/K/BRIT/965, Sgt W. H. Tuggey, 1.

[45] Large, *One Man's War in Korea*, 87.

how long we'd been in Korea, civil occupation, [and] next of kin', Private J. E. Wiseman remembered. When prisoners voiced concerns about going beyond name, rank, and number, the Chinese indicated that if the forms were not completed then families would not be informed that they were still alive. Some men held out, but others accepted the idea that getting one's name out was paramount.[46]

Such behaviour might suggest that those taken in April were starting to bend to the enemy's will. In fact there is a good deal of evidence to suggest that the Glosters and men from other units captured on the Imjin were a good deal more difficult to control at times than perhaps anticipated.

The Chinese had been doing everything they could to undermine British Army discipline and impose their own will. From the start, officers were informed in no uncertain terms that they no longer had any authority, and were soon segregated at the head of each column. The rest of the captives were to be organized into squads of a dozen or so men, to be headed by a democratically elected representative. The idea evidently was to create a new, more malleable chain of command, but things did not always work out this way. The men grouped themselves along existing squad and platoon lines, and according to Sergeant Frank Cottam the open vote 'took all of ten seconds, and surprise, surprise, resulted in a senior NCO as the leader of each squad'.[47] Once this started happening, the Chinese short-circuited the process and themselves chose squad leaders, often the youngest men. 'One prisoner in each squad was appointed "leader"', recalled Private R. F. Matthews, 'and was told that if any of his men escaped he would be shot.'[48]

There were plenty of men who did indeed discard the idea of trying to make their way back to UN lines as they moved north. As Matthews admitted:

> I didn't escape. Perhaps like the majority, I was too tired to begin with, and hadn't got back enough strength to make the effort seem worth while. A diet of rice and bug-dust doesn't build you up. Perhaps, too, my determination wasn't all it might have been. Escaping is a specialized pastime, and needs fitness, resoluteness of a high order, and a fair amount of initiative to cope with items such as food and which route to follow. I had no food, and hadn't the remotest idea where I was, or where the enemy was, either. In short I didn't try.[49]

Nevertheless dozens of British captives made bids for freedom in the first ten days or so of the march. It proved easy enough to drop away in the darkness when guards were not looking or when the columns took cover from potential air strikes. Everyone was picked up within a few days—men had few resources and it was impossible as Caucasians to avoid recognition by locals—and usually strung up or

[46] IWMDS, 30075/4, J. Wiseman.

[47] IWMDS, 21729/4, F. Cottam; see also ibid. 17929/4, D. Sharp; NAA, Part 3, AI9/K/BRIT/82, Sgt T. F. Clayden, 1. On the men sticking with their British Army squad and platoon mates see Green, *Captured at the Imjin River*, 110.

[48] Matthews in Francis S. Jones, *No Rice for Rebels*, 28; see also e.g. IWMDS, 30075/4, J. Wiseman.

[49] Matthews in Francis S. Jones, *No Rice for Rebels*, 29.

otherwise punished, but the mere effort proved that at least some prisoners did not wish to sit out the war in Chinese hands.[50]

The officers, though separated much of the time, did their best to set an example to the men and remind them that they were still soldiers, Colonel Carne telling his subordinates that he expected those who held the King's commission to uphold the highest standards of behaviour.[51] In between escape bids Farrar-Hockley continued to act as if he was adjutant, angrily telling a guard who was pushing him back into line at one point to keep his dirty hands off the King's uniform and at another juncture upbraiding a fusilier for not thinking of others and for giving away a piece of personal information to an interrogator.[52] Placing the officers at the head of the two columns where there were more guards gave them less chance to escape but also produced the impression that they were leading. 'The Colonel and Major [Denis] Harding were at the head of the column all the way', Private Keith Godwin later wrote of his CO and one of the company commanders, adding that Carne 'was a continuous source of inspiration to us all'. Such admiration was by no means confined to the Glosters. 'I always especially admired how the Colonel kept himself erect as he marched along, and the way he completely ignored the Chinese who tried to push him on to one path or another', remembered a fusilier.[53] Even the padre did his bit, encouraging the men to sing *Onward, Christian Soldiers* and getting struck for his efforts.[54]

Even without such encouragement the men were inclined to lift up their voices, reacting to yet another loss of orientation on the part of the escort with the chorus 'We are poor little lambs who have lost our way, baa, baa, baa' or whistling like canaries because they were being fed millet.[55] Passing through a village at one point where a North Korean army choir was practicing, Corporal Bill Westwood noted that without any prompting 'all the chaps got in step, and started singing army songs and drowned them out, quite honestly', adding: 'I think it did our morale a lot of good.'[56]

Of course even in the early days of the march not everyone stuck together, some men from the first refusing to help carry along those less physically able than themselves, for instance.[57] Fatigue and privation also took their toll as the columns set off

[50] See ibid.; Walters in *The Back Badge*, 229; Kinne, *The Wooden Boxes*, 32; IWMDS, 17283/4, A. Eagles; 26353/3, A. Hawkins (see also Tom Hickman, *The Call-Up* (London, 2004), 97); IWMDS, 17929/4, D. Sharp; 15557/3, G. Temple; 19871/1, W. Westwood; NAA, Part 4, AI9/K/BRIT/824, Pte R. B. Allum, 1; ibid. AI9/K/BRIT/875–876, Sgt F. W. Cottam and Sgt J. M. Hale, 3; Part 4, AI9/K/BRIT/390, Pte S. Foster, 1; ibid. AI9/K/BRIT/823, Fus. K. Fowler, 1; ibid. AI9/K/BRIT/108, Pte W. Kear, 2; Part 5, AI9/K/BRIT/894, Pte A. Marsh, 1; Part 6, AI9/K/BRIT/852, Sgt P. V. Petherick, 1; ibid. AI9/K/BRIT/377 et al. Part II, Pte D. C. Stocking et al., 1.

[51] C. Cunningham, *No Mercy, No Leniency: Communist Mistreatment of British Prisoners of War in Korea* (Barnsley, 2000), 76.

[52] Kinne, *The Wooden Boxes*, 44, 52–3; K. V. Godwin in *The Back Badge*, 231. On Farrar-Hockley taking a more shepherd-like attitude to leadership see e.g. IWMDS, 16618/3, C. Papworth.

[53] Kinne, *The Wooden Boxes*, 57; Godwin in *The Back Badge*.

[54] IWMDD, F. Carter, 40.

[55] Green, *Captured at the Imjin River*, 111; see IWMDS, 21729/5, F. Cottam.

[56] IWMDS, 19871/1, W. Westwood.

[57] See Davies, *In Spite of Dungeons*, 30; G. Hobson in Brian Catchpole, *The Korean War, 1950–53* (London, 2000), 211.

from Halfway House on the second leg of the journey. Derek Kinne, who after escaping and being recaptured had been away for some weeks, noticed a distinct change:

> A lot of the 'mucking in' spirit seemed to have disappeared. Men didn't help one another unless they happened to be particular friends. Nearly everyone would try to get away with getting food at the expense of other men. Individual troubles were not shared. There was general depression and apathy. Most of the sergeants and a few of the corporals tried to keep things on an organized basis, but it was an uphill job, often a failure. It seemed that so many of us were drugged—drugged by the shock of capture; the lack of food; the drain on our strength imposed by the long marches; the dark, obscure future in the hands of captors who plainly were not concerned with dispensing even the basis necessities of life.[58]

The Chinese escorts once again varied in their behaviour: some were sympathetic characters, others thoroughly detestable. For some friendly guards the march could be almost as taxing as it was for the prisoners, and enough mutual sympathy developed for the stronger captives to carry the packs of their captors.[59] Other characters were rather less sympathetic. Corporal Cyril Papworth, frustrated by the bullying and kicking inflicted by one particular guard at a stopping place made the mistake of striking him back. 'He was immediately pounced upon by several guards, his arms lashed behind his back, then, with his arms straight out behind him he had a rope tied around his wrists, and was hoisted off the ground to dangle from the branch of a tree for two or three hours', Lofty Large later wrote. 'We watched, helpless to do anything, as he went in and out of consciousness, the dysentery dripping from his feet, and the guards glaring at us over their guns.'[60] This was a relatively isolated incident, the corporal apparently being made an example of to remind prisoners who was in charge, though it certainly did nothing to win hearts and minds. 'The treatment they handed out showed us that the Chinese had nothing to learn about savagery', R. F. Matthews reflected.[61]

Among the non-walking wounded who were ferried northward through a succession of transit camps and medical facilities, treatment could vary from quite appalling—not least for those, like some of the escapees, snaffled as potential collaborators in the Pyongyang area by the North Koreans[62]—to fully professional. One sick British soldier fervently believed that a Chinese doctor saved his life, making him a prime candidate for indoctrination and service as a propagandist.[63] This tended not to be the case among the walking wounded or those in the carts trailing the columns, whose tribulations continued right up until early May–June 1951 when the columns arrived at Camp 1—and indeed, as we shall see, for some

[58] Kinne, *The Wooden Boxes*, 56.   [59] IWMDD, F. Carter, 39–40.

[60] Large, *One Man's War in Korea*, 90; see IWMDS, 16618/4, C. Papworth.

[61] Matthews in Francis S. Jones, *No Rice for Rebels*, 30; see Large, *One Man's War in Korea* (Matthews misidentified Papworth as 'Primrose'.)

[62] See ch. 4.

[63] See NAA, Part 6, AI9/K/BRIT/90, Tpr P. F. Rowley, 4; *Daily Worker*, 15 January 1952, 3; Chen Zhiyong, 'The Doctor and the Prisoner', *China Pictorial*, October 2003, <http://www.china-pictorial.com/chpic/htdocs/English/content/200310/3-2.htm> (accessed 19 April 2005). On decent medical treatment see e.g. NAA, Part 3, AI9/K/BRIT/954, Lt T. Conneeley, 3. On lack of medication see e.g. IWMDS, 19387/5, A. Perrins.

months further. One soldier, with several bullets in his chest, spat blood every night as he marched the first 200 miles northward. Eventually, he was put on an ox cart, but died on the last day. Private W. J. Donaldson was left to die by the side of the road within walking distance of his column's final destination.[64] In all 130 wounded and sick captives would die en route to the Yalu, most from a combination of poor treatment and lack of medical attention.[65] Those who survived were, in the words of one rifleman, 'a decrepit looking lot' by this point, '—our hair and beards were long, many of our boots were falling apart, clothing was torn, and most men looked emaciated'.[66]

Like the men taken prisoner in the winter, those moving north in the spring had managed to keep going in part because of the promise of a destination where everyone could finally stop permanently and where conditions would be better. Once again the reality turned out to be a world away from dreams of an all-inclusive Stalag.[67]

On 20 May the first column—followed by the second column twenty days later—turned a corner into a valley and saw their new home, adorned according to one prisoner with a sign that read 'Welcome to Chongson POW Camp No. 1.'[68] Some 25 miles away from Pyoktong as the crow flies, located on the south bank of a tributary stream 10 or so miles south of the Yalu River itself, the camp consisted for the most part of large numbers of Korean-style huts at the northern end of a village, framed with timber but with mud-and-straw walls, dirt floors, and thatched roofs. There was no running water and the common latrine was a simple open trench affair. There were no guard towers or even barbed wire, except for barriers at each end of the road that ran through the camp.[69]

These features, however, was not what forcibly struck the Imjin survivors as they moved down the road; it was the state of the inhabitants already in residence. Camp 1 had opened in March 1951 to accommodate hundreds of US prisoners captured after the CPV first intervened in the Korean War. Disease, starvation, and despair had taken terrible toll on the emaciated and zombie-like Americans, who to the British looked like concentration-camp victims: 'Belsen' was a common metaphor used by British ex-captives remembering the scene decades later.[70] Over

---

[64] Kinne, *The Wooden Boxes*, 578–9; NAA, Part 7, AI9/K/BRIT/870, Pte E. Viney, 2; Large, *One Man's War in Korea*, 81.

[65] Cyril Cunningham, *No Mercy, No Leniency*, 82; see, e.g., NAA, Part 7, AI9/K/BRIT/545, Pte H. Wheeler, 2.

[66] O'Kane, *O'Kane's Korea*, 79.

[67] See L/Cpl J. King in Tony Strachen (ed.), *In the Clutch of Circumstance* (Victoria, BC, 1985), 97; O'Kane, *O'Kane's Korea*, 75; IWMDS, 19664/3, V. Whitamore; 30075/4, J. Wiseman.

[68] On the sign see Green, *Captured at the Imjin River*, 114. On the arrival dates see e.g. NAA, Part 4, AI9/K/BRIT/390, Pte S. Foster, 1; ibid. AI9/K/BRIT/975, 981, Part I, WOII H. Gallagher and WOII A. E. Morton, 1.

[69] On the layout of the camp see J. King in Strachen, *In the Clutch of Circumstance*, 98; Green, *Captured at the Imjin River*, 115; Large, *One Man's War in Korea*, 90; Matthews in Francis S. Jones, *No Rice for Rebels*, 31; O'Kane, *O'Kane's Korea*, 80; IWMDS, F. Carter, 41; 16850/6, W. Gibson. On the latrines see e.g. Large, *One Man's War in Korea*, 104.

[70] See e.g. IWMDS, 21729/5, F. Cottom; 18544/2, C. Sharpling; 18439/2, A. Tyas; 19871/1, W. Westwood; 19664/3, V. Whitamore; King in Strachen, *In the Clutch of Circumstance*, 99.

the following weeks the horror of the scene only deepened, it becoming clear that up to twenty Americans or more were dying each day. 'Every day you would see their burial squad,' wrote David Green, 'shovels in hand, making two or three trips up the little hill to the cemetery, which was known as "Boot Hill".'[71]

Initial conditions were very poor indeed. Serious overcrowding was the norm, with squads assigned to hut rooms in which each man had to occupy under a square yard of space. 'You had to lie head to foot,' recalled Ronald Norley, 'just packed in like sardines for sleeping.' As Tony Eagles explained, this meant 'if one turned, you all had to turn'.[72] Rations mostly consisted of small quantities of boiled sorghum, and more occasionally boiled millet, served twice a day. Both tasted foul and the sorghum was, according to Dr Douglas Patchett, 'about the best laxative that I know of—it just went straight through you'.[73] Soon beriberi, night blindness, and other diseases related to malnutrition or to lice began to appear, while dysentery, sometimes accompanied by worms, reached near-epidemic proportions. 'Men had to rush out in the night several times', Lofty Large remembered, 'heading for the latrines.' Night blindness became so widespread that it was common enough for one man who could still see in the darkness to lead a column of five or six who could not on such excursions.[74] There was a camp infirmary of sorts; but there were almost no medical supplies or treatment and virtually no one came out alive, so men came to dread the place. 'I visited the "hospital" in the old temple after a few days', wrote Derek Kinne. 'Here their only comfort was a stoutly timbered floor. But the floor was already saturated with excrement from the sick men with dysentery who had lain and died upon it; soaked too, with pus that ran out from wounds for which there were no proper dressings.' Tablets made from ground-up bone or charcoal, along with the occasional aspirin, were the only medicines on offer, and were issued only *in extremis*. According to Gunner E. G. Bushy and Bombardier E. W. Maryan, 'charcoal tablets were virtually the only medicine available and then only issued if a man had to make about 24 visits to the latrine nightly'.[75] Under such conditions it

---

[71] Green, *Captured at the Imjin River*, 116; see Walters in *The Back Badge*, 230; Kinne, *The Wooden Boxes*, 62; Large, *One Man's War in Korea*, 91; IWMDS, 16618/4, C. Papworth. On the estimated death rate see NAA, Part 3, AI9/K/BRIT/340–341, Gnr E. G. Bushby and Bdr E. W. Maryan, 2; Part 4, AI9/K/BRIT/14–18, Pte A. E. Hunt et al., 3; Part 5, AI9/K/BRIT/4, Part I, Sgt W. A. Lucas, 2; IWMDS, 18262/6, F. Carter; 21729/5, F. Cottam; 17283/6, A. Eagles; 15539/3, E. Norley; 18439/2–3, A. Tyas.

[72] IWMDS, 12783/5, A. Eagles; 15539/3, E. Norley; see Matthews in Francis S. Jones, *No Rice for Rebels*, 32; O'Kane, *O'Kane's Korea*, 80; IWMDS, 16850/6, W. Gibson; 16618/4, C. Papworth; 18439/3, A. Tyas; 19871/2, W. Westwood.

[73] IWMDS, 16759/1, D. Patchett; see e.g. Walters in *The Back Badge*, 230; Godwin in *The Back Badge*, 231; Large, *One Man's War in Korea*, 101; O'Kane, *O'Kane's Korea*, 81; IWMDS, 16850/6, W. Gibson; King in Strachen, *In the Clutch of Circumstance*, 99.

[74] Large, *One Man's War in Korea*, 104. On night blindness see IWMDS, 26353/4, A. Hawkins; 16337/2, J. Grosvenor. On beriberi see ibid. 21729/6, F. Cottam; 16850/6, W. Gibson; 16618/4, C. Papworth. On other diseases associated with malnutrition see e.g. O'Kane, *O'Kane's Korea*, 81; J. Hart in Richard Peters and Xiaobang Li, *Voices from the Korean War* (Lexington, Ky., 2004), 238. On dysentery see ibid.; IWMDS, 21729/6, F. Cottam; 16850/6, W. Gibson; 16337/2, J. Grosvenor; 16618/4, C. Papworth; 18439/2, A. Tyas. On worms see ibid. 18262/4, F. Carter; 19871/2, W. Westwood.

[75] NAA, Part 3, AI9/K/BRIT/340–341, Gnr E. G. Bushby and Bdr E. W. Maryan, 2; Kinne, *The Wooden Boxes*, 64. On the 'hospital' see also Large, *One Man's War in Korea*, 97; IWMDS, 18262/6,

was hardly surprising that somewhere between ten and fifteen British prisoners died in the first weeks through a mixture of untreated wounds, sickness, malnutrition, and despair.[76]

Nevertheless members of the British contingent at Chongson often believed that they were coping far better than their American cousins. Some could recognize that the US prisoners had been suffering extreme privations, often in atrocious weather, for months longer than the men captured on the Imjin.[77] But even they might share the widespread British perception that the Yanks were both too soft (a higher standard of living sometimes leading them to refuse to eat what little was provided and succumb to give-up-itis) and too individualistic (a dog-eat-dog mentality which undermined discipline and prevented men from helping one another). 'The men didn't seem able to help themselves, and help each other, like the British troops did', remarked Albert Tyas. According to Ron Norley 'they were so used to home comforts, [that] when they had to rough it a bit they sort of gave up'.[78]

Such stereotyping was doubtless based on the fear that what had happened to the Americans could happen to the British. 'If we were scared before,' Jim King wrote, 'the sight of these poor guys frightened us even more. Would we be like that in a few weeks?' Frank Cottam was equally worried: 'I thought, "My God, how long is it going to take us to get like this?"'[79] The desire to avoid such a fate, however, helped the men accept the efforts of British officers and NCOs to maintain discipline and impose order to everyone's benefit.[80] Major 'Sam' Weller of the Glosters, the senior officer in the first column, immediately took charge, as R. F. Matthews related:

> The weary ones, who'd thought that after that long march surely to God there'd be a week or two's rest, soon learnt that they were still in the Army. The Major, now sport-

---

F. Carter. On the nature and shortage of medicines see Kinne, *The Wooden Boxes*; O'Kane, *O'Kane's Korea*, 82; NAA, Part 3, AI9/K/BRIT/955, Lt S. W. Cooper, 3; ibid. AI9/K/BRIT/979. Sgt S. J. Brisland, 2; Part 4, AI9/K/BRIT/981, Capt. R. P. Hickey, 2; Part 5, AI9/K/BRIT/4, Sjt W. A. Lucas, 2.

[76] On estimates concerning the number of British prisoners who died in this period see NAA, Part 4, AI9/K/BRIT/14 et al., Pte A. E. Hunt et al., 3; IWMDS, 18439/2, A. Tyas. On despair see Large, *One Man's War in Korea*, 97; IWMDS, 16618/4, C. Papworth.

[77] See e.g. Walters in *The Back Badge*, 230; King in Strachen, *In the Clutch of Circumstance*, 99; Green, *Captured at the Imjin River*, 115; Matthews in Francis S. Jones, *No Rice for Rebels*, 36; IWMDD, F. Carter, 44; IWMDS, 15539/3, R. Norley; 16618/4, C. Papworth. On the trials and tribulations of the Americans before they even reached Chongson see e.g. G. Matta in US Senate, Subcommittee on Investigations on Government Operations, *Korean War Atrocities* (Washington, DC, 1954), 113–19; D. Griffith, <http://www.loc.gov/vets/stories/pow-korea.html#stories> (accessed 15 November 2010); J. Smith in Arthur W. Wilson (ed.), *Korean Vignettes* (Portland, Oreg., 1996), 129.

[78] IWMDS, 15539/3, R. Norley; 18439/2, A. Tyas; see also e.g. ibid. 18459/2, W. Clark; 12783/6, A. Eagles; 15338/5, B. Murphy; 16850/6, W. Gibson; 19664/3, V. Whitamore; IWMDD, F. Carter, 44; NAA, Part 4, AI9/K/BRIT/14 et al., Pte A. E. Hunt et al., 3; Matthews in Francis S. Jones, *No Rice for Rebels*, 36.

[79] IWMDS, 21729/5, F. Cottam; King in Strachen, *In the Clutch of Circumstance*, 99.

[80] See Green, *Captured at the Imjin River*, 116; NAA, Part 4, AI9/K/BRIT/14 et al., Pte A. E. Hunt et al., 3. It should be noted that the British, including the officers, were not immune from 'give-up-itis'. 2/Lt Beverley Gale, for instance, though not badly wounded, appears to have more or less willed himself to die through despair at the thought of a rival having the opportunity to woo exclusively the young woman they were both interested in. Ironically the rival in question, a Fleet Air Arm pilot, was shot down over North Korea and taken prisoner too. IWMDS, 19387/5, A. Perrins.

ing a ferocious red beard, went the orderly-officer rounds, had plenty to say to incipient slackers, and found enough work to keep all idle hands busy. He made us dig proper latrines, and fill in unsanitary holes in the ground that were extending a warm welcome to dysentery and other unpleasant ailments.[81]

The sick were nursed by their fellows, while huts and bodies were kept as clean and (in the latter case) active as circumstance allowed.[82]

The Chinese camp authorities were happy enough to see actions that would improve hygiene and inmate survivability in Camp 1, and may indeed themselves have fostered the idea that the British were setting a good example to the Americans as part of a not entirely unsuccessful effort to develop anti-Americanism.[83] What they were far less happy with was the way in which this was carried out through the British Army chain of command. When the two columns arrived they were addressed about the impossibility of escape and the Lenient Policy—that is, instead of being killed for their crimes against the peace-loving peoples they would be treated as mere dupes of the capitalist warmongers who would now be given the opportunity to learn the truth. Those who resisted, it was implied, would be viewed as 'reactionaries' and treated accordingly.[84] It was rightly assumed that officers might seek to counteract this process, which was why when Weller tried to insist on his rights as Senior British Officer he was brusquely told that the British rank structure had ceased to exist and that 'we will give orders, not you'.[85]

As a private in the Glosters later explained, 'the general attitude of the Chinese' was that 'there was no need to pay respect to officers and NCOs, and that we could do what we liked. Now was our chance to get our own back on our officers.' It soon became evident 'that this didn't work, respect was still paid to officers, saluting continued within the camp' and that a competing command structure still functioned.[86]

The Chinese authorities remained interested in whatever military information the prisoners might possess, and sometimes engaged in intensive interrogation in the coming months of captives at Chongson whom it was thought might have

---

[81] Matthews in Francis S. Jones, *No Rice for Rebels*, 32–3; see TNA, WO 373/119, citation for Maj. P. W. Weller, f. 188.

[82] See e.g. Green, *Captured at the Imjin River*, 116–18; King in Strachen, *In the Clutch of Circumstance*, 100; Large, *One Man's War in Korea*, 97; NAA, Part 4, AI9/K/BRIT/14 et al., Pte A. E. Hunt et al., 3.

[83] On setting an example see e.g. IWMDD, F. Carter, 44; Green, *Captured at the Imjin River*, 117. On the Chinese trying to foster anti-American sentiment among the British see Edward Hunter, *Brainwashing* (New York, 1956), 189; see also e.g. *Daily Worker*, 18 December 1951, 2. On the success of this effort see e.g. NAA, Part 4, AI9/K/BRIT/14 et al., Pte A. E. Hunt et al., 9. A number of Americans *did* think the British set a good example (see Hunter, *Brainwashing*, 190), though others believed the Chinese favoured the British at their expense (see NARA, RG 319, entry 85, Phase III summaries, box 1026, Clyde E. Barton, Donald R. Bitner; box 1033, Henry M. Lyman; box 1034, William Miller, Wilmer Norman; box 1035, Christopher Papagopoulos, Donald E. Paul).

[84] See Large, *One Man's War in Korea*, 98; O'Kane, *O'Kane's Korea*, 79; IWMDD, F. Carter, 41; NAA, Part 6, AI9/K/BRIT/2, Sgt S. Robinson, Part I, 8–9.

[85] IWMDS, 19871/2, W. Westwood.

[86] Ibid. 30075/4, J. Wiseman; see ibid. 18262/6, F. Carter; TNA, WO 373/119, citation for Maj. E. D. Harding, f. 243.

knowledge of specialist forces or branches.[87] Even more important, judging by the effort put into it, was the goal of collecting as much personal information as possible on each individual man as part of the re-education effort. Questionnaires were issued at various stages asking for the socio-economic background—everything from religion and education to wages and street addresses—of not only the man concerned but also his family and friends, and whatever was put down was usually subject to rigorous cross-checking and verbal or written repetition.[88] The officers were not keen on going beyond name, rank, and number, and the NCOs only did so when they were given the false impression that Colonel Carne had done so himself. As for the rank and file, they too refused to do so until threatened with dire consequences.[89]

This recalcitrant attitude was at least in part the result of semi-clandestine efforts by the officers to bypass Chinese insistence that British Army rank no longer counted. Thus when the camp authorities tried to dissolve the traditional hierarchy among the officers by making the youngest their squad leader, 22-year-old Lieutenant A. F. Blundell refused to give orders on their behalf, and deliberately made himself so objectionable to the Chinese that he was eventually relieved.[90] As for the rank and file, the senior officers reminded men of their duty and pointed out the likely consequences of collaboration. 'It was made quite clear by Major Weller', reported Second Lieutenant D. J. English, 'that all prisoners of war were subject to military law, and that on their return to freedom, a court of inquiry would be held on each one of them, to determine how they behaved themselves, at the time of capture, and whilst a P. O.W.'[91]

Undeterred, the Chinese, within weeks of the British arriving, selected some the youngest men to be squad leaders among the rank and file and took many of them off for an intensive course of political indoctrination in what would become known to some as 'Chong-Song University'.[92] In the summer the full-scale programme got underway for the general population at Camp 1 with a mixture of compulsory morning lectures followed by topical squad discussions on Marxist-Leninist subjects of a kind familiar to inhabitants of Camp 5. As a British captain reported after questioning three soldiers from Chongson in the wake of their eventual release,

[87] See e.g. NAA, Part 3, AI9/K/BRIT/178 et al., Pte L. Allen et al., 17; ibid. AI9/K/BRIT/825, Tpr K. M. Bielby, 1; Part 4, AI9/K/BRIT/390, Pte S. Foster, 2; ibid. AI9/K/BRIT/160, Sgmn H. Jennings, 2; Part 6, AI9/K/BRIT/392 et al., Pte T. Pink et al., 2; TNA, WO 373/119, f. 249.

[88] On the extent of personal questioning see e.g. NAA, Part 4, AI9/K/BRIT/296, Cpl J. T. Green; Part 5, AI9/K/BRIT/4, Part I, Sgt W. A. Lucas, 8. On cross-checking see e.g. Part 6, AI9/K/BRIT/2, Sgt S. Robinson, Part I, 7; ibid. AI9/K/BRIT/549, Sgt B. M. Smith, 4. On repetition see e.g. Part 7, AI9/K/BRIT/449, Cpl S. H. Truan, 1; O'Kane, *O'Kane's Korea*, 90.

[89] On Carne, the NCOs and rank and file see NAA, Part 3, AI9/K/BRIT/82, Sgt T. F. Clayden, 2. On the officers refusing, see e.g. Part 6, AI9/K/BRIT/977, Lt A. Peal, 2.

[90] Ibid. Part 3, AI9/K/BRIT/849, 842, Lt A. F. Blundell and 2/Lt J. A. Haggerty, 1–2; ibid. AI9/K/BRIT/955, Lt S. W. Cooper, 3.

[91] Ibid. Part 4, AI9/K/BRIT/958, 2/Lt D. J. English, 3.

[92] On selection of the young for squad leadership and the preliminary course see Matthews in Francis S. Jones, *No Rice for Rebels*, 47; NAA, Part 3, AI9/K/BRIT/178 et al., Pte L. Allen et al., 22; ibid. AI9/K/BRIT/340–341, Gnr E. G. Bushby and Bdr E. W. Maryan, 3; Part 7, AI9/K/BRIT/157, Cpl W. K. Westwood, 3. On the 'university' label see IWMDS, 21729/5, F. Cottam; L. Jimenez in Robert E. Davis, *Ex-POWs of Alabama* (Montgomery, Ala., 1984), 450.

'instructional classes were given which led the students through the ages from the Feudal system to the present day, pointing out the evils of private enterprise, capitalism, imperialism, and the basic reasons for the Korean war'.[93]

The senior officers tried to set an example to the men by insisting that those with commissions all form up and move in step smartly to the parade ground where prisoners were assembled for the morning lectures 'because marching seemed to be a soldierly thing to do and we wanted to show that we were still soldiers, come what may', as Lieutenant Peter Whitamore explained many years later.[94] They were also not slow to ask awkward questions during the lectures, something made easier by the inadequate knowledge and verbal skill of the speakers compared to those who held the King's commission. Second Lieutenant Arthur Peal later reported that 'his brief study of politics and economics at RMA Sandhurst was a great help in counter-acting the Communist indoctrination'.[95]

With the rank and file having taken to singing *Land of Hope and Glory* on the way to the lectures and, taking their lead from the officers, refusing to take the bait of a letter home in return for signing a peace petition, it was clear to the camp authorities that the men would have to be separated from their leaders. Weller was arrested and then removed after being caught red-handed giving a soldier a direct order, followed by Carne himself because, as he later put it, his presence was affecting junior officers 'and preventing them from absorbing the Communist propaganda'.[96] The entire officer contingent was relocated to a distant part of the camp, and the senior NCOs segregated from the men.[97]

It was also made clear to the rank and file that there would be negative consequences for anyone who voiced dissent in the lectures or during squad discussions. Vocal reactionaries of this kind would be subjected to lengthy quiz sessions by Chinese staff, which often meant a meal was missed by men already in a state near starvation.[98] Those who still did not get the message could find themselves, like Private Keith Godwin and fourteen other 'backward students', isolated and forced to study six hours daily for six days a week for twelve weeks.[99] Really hard cases could find themselves relegated to solitary confinement under extremely unhygienic conditions for weeks or months until they made a public confession that

---

[93] NAA, Part 4, AI9/K/BRIT/14 et al., Pte A. E. Hunt et al., 9; see also e.g. IWMDS, 21729/5, F. Cottam.

[94] IWMDS, 19664/3, V. Whitamore.

[95] NAA, Part 6, AI9/K/BRIT/977, Lt A. Peal, 2. On the limited knowledge and poor oratorical skills of the lecturers see Part 5, AI9/K/BRIT/67, Capt. A. M. L. Newcombe, 2. On asking awkward questions see Cunningham, *No Mercy, No Leniency*, 85–6.

[96] TNA, WO 208/4021, Verbatim Transcript of the Re-Interrogation of Lt Col. J. P. Carne, f. 2. On the arrest of Weller see Cunningham, *No Mercy, No Leniency*, 85. On 'Land of Hope and Glory' see Large, *One Man's War in Korea*, 133. On refusing to sign the peace petition at the behest of the officers see Kinne, *The Wooden Boxes*, 93–4; see also NAA, Part 5, Sjt W. A. Lucas, Part I, 5.

[97] See Kinne, *The Wooden Boxes*, 90–1; NAA, Part 3, AI9/K/BRIT/955, Lt S. W. Cooper, 2; Part 4, AI9/K/BRIT/14 et al., Pte A. E. Hunt et al., 4; IWMDS, 21729/5, F. Cottam; 15338/5, B. Murphy.

[98] See e.g. IWMDS, 12783/4, A. Eagles; Matthews in Francis S. Jones, *No Rice for Rebels*, 56–8; Kinne, *The Wooden Boxes*, 84–5; Andy McNab, *Immediate Action* (London, 1995), 142.

[99] Godwin in *The Back Badge*.

they had been wrong to engage in 'frivolous and insulting behaviour during study periods'.[100]

In addition, in a more subtle fashion, it was made evident that a progressive attitude arising from indoctrination would be rewarded. Those who cooperated would be more likely to be able to send and receive mail or get extra food and cigarettes. There was also a widely believed rumour that if someone showed himself to be sufficiently progressive he could expect to be released early.[101]

The Chinese also sought to instill gratitude and thereby cooperation by highlighting the ways in which camp conditions under their supervision gradually improved through the latter months of 1951 and on into 1952. Among the first advances was the regular issue of limited amounts of tobacco and sugar.[102] In the summer months the disintegrating clothing and boots in which men had been captured were replaced by blue cotton high-neck jackets and trousers plus a blue peaked soft cap, a white shirt, cotton underwear, and rubber-soled shoes. In the winter months this suit was in turn exchanged for padded, kapok-filled blue jackets, caps with earflaps, and canvas boots with foot-wrappings.[103] Each man was also issued with a bowl, a small amount of soap, a towel, toothbrush plus razor, and bathing was allowed in the river.[104] Straw mats replaced bare floors, in time quilts were issued in place of sacking as sleeping covers in the cold, and eventually some bunk-beds and stools were constructed.[105] The camp authorities could not take credit for the traditional Korean under-floor heating that existed in the huts prior to their occupation, but they had insisted the prisoners go out wood-gathering in the surrounding hills prior to the onset of cold weather to build up a fuel supply for the winter months that proved vital to survival.[106]

Just as important as improvements in clothing and shelter were advances in nutrition and medical care. By the end of 1951 and more commonly in 1952 prisoners were getting some rice, eggs, steamed corn bread, vegetables, and even small amounts of meat. As Frank Cottam put it, while the food 'was never what you got at the Dorchester, it was reasonable'.[107] Medicines remained in short supply, but

[100]　NAA, Part 3, AI9/K/BRIT/246 et al., Pte A. J. Allum et al., 3; see e.g. King in Strachen, *In the Clutch of Circumstance*, 102–3.

[101]　On the early release rumour see NAA, Part 7, AI9/K/BRIT/157, Cpl W. K. Westwood, 4; Matthews in Francis S. Jones, *No Rice for Rebels*, 48. On the lure of better treatment see e.g. Jones in Knox, *The Korean War*, 335; Kinne, *The Wooden Boxes*, 75; NAA, Part 6, AI9/K/BRIT/156 Part II, L/Cpl H. C. Sharpling, 2. On mail see e.g. IWMDD, F. Carter, 49.

[102]　On tobacco being issued see e.g. Green, *Captured at the Imjin River*, 64; Large, *One Man's War in Korea*, 119; Matthews in Francis S. Jones, *No Rice for Rebels*, 34; IWMDS, 16337/2, J. Grosvenor; 19871/2, W. Westwood. On sugar see Large, *One Man's War in Korea*, 101; Matthews in Francis S. Jones, *No Rice for Rebels*.

[103]　On the issuing of summer clothing see Green, *Captured at the Imjin River*, 146; O'Kane, *O'Kane's Korea*, 87; IWMDS, 19871/2, W. Westwood; NAA, Part 6, AI9/K/BRIT/2, Part I, Sgt S. Robinson, 3. On the issue of winter clothing see Green, *Captured at the Imjin River*, 146; O'Kane, *O'Kane's Korea*, 92–3; IWMDS, 18439/3, A. Tyas.

[104]　See IWMDS, 16850/7, W. Gibson; 16337/2, J. Grosvenor; 16618/4, C. Papworth; 19871/2, W. Westwood.

[105]　See e.g. ibid. 19871/2, W. Westwood; Green. *Captured at the Imjin River*, 147.

[106]　See e.g. IWMDS, 18439/3, A. Tyas; O'Kane, *O'Kane's Korea*, 93.

[107]　IWMDS, 21729/6, F. Cottam; see Walters in *The Back Badge*, 230; Green, *Captured at the Imjin River*, 119–20; Large, *One Man's War in Korea*, 134; Matthews in Francis S. Jones, *No Rice for Rebels*, 34; IWMDS, 18262/7, F. Carter; 12783/5, A. Eagles; IWMDD, F. Carter, 50–1.

prisoners were impressed by the efforts of a Dr Wu, an Edinburgh-trained woman surgeon, to do what she could for them, and by Chinese efforts to eradicate germ-carrying flies and inoculate against typhoid.[108]

The Chinese also encouraged recreational diversions. Men were allowed to make chess sets and packs of cards, even a dart board and darts (until the latter were banned as potential weapons). Above all a soccer ball was eventually provided: 'Football now played a large part in the lives of the men', according to Keith Godwin.[109]

With the leaders removed and conditions improving, compulsory lectures and study thereafter did yield some superficially quite positive results from the Chinese perspective down into the first months of 1952. Ordinary soldiers were often not as well educated as the officers and senior NCOs from whom they had been separated, and thus a bit more likely to fall prey to the arguments of the more articulate instructors. The pent-up resentments of some of the reservists at having been called back to the colours might also play into Chinese hands.[110] Some men were flattered by the interest taken in them; some became partial converts, including an occasional NCO; and once all the overt troublemakers had been identified and removed one soldier estimated that just over half the British in Camp 1 were affected to a greater or lesser degree by enemy efforts.[111] Furthermore, while only a few British soldiers at Chongson proved willing to make broadcasts, once the officers were gone many signed peace petitions if bait was offered, and most accepted the need to insert anti-war slogans and comments praising their treatment by the CPV in order to get news of their capture home in letters.[112]

---

[108] On Dr Wu see Large, *One Man's War in Korea*, 139; IWMDD, F. Carter, 48; NAA, Part 3, AI9/K/BRIT/907 et al., Fus. J. Aitkin et al., 9; Part 4, AI9/K/BRIT/14 et al., Part I, Pte A. E. Hunt et al., 7; Part 5, AI9/K/BRIT/894, Pte A. Marsh, 3. On the 1952 fly eradication campaign, in which the prisoners took a leading role in exchange for cigarette paper, see Green, *Captured at the Imjin River*, 127; Large, *One Man's War in Korea*, 129; Matthews in Francis S. Jones, *No Rice for Rebels*, 62; IWMDS, 16618/4, C. Papworth; 18439/3, A. Tyas.

[109] Godwin in *The Back Badge*, 231. On football see also IWMDS, 17283/5, A. Eagles; NAA, Part 3, AI9/K/BRIT/971 et al., Sgt P. C. Crompton et al., 2. On darts see Green, *Captured at the Imjin River*, 125; Large, *One Man's War in Korea*, 119; IWMDS, 18262/7, F. Carter. On chess see O'Kane, *O'Kane's Korea*, 93. On cards see Green, *Captured at the Imjin River*, 145; Large, *One Man's War in Korea*; IWMDD, F. Carter, 48. On music and shows see Large, *One Man's War in Korea*, 121; Green, *Captured at the Imjin River*, 151; O'Kane, *O'Kane's Korea*, 94.

[110] On effective instructors see e.g. IWMDS, 18262/6, F. Carter. On the men being ill-equipped educationally to counter-argue with the instructors and the problem of reservist disgruntlement see e.g. ibid. 30075/2, J. Wiseman; Matthews in Francis S. Jones, *No Rice for Rebels*, 103.

[111] NAA, Part 4, AI9/K/BRIT/160, Sgmn H. Jennings, 2; see also ibid. AI9/K/BRIT/14 et al., Pte A. E. Hunt et al., 9; Part 3, AI9/K/BRIT/423 et al., Rfn H. Burton et al., 3; ibid. AI9/K/BRIT/875–876, Sgt F. W. Cottam and Sgt J. M. Hale, 2; ibid. AI9/K/BRIT/606, Gnr J. C. Dabbs, 3. On flattery producing cooperation see e.g. ibid. AI9/K/BRIT/824, Pte R. B. Allum, 2; Matthews in Francis S. Jones, *No Rice for Rebels*, 132.

[112] On letters see NAA, Part 3, AI9(a)/S/150/87, Interrogation Report on British Ex-PW Released in Korea, Batch 2 (Supplementary), 2D, Pte M. E. Boundin, 1; ibid. AI9/K/BRIT/690 et al., Pte L. Allen et al., comments *re* Pte T. Barry and Pte T. R. Bingham, 23, 26; Part 6, AI9/K/BRIT/2, Part I, Sgt S. Robinson, 11; ibid. AI9/K/BRIT/469, Pte M. Pendle, 2; IWMDS, 30075/4, J. Wiseman; Large, *One Man's War in Korea*, 105; see also e.g. IWMDD, letters of D. Kaye. On peace petitions see NAA, Part 4, AI9/K/BRIT/421, Cpl D. W. Hansford, 5; Part 5, AI9/K/BRIT/469, Pte M. Pendle, 2; Kinne, *The Wooden Boxes*, 70; *Daily Worker*, 1 July 1953, 1. On broadcasts see NAA, Part 3, AI9/K/BRIT/463 et al., Rfn R. Boyd et al., 4; Part 4, AI9/K/BRIT/441, Pte R. Foster, 2; ibid. AI9/K/BRIT/421, Cpl D. W. Hansford, 5; Part 6, AI9/K/BRIT/549, Sgt B. M. Smith, 2 and Annex A.

Overall, however, the Chinese compulsory indoctrination effort at Camp 1 among the British cannot be judged a success. Men were baffled and alienated far more often than they were engaged by what was taught and how improvements in living conditions were always only relative, and even when reactionaries were removed the bulk of the Imjin prisoners still proved remarkably resistant to becoming willing tools of communism. Even without officers and senior NCOs, a remarkable number of figures played along with the Chinese without seriously collaborating and engaged in highly subversive activities such as escaping.

The lectures, usually delivered in Chinese and then translated into English by an interpreter, were universally considered long, boring, and often incomprehensible. Careful to avoid the attentions of roving guards, men surreptitiously slept or even played cards to pass the time.[113] As for the discussion groups, while men learned to give the Chinese what they wanted in terms of written or verbal responses from the appointed monitor, only when a Chinese instructor or guard was about did squads actually talk politics (and sometimes not even then if it was clear that lapsing into broad regional accents and using local colloquialisms made it impossible for the enemy to understand what was being said). Most of the time was given over to playing games and chatting about football and other personal interests.[114] For many the subject matter was in any case too abstract to comprehend, former corporal Jim Bateman commenting many years later that even if the Chinese had persevered for decades, ordinary soldiers 'still wouldn't have grasped the fundamental contradictions between capitalism and socialism'. Ex-private David Kaye agreed: 'if we'd stopped there for fifty years I don't think it would have worked'.[115] Even for those who did understand, the fact that enlightenment was being peddled by the King's enemies meant that, as Bill Gibson explained, 'it was like water off a duck's back'.[116]

Some of the instructors did themselves no favours by betraying their extreme ignorance of life in contemporary Britain. 'I mean,' Kaye explained, 'they just did not believe us when we said we had cars, shops.' At best their conception was laughably Dickensian. At worst, as Ron Norley put it, 'they thought we still lived in the Middle Ages, under feudal landlords'.[117] Running water piped into homes, not to speak of flush toilets, were beyond them. Frank Cottam was baffled when

[113] Green, *Captured at the Imjin River*, 124; IWMDS, 26353/3, A. Hawkins; NAA, Part 3, AI9/K/BRIT/971 et al., Sgt P. C. Crompton et al., 4.

[114] Green, *Captured at the Imjin River*, 122, 125; Matthews in Francis S. Jones, *No Rice for Rebels*, 54, 59 ff.; IWMDS, 18459/2, W. Clark; 26353/3, A. Hawkins; 17468/2, D. Kaye; 16618/5, C. Papworth; 30075/4, J. Wiseman; NAA Part 3, AI9/K/BRIT/92, Pte D. R. Butcher, 3; Part 6, AI9/K/BRIT/479, Cpl J. W. Peskett, 4; ibid. AI9/K/BRIT/2, Part I, Sgt S. Robinson, 9. On regional accents and colloquialisms see A. Tyas in Hickman, *The Call-Up*, 98.

[115] IWMDS, 17468/3, D. Kaye; J. Bateman in *Korea: The Unknown War* (Thames Television, 1988). On material being beyond the comprehension of even some senior NCOs see NAA, Part 6, AI9/K/BRIT/961, WO II F. G. Strong, 3.

[116] IWMDS, 16850/6, W. Gibson. It was even claimed that one squad managed to counter-argue so successfully that their instructor had to be removed. NAA, Part 3, AI9/K/BRIT/346 et al., Pte W. J. Cooke et al., 2; see also IWMDD, F. Carter, 47–8.

[117] IWMDS, 15539/3, R. Norley; 17468/2, D. Kaye. On Dickens as a source for the Chinese see e.g. ibid. 16850/11, W. Gibson; 16759/1, D. Patchett.

asked: 'what will your family do now the rainy season has arrived and you're not home to plant the rice?'[118] Jim Bateman was doubtless right when he opined that the Chinese could never convince him and his mates 'that their way of life was better than ours'.[119]

The cultural gulf could be great. Unlike their Chinese counterparts, British soldiers considered it effeminate for men to hold hands, and at least some thought the habit among the guards of publicly and loudly collecting and spitting out phlegm rather disgusting.[120] Ideas concerning what was, and what was not, a 'crime' could differ radically; prisoners, for example, sometimes finding themselves charged with destroying the people's property after having innocently torn up pages from the *Shanghai News* in order to roll cigarettes and smoke their tobacco ration.[121] In one notorious instance the Chinese mistook the significance of a student-soldier giving a passing woman a visual once-over accompanied by a wolf-whistle, and from a Western perspective massively overreacted by charging the man with rape.[122] When a loudspeaker system was eventually installed, the recorded music played often grated on Western ears—'banging cymbals, drums going on, someone screeching at the top of their voice'[123]—while the staff seem to have entirely missed the irony involved in prisoners hearing Paul Robeson singing *The Internationale* with verses such as 'arise, ye prisoners of starvation'.[124]

In such circumstances gratitude was in short supply. The rations may have improved, but men were still thin and hungry. 'If you could have seen our daily diet,' wrote David Green, 'you never would have believed that a man could live on it.' Malnutrition remained a problem through the winter of 1952–3.[125] Despite the ministrations of Dr Wu and the efforts of the British medical orderlies, moreover, drugs remained in short supply and treatment crude. Everything from shrapnel to rotten molars had to be extracted without benefit of proper anesthetics using whatever substitute painkillers and tools were at hand. For the pulling of teeth, for example, for which rusty pliers had to be used, patients might be bear-hugged into brief unconsciousness or advised to smoke marijuana, which grew wild in the surrounding hills, before being held down.[126] 'Conditions improved gradually,' Lofty

---

[118] Ibid. 21729/6, F. Cottam; see also e.g. ibid. 18262/9, F. Carter. On indoor plumbing see Matthews in Francis S. Jones, *No Rice for Rebels*, 136.

[119] J. Bateman in *Korea: The Unknown War* (Thames Television, 1988).

[120] On spitting see IWMDS, 17468/2, D. Kaye. On holding hands see Green, *Captured at the Imjin River*, 139.

[121] Matthews in Francis S. Jones, *No Rice for Rebels*, 49–50; see also Jones in Knox, *The Korean War*, 335–6; Green, *Captured at the Imjin River*, 122.

[122] See Large, *One Man's War in Korea*, 128; IWMDD, F. Carter, 53.

[123] IWMDS, 16850/9, W. Gibson; see IWMDD, F. Carter, 53. Sometimes Russian classical music was played, though this too could grate after a while. See ibid. 53–4.

[124] O'Kane, *O'Kane's Korea*, 93; Green, *Captured at the Imjin River*, 155.

[125] Green, *Captured at the Imjin River*, 153, 145–6.

[126] See ibid. 149; IWMDS, 18262/7, F. Carter; 16850/7, W. Gibson; Large, *One Man's War in Korea*, 106–7. Marijuana was also smoked by some British prisoners for recreational purposes, but the alterations in behaviour this produced—e.g. L/Cpl Jack Spence ran around with his arms outstretched imagining he was an aeroplane until he crashed into something—caused the Chinese and even some British users to ban it. Green, *Captured at the Imjin River*, 154; NAA, Part 6, AI9/K/BRIT/2, Part I, Sgt S. Robinson, 3; IWMDD, F. Carter, 51. On Spence see O'Kane, *O'Kane's Korea*, 99.

Large remembered, 'with the Chinese trying to gain the maximum Commie propaganda out of each step. The more they tried the more they failed, of course, such
is the British nature.'[127]

This may not have been clear to the Chinese over the winter of 1951–2. As
noted, prisoners had become adept at saying or writing things in praise of communism while mentally dismissing them, in the words of one corporal, as 'a load
of codswallop'.[128] Yet there existed a number of indications that the British rank
and file at Chongson remained far less accommodating than their counterparts at
Pyoktong.

To begin with, despite the twin dangers of misidentification and retribution by
the Chinese, groups of other-rank de facto vigilantes took to hunting down those
they suspected of collaboration in the late summer of 1951. According to Dave
Green they were 'a bunch of hooligans who specialized in bullying the so-called
"Reds" ', usually only those smaller than themselves. 'We caught several of them,'
R. F. Matthews recalled, 'stripped off their trousers, and daubed their buttocks
bright blue with an indelible dye from the medical room.' He recognized, though,
that boredom and restlessness rather than cool calculation increasingly lay behind
what was going on: 'Men who were normally rational acted wantonly and sometimes visciously, and with every real and suspected collaborator equipped with a
bright blue bottom, innocents began to fall foul of the mob.' Threats of dire consequences from the Chinese, and a shocked realization that things were getting out
of hand among the patriots themselves, led to the abandonment of such
tactics.[129]

Efforts to defeat collaboration, however, continued. Independently of one
another Corporal Frank Upjohn and Corporal Bill Westwood, though chosen as
members of the camp peace committee by the Chinese, were in fact only posing as
progressives in order to gather intelligence on who really was cooperating with the
enemy.[130] When it became known that one of the identified progressives was writing a scurrilous manuscript under Chinese supervision about the Glosters in Korea,
Private D. 'Fingers' Haines and other reactionaries stole it before it could be used
for propaganda purposes and made plans to bring it home when repatriation took
place to use as evidence against the author.[131] Lance Corporal H. C. Sharpling and
Private N. A. Ward meanwhile surreptitiously put up notices reminding prisoners
of their duty to King and Country and the consequences of collaboration when
repatriation eventually occurred.[132] In addition, as another soldier recalled:

[127] Large, *One Man's War in Korea*, 113.
[128] IWMDS, 155349/3, R. Norley; see e.g. Green, *Captured at the Imjin River*, 120; Matthews,
Francis S. Jones, *No Rice for Rebels*, 59 ff.; IWMDS, 18459/2, W. Clark; 26353/3, A. Hawkins.
[129] Matthews in Francis S. Jones, *No Rice for Rebels*, 64–5; Green, *Captured at the Imjin River*,
136.
[130] NAA, Part 7, AI9/K/BRIT/157 Part II, Cpl W. K. Westwood, 2–4.
[131] Ibid. Part 3, AI9/K/BRIT/246 et al., A. J. Allum et al., 7; see also ibid. AI9/K/BRIT/907, Fus.
J. Aitken et al., 11; ibid. AI9/K/BRIT/483 et al., Pte A. Anderson, 6. On some of the leading individuals involved in resisting enemy subversion efforts see TNA, WO 373/119, ff. 195, 197,199, 201,
203, 205, 207.
[132] NAA, Part 6, AI9/K/BRIT/156 Part II, L/Cpl H. C. Sharpling, 3.

Little hangman's nooses would appear as if by magic in all sorts of places. On the notice boards. Over the doorway to the Chinese Office. At the end of the office verandah, right under the noses of the guards. One of the sentries nearly went off his head when he saw a noose hanging from a tree opposite his sentry box. But he looked even more shaken when he returned to his sentry box and found one hanging over the doorway.[133]

This particular effort indicates that prisoners were interested in ragging the enemy as well as deterring collaborators. British captives at Chongson, whether they were hard-core reactionaries or the far more common individuals just trying to survive,[134] were happy to try and generate confusion and bafflement among the Chinese.

Several among the British contingent had been POWs in the Second World War, and it was through them that techniques once used on the Germans were revived. Individually or in groups, prisoners took to engaging in activities with invisible props: walking an imaginary dog on an invisible lead, kicking around an imaginary football, staging a tug of war with no rope, or perhaps sewing with imaginary needle and thread. The table tennis version, according to Lofty Large, was particularly effective in inducing uncertainty among the guards:

> Two men would go through the motions of playing a fast game of table tennis, in an open area between the huts, or in the road. A crowd of persons would gather and all heads would move together as the 'ball' went from end to end. The Chinese would notice the crowd and inevitably investigate. From behind the crowd it would look very realistic, but as soon as the Chinese tried to push through to see what was going on everyone would turn and move silently away.[135]

The guards showed satisfying signs of being utterly mystified by this kind of behaviour; though sometimes—as when men ordered to engage in exercise began thumb-twiddling, eyebrow twitching, and finger waggling—they recognized that they were being made fools of and retaliated.[136]

The happy sense that the wool was being pulled over the enemy's eyes, that they were demonstrably foolish and gullible, and by extension had nothing worth paying attention to in the way of political ideas, could be augmented by providing erroneous answers to Chinese queries; preposterous responses which were, apparently, believed more often than not. Thus, as another Gloster recalled, one day a political instructor 'saw a group of about twenty men prancing around the compound, stamping their feet, uttering "Indian" war cries, and waving imaginary tomahawks'. When he asked why, he was told that this was an 'English tribal custom' and that the men involved were 'pacifying the spirits of our ancestors'.[137] Then

---

[133] Large, *One Man's War in Korea*, 133.

[134] TNA, WO 208/4012, Report on the Success of Communist indoctrination among British PW in North Korea, with particular reference to after effects on their return to the United Kingdom, 22 October 1953, 3.

[135] Large, *One Man's War in Korea*, 120.

[136] See ibid. 120; Green, *Captured at the Imjin River*, 125; IWMDS, 21729/6, F. Cottam; 26353/4, A. Hawkins; Hunter, *Brainwashing*, 185–6.

[137] Matthews in Francis S. Jones, *No Rice for Rebels*, 64. On 'Apache' war dances see also IWMDS, 21729/6, F. Cottam.

there was the admittedly.rather over-the-top day in the summer of 1951 when an instructor known as Hedgehog ('because his hair was cut very short and it stood up spiky', according to Ron Norley[138]) came across Lance Corporal W. 'Jungle' Aylward tied to a stake with a fire burning at his feet surrounded by a gang of his fellow Glosters dancing, whooping, and apparently all set to make a human sacrifice. A horrified Hedgehog, after ordering that the fire be put out, Aylward be released, and an explanation be given, apparently believed Sergeant S. J. Brisland when he told the instructor that it was a British tribal custom to incinerate people who were not liked. A written warning was thereafter posted banning this custom: 'This is an inhuman bourgeois practice that will not be tolerated.'[139]

If the Chinese really did fall for this sort of thing then they would not have realized the implications with regard to the respect, or lack thereof, in which they and by extension the ideas they were peddling were held. The number of incidents in which efforts to win men over and produce propaganda through mass participation in staged events or campaigns were met with a certain amount of resistance was a warning—albeit not always understood—that students were not truly absorbing what they were being taught in terms of a politically correct outlook.

In the late summer 1951 the inmates of Camp 1 were made to watch an outdoor six-hour performance of *The White Haired Girl*. 'I can only think that this opera was part of the brainwashing we were supposed to be succumbing to and meant to show the evils of capitalism and the ownership of private property', David Green reflected, adding: 'What a hope!' He was far from alone in rejecting this rather alien and very long piece of propaganda. 'We applauded joyfully every time the girl got raped by the landlord and hissed at the wrong places much to the disgust of the Chinese', Henry O'Kane remembered.[140]

The second anniversary of the founding of the People's Republic of China, which fell on 1 October 1951, was an event which the Chinese wanted to see turned into a propaganda exercise in Chongson. There would be a parade down the road in which prisoners would march and be photographed carrying banners with slogans such as, in the case of the British, 'Down with Churchill'.[141] Thanks to the promise of a 'feast' on the day in question, most of the rank and file agreed to go along with this. 'By and large,' R. F. Matthews observed, 'the prisoners at Chongson didn't care what they carried or waved on Revolution Day so long as they got a decent meal at the end of it.'[142]

However, a number of men who were at this point thought by the Chinese to be progressive but were in fact only going through the motions managed marginally to dilute the propaganda message through leaving out key words from banners—thus 'Down with the Imperialist Warmongers' became 'Down with the

[138] IWMDS, 15539/3, R. Norley; see also ibid. 26353/3, A. Hawkins.
[139] Matthews in Francis S. Jones, *No Rice for Rebels*, 65–6, see also 136–7. The British also enjoyed imparting fake British slang and fake culinary customs to the Chinese: see IWMDS, 15338/6, B. Murphy; 16618/5, C. Papworth; Large, *One Man's War in Korea*, 132.
[140] O'Kane, *O'Kane's Korea*, 95; Green, *Captured at the Imjin River*, 152.
[141] See NAA, Part 3, AI9/K/BRIT/76 et al., Drm Maj. P. E. Buss et al., 3.
[142] Matthews in Francis S. Jones, *No Rice for Rebels*, 71–2.

Warmongers' and 'Long Live the Peace-Loving Chinese People' came out as 'Long Live the Peace-Loving People'—and by using double entendres which the Chinese did not spot such as a painted double-size scroll of a busty woman with a peace dove on her arm captioned 'We Want A Firm Front'.[143] The officers and senior NCOs, meanwhile, were warned that 'future living conditions will be imperiled' if they did not cooperate. Nevertheless neither the British officers nor all but two or three of the British sergeants would agree to march either with or without banners.[144] Among the British who did parade there was a certain amount of subversive comment. 'The column marched along briskly, waving banners and warming up with "Peace!" "Down with War!" and "Asia for the Orientals!"', Matthews wrote. 'By the time we neared the Communist aristocracy [on the reviewing stand], we were in good fettle, but alien calls were already creeping in. "Up the Peace-Loving People!" and "Down with Warmongers!" were now contending with irreverent cries of "Beer is Best!" and "Everton for the Cup!"' Thankfully the Chinese officials did not pick up on these irreverent slogans, nor hear the man who roared out 'down with you enameled bastards!' and 'You slant-eyed sons of whores!', so the men got to eat their extra rations.[145]

Another indication that the British could not be counted upon for propaganda purposes occurred later the same month. On 13 October 1951 the camp, the location of which the Chinese had hitherto kept secret from the UN and allowed no sign visible from the air to indicate its function, was hit by a USAF B-26, wounding several British officers and killing one American.[146] A few days later the camp authorities suggested that a petition be drawn up and sent to the UN armistice delegation at Panmunjom protesting such attacks. Among the other ranks a few men refused to sign under any circumstances, arguing either that the aircraft had been Chinese or that so long as the village was used as a staging area by the Chinese People's Volunteers it was a legitimate target.[147] The majority, though they wanted to get their names out, would only do so once the initial language—which claimed the attack had been deliberate—was watered down.[148] Meanwhile dozens of the sergeants proved unwilling to sign even when the Chinese made clear their wishes. The camp authorities pressed Sergeant W. P. M. O'Hara, one of the leaders, to approach his fellow senior NCOs again on the matter. O'Hara returned the petition to the Chinese unsigned, saying that nobody was interested. Unfortunately

[143] Ibid. 72.

[144] NAA, Part 6, AI9/K/BRIT/2, Sgt S. Robinson, 10; see Part 3, AI9/K/BRIT/1000, Sgt S. F. Baxter, 2; Part 5, AI9/K/BRIT/999, Sgt W. P. O'Hara, 5; ibid. AI9/K/BRIT/4, Sgt W. A. Lucas, 5.

[145] Matthews in Francis S. Jones, *No Rice for Rebels*, 75–6.

[146] IWMDS, 19664/3, V. Whitamore; NAA, Part 6, AI9/K/BRIT/2, Sgt S. Robinson, 11; AI9/K/BRIT/156 Part II, L/Cpl H. C. Sharpling, 2.

[147] See ibid. AI9/K/BRIT/156 Part II, L/Cpl H. C. Sharpling, 2; AI9/K/BRIT/549, Sgt B. M. Smith, 2. This was not the first air attack. One night a truck passing through the village with its lights on had been strafed, killing several Chinese. The prisoners were asked to sign a petition protesting such action: some refused (see ibid. AI9/K/BRIT/156 Part II, L/Cpl H. C. Sharpling, 2) while others signed only on condition that an American sergeant who had lost both legs be sent back across the lines (IWMDS, 19871/2, W. Westwood).

[148] Large, *One Man's War in Korea*, 123. On the desire to get names out see also e.g. NAA, Part 3, Rfn J. W. Cooke, 2.

for him this was not entirely true, as a handful of British NCOs under the leadership of a Royal Artillery sergeant had decided to go along with the petition. This was made known to the camp authorities, who promptly arrested O'Hara.[149] Still, forty NCOs had refused to sign at all, the Chinese only managed to obtain the document they desired by adding a paragraph to the petition *after* the prisoners had provided their signatures, and when the camp authorities made a propaganda film of the incident the following month only one British soldier said he would participate.[150] A new petition protesting another attack in March of the following year garnered a grand total of nine British signatures.[151]

As for the officers, they all refused to sign any petitions, despite a veiled threat—which did not turn out to be idle—that treatment of those wounded in the first attack would be delayed by such action. Shortly thereafter the officers were moved from Chongson to their own camp at Pinchon-ni.[152]

That this, along with efforts to segregate troublemakers among the rank and file by setting up a separate labour unit where living conditions were tougher,[153] had only a limited effect in terms of dampening resistance was dramatically highlighted in the spring of 1952. Supposedly in order to ease racial tensions but in reality to play on them, the Chinese announced that black and white prisoners would be split into separate companies in all camps.[154] This primarily affected the Americans, but when a black Army Catering Corps cook, who had been captured with the Glosters at the Imjin, was told he was leaving the rest of the British reacted strongly. 'There were shouts of "He's a Brit, he belongs with us"', Lofty Large wrote, followed by several hundred voices chanting 'We want Steve.' The Chinese, to everyone's relief, decided that Private F. H. Stevens could stay with his mates.[155]

A united front was also used with effect when the camp authorities tried to use one of the things the British soldier loved most—football—to enhance levels of obedience. A plan to make observers sit according to platoons, rather than as men chose, and another, more localized effort to get men to agree to do PT under Chinese supervision, both collapsed when the British prisoners concerned proved willing to forgo the sport until the camp authorities compromised.[156]

[149] NAA, Part 5, AI9/K/BRIT/999, Sgt W. P. O'Hara, 5; Part 6, AI9/K/BRIT/852, Sgt P. V. Petherick, 2; ibid. AI9/K/BRIT/2. Sgt S. Robinson, 11; Part 3, AI9/K/BRIT/971 et al., Sgt P. C. Crompton et al., 3; ibid. AI9/K/BRIT/983, Sgt S. E. Aselby, 2–3.

[150] On the propaganda film see ibid. Part 6, AI9/K/BRIT/2, Sgt S. Robinson, 11; Part 7, AI9/K/BRIT/157 Part II, Cpl W. K. Westwood, 3. On adding a paragraph to the petition after the signing, see Westwood above. According to the progressive private who did the typing, this was a common Chinese trick. See Part 3, AI9/K/BRIT/824, Pte R. B. Allum, 2.

[151] *Daily Worker*, 2 April 1952, 4.

[152] IWMDS, 19664/3, V. Whitamore; Kinne, *The Wooden Boxes*, 95; NAA, Part 3, AI9/K/BRIT/955, Lt S. W. Cooper, 2.

[153] See e.g. NAA, Part 3, AI9/K/BRIT/690 et al., Pte L. Allen et al., 15–16; Green, *Captured at the Imjin River*, 138.

[154] For the justification that this was to ease racial tensions see Clarence Adams, *An American Dream* (Amherst, Mass., 2007), 54. On suspecting that the Chinese were in fact trying to play on racial tensions see Lewis H. Carlson, *Remembered Prisoners of a Forgotten War* (New York, 2002), 191.

[155] Large, *One Man's War in Korea*, 128–9; see Gaston, *Korea 1950–1953*, 27.

[156] IWMDS, 16618/5, C. Papworth.

Rather more worrying to the camp authorities was the outcome of the May Day celebrations. When at the last moment it was announced that the inhabitants of the camp would parade in review carrying banners and the red flag, the prisoners flatly refused to participate.[157] Some men did prove willing to compete in singing songs such as *The East is Red* in order to win a bit more food;[158] but the politically correct image the camp authorities were trying to cultivate for propaganda purposes was subsequently undone by what happened at the concert party that the prisoners had organized. The Chinese insisted that everything be vetted ahead of time, but could not know that the cockney master of ceremonies, Sergeant A. B. 'Bill' Sykes of the Glosters, planned to depart from the approved script once on stage.[159] In best music-hall style Sykes, with assistance from a sidekick in the audience, Private Keith Godwin, told a series of rapid-fire jokes sending up communist jargon that sent the audience into hysterics but were too fast for the interpreters to keep up with. Sykes then started to recite his own version of the poem from *The Scarlet Pimpernel*:

> They seek him here, they seek him there.
> They seek the (so and so) everywhere;
> Should he be shot, or will he be hung?
> That dirty old (so and so) Mao Tse-tung?

After a second of total silence the audience collapsed with laughter at this blatant act of *lèse-majesté*. Sykes was marched in front of an enraged interpreter, who demanded to know why he was mocking the Chairman. The sergeant replied 'Don't be silly. I am only paying compliments to your big nob, Mr Mao.' He was allowed back on stage, where he added insult to injury with another Mao joke involving an exchange at the Pearly Gates in which St Peter refuses Mao entry into Heaven on the grounds that it was too much trouble to cook rice for one. The interpreters caught this even as the audience began to laugh uproariously. The Chinese moved in and arrested the comedian; but the sergeants, followed by the rank and file, began to chant 'We want Bill Sykes!' and tried to rescue him even as the guard company was called out. A bloodbath might have ensued, but luckily a Chinese officer agreed to release the struggling sergeant as he was being carried away and the men returned to their huts.[160]

The sergeants, though segregated, were clearly still a problem for the camp authorities; so they were all transferred to Camp 4 at Kuuptong in the summer.[161] The British

---

[157] Kinne, *The Wooden Boxes*, 104–5; NARA, RG 319, entry 85, Phase III summaries, box 1027, Frank J. Celusniak, 4.

[158] NAA, Part 3, AI9/K/BRIT/1000, Sgt S. F. Baxter, 2; see also Green, *Captured at the Imjin River*, 147.

[159] Green, *Captured at the Imjin River*, 124; O'Kane, *O'Kane's Korea*, 94.

[160] Sykes in *Daily Express*, 28 February 1955, 1; Kinne, *The Wooden Boxes*, 106–9; see Green, *Captured at the Imjin River*, 124; Large, *One Man's War in Korea*, 124–5; O'Kane, *O'Kane's Korea*, 94–5; IWMDS, 16618/5, C. Papworth; 30075/4, J. Wiseman; NAA, Part 3, AI9/K/BRIT/971 et al., Sgt P. C. Crompton et al., 2; Part 6, AI9/K/BRIT/156 Part II, L/Cpl H. C. Sharpling, 3.

[161] On the connection between the concert party and the move of the senior NCOs to Camp 4 see NAA, Part 3, AI9/K/BRIT/824, Pte R. B. Allum, 2; Sgt G. J. Matta in US Senate, Subcommittee on Investigations of the Committee on Government Operations, *Korean War Atrocities* (Washington, DC, 1954), 123.

nevertheless continued to cause problems for the Chinese at Chongson, not least because the leading progressives were a lot less inspiring than their counterparts at Pyoktong while some of the reactionaries were rather more subtle. Belatedly the camp authorities woke up to the fact that a number of apparently cooperative men taken into Chinese confidence, above all the chairman of daily life committee, Corporal Frank Upjohn of the Glosters, were in fact working as double agents for the reactionary cause: indeed, Upjohn himself turned out to be a driving force in the formation and operation of an escape committee.[162] That left figures such as a particular corporal and a well-known private each willing to hold office on the peace committee and do anything the camp authorities demanded: but as other prisoners knew, out of a desire to better their material condition rather than through political conviction. The private soldier was described by an AI9 officer as 'completely cynical and unscrupulous', while the corporal was widely believed to be an informer: he certainly had no compunction about telling the Chinese that the former 'paid only lip service to communism, and ridiculed it behind their backs'. They were despised by the rest of the British contingent, and threats to their lives plus their manifest ineffectiveness as role models led to their transfer to Pyoktong in the summer of 1952.[163]

The absence of an effective progressive element made forays to Camp 1 by Western pro-communists much less comfortable affairs than visits to Camp 5. Some prisoners were happy enough to receive news, however biased, on the progress of the armistice talks, and at least one found Wilfred Burchett 'quite a pleasant fella'.[164] The majority, however, were openly hostile to the likes of Burchett and Alan Winnington, singing patriotic anthems and shouting things like 'traitor' or 'you'll hang, you bastard', with some men dangling little nooses they had made to emphasize the point.[165] So great was the tumult that during a subsequent visit the men were confined to their huts while Winnington spoke only to a select group of progressives. Not surprisingly it was Pyoktong rather than Chongson that featured in what they wrote concerning their visits to the Yalu camps.[166]

[162] See NAA, Part 1, Encl. 2D, Interrogation Report on British Ex-PW Released in Korea, Batch 2 (Supplementary), Pte Bounden, 2; Part 7, AI9/K/BRIT/157 Part II, Cpl W. K. Westwood, 2–4; Cunningham, No Mercy, No Leniency, 86–7. On Upjohn and the escape committee see Matthews in Francis S. Jones, No Rice for Rebels, 138 ff. He was arrested in June 1952 (NAA, Part 3, AI9/K/BRIT/690 et al. Part II, Pte L. Allen et al., 1).

[163] NAA, Part 3, AI9/K/BRIT/824, Pte R. B. Allum, 2–3; see Part 6, AI9/K/BRIT/302, Cpl W. H. Smith, 2–3; Part 7, AI9/K/BRIT/157, Cpl W. K. Westwood, 2. Both men took leading roles on the camp peace committee (see ibid. AI9/K/BRIT/549, Sgt B. M. Smith, 4; ibid. AI9/K/BRIT/156 Part II, L/Cpl H. C. Sharpling, 3).

[164] IWMDS, 18439/3, A. Tyas; see e.g. IWMDD, F. Carter, 58; IWMDS, 18262/8, F. Carter.

[165] See Kinne, The Wooden Boxes, 113–14; O'Kane, O'Kane's Korea, 109–10; IWMDS, 18459/2, W. Clark; 17283/5, A. Eagles; 17468/2, D. Kaye; 16618/5, C. Papworth; 18439/3, A. Tyas; 19871/2, W. Westwood; NAA, Part 3, AI9/K/BRIT/907 et al., Fus. J. Aitken et al., 12; Large, One Man's War in Korea, 135–6.

[166] See e.g. Daily Worker, 25 June 1952, 1; Wilfred G. Burchett, This Monstrous War (Melbourne, 1953), 300–1; Alan Winnington, Breakfast with Mao (London, 1986), 160–5; NAA, Part 4, AI9/K/BRIT/14 et al., Pte A. E. Hunt et al., 9. The same was true for Monica Felton: she visited Camp 1 (see ibid.; IWMDS, 12783/5, A. Eagles) as well as Camp 5, but only wrote about the latter (Daily Worker, 2 October 1952, 2). The communist lawyer Jack Gaster, who visited both camps and wrote a glowing account of his experiences (see Farrar-Hockley, British Part, II, 275–6) got round the problem by only exposing himself to select progressives (IWMDS, 18439/3, A. Tyas).

Yet another indication by this point that students were not accepting the party line was the eagerness with which some of them tried to escape. Many of the British other ranks, and indeed some of the sergeants, accepted the Chinese contention that such attempts were futile because of the extreme terrain, a hostile civilian population, and above all their Caucasian appearance.[167] A minority, on the other hand, considered it their duty to try, aided and abetted by a succession of small and rather improvisational escape committees. An unwillingness to believe that anyone other than an overt progressive would inform on them and poor security measures in general meant that many attempts were nipped in the bud. 'If anyone was going to escape,' as an AI9 investigator put it, 'everyone appeared to know in advance.'[168] Some men did get beyond Chongson, but all were recaptured within a matter of days and promptly thrown into holes or wooden cages, strung up, or beaten until they agreed to publicly confess the error of their ways.[169] Despite the odds against success and consequences of failure prisoners continued to try and get away through the summer of 1952, and even after half a dozen or so of the hard cases were transferred to a penal camp at Song-ni (Camp 2, Branch 2) at the end of the year, there were still men willing to try again in the spring of 1953. In all at least a dozen attempts involving over thirty British soldiers were made between the time men arrived at Chongson and repatriation: not exactly a vote of confidence in the beneficence of the Lenient Policy.[170]

The extent to which 'the great majority' of British prisoners remained solidly 'anti-communist', as a British intelligence officer put it, became abundantly clear once compulsory indoctrination gave way to voluntary study in the course of 1952.[171] Though there is some evidence to suggest that ongoing exposure to back issues of the *Daily Worker*—the only source of news about what was happening in

---

[167] See e.g. Green, *Captured at the Imjin River*, 123–4; Matthews in Francis S. Jones, *No Rice for Rebels*, 68; IWMDS, 18262/6, F. Carter; 18459/2, W. Clark; 21729/6, F. Cottam; 16337/2, J. Grosvenor; 15539/3, R. Norley; 26353/3, A. Hawkins; 18544/2, C. Sharpling; 18439/3, A. Tyas.

[168] NAA, Part 3, AI9/K/BRIT/907 et al., Fus. J. Aitkin et al., 8; see ibid. AI9/K/BRIT/690 et al. Part II, Pte L. Allen at al., 1–4; ibid. AI9/K/BRIT/13 Part II, Pte M. L. Bounden, 3; Part 4, AI9/K/BRIT/14 et al. Part II, Pte A. E. Hunt et al., 7; Part 7, AI9/K/BRIT/157 Part II, Cpl W. K. Westwood, 1; Matthews in Francis S. Jones, *No Rice for Rebels*, 146–7; Green, *Captured at the Imjin River*, 132; Kinne, *The Wooden Boxes*, 111.

[169] See e.g. NAA, Part 3, AI9/K/BRIT/134, Fus. D. G. Kinne, 2; Kinne, *The Wooden Boxes*, 132 ff.; Green, *Captured at the Imjin River*, 133 ff.; Large, *One Man's War in Korea*, 128; Matthews in Francis S. Jones, *No Rice for Rebels*, 41 ff.

[170] Col. Carne had ordered a halt to escape attempts in July 1951 when it looked as if there would be an armistice in the near future (see Kinne, *The Wooden Boxes*, 78: O'Kane, *O'Kane's Korea*, 85), but there had been attempts before this and once it was clear that the armistice talks were in stalemate activity resumed on a larger scale in the spring of 1952 (see Kinne, *The Wooden Boxes*, 111). On the attempts see Green, *Captured at the Imjin River*, 132 ff.; Matthews in Francis S. Jones, *No Rice for Rebels*, 41 ff., 67, 70 ff., 146–7, 154 ff.; IWMDS, 17929/5, D. Sharp; NAA, Part 3, AI9/K/BRIT/134, Fus D. G. Kinne, 2; ibid. AI9/K/BRIT/690 et al., Pte L. Allen et al., 2–4; ibid. AI9/K/BRIT/596, Pte C. Baker et al., 5; ibid. AI9/K/BRIT/979 Part II, Sgt S. J. Brisland, 1–2; ibid. AI9/K/BRIT/811, 816, Bdr L. Bristow and Gnr R. Thompson, 3; Part 4, AI9/K/BRIT/482 Part II, Mne S. D. Hicks, 2; Part 6, AI9/K/BRIT/377 et al. Part II, Pte D. C. Stocking et al., 1–2. On the transfer of hard cases to Camp 2 (Branch 2) at Song-ni see Kinne, *The Wooden Boxes*, 167 ff.

[171] NAA, Part 3, AI9/K/BRIT/907 et al., Fus. J. Aitkin et al., 10. A USMC corporal estimated that at most only about a third of the British could 'be possibly pro communist.' NARA, RG 38, entry 1015(a1), Phase II Questionnaire, Joe E. Saxon, question 46a response.

the UK—did affect at the time how at least some of the British rank and file viewed British politics,[172] and that Chinese reports blaming the US for delaying completion of the armistice talks fanned anti-Americanism,[173] the number of British captives at Chongson who chose to continue their political education on a voluntary basis was extremely disappointing from the Chinese perspective. They numbered only about a third of those who signed up at Pyoktong, which translated into a mere 6 per cent of the British population at Camp 1 as against around 20 per cent of the British inhabitants of Camp 5.[174] Some were bored and simply looking for something to do, others genuinely interested in politics; but the main group, according to an intelligence estimate, was made up of opportunists simply hoping to better their condition—and in the case of a couple of medical orderlies that of their fellows—through cooperation with the enemy.[175] Moreover, one or two attendees at Chongson appear to have been acting as double agents: that is, going to discussions in order to discover what the party line on a particular issue was, who was listening, and thereafter arguing with or even threatening potential converts to the enemy cause.[176]

There were limits to the British rejection of Chinese desires at Camp 1. Though there was some initial group resistance, and the sergeants mostly refused to cooperate, only a very few soldiers were not eventually willing to include the required positive statements about their treatment and desire for peace in order to send and receive letters, a key element in sustaining morale that the camp authorities were not slow to exploit.[177] Nobody from Chongson seems to have understood that participating in an inter-camp Olympic Games staged by the Chinese in November

---

[172] See NAA, Part 4, AI9/K/BRIT/14 et al., Pte A. E. Hunt et al., 9; ibid. AI9/K/BRIT/372, L/Cpl H. W. Johnstone, 2; Hunter, *Brainwashing*, 189. On the other hand, as a naval officer had occasion to observe at the end of the war, a significant number of the rank and file were pretty much illiterate (D. Mather in John R. P. Lansdowne, *With the Carriers in Korea* (Southside, 1997), 391), and therefore unlikely to be swayed by the written word.

[173] See e.g. Green, *Captured at the Imjin River*, 151; IWMDS, 15539/4, R. Norley; NAA, Part 7, AI9/K/BRIT/449, Cpl S. H. Truan, 1.

[174] Estimates of the number of regular attendees at voluntary discussion at Pyoktong ranged between ten and thirty-seven (see NAA, Part 3, AI9/K/BRIT/118 et al., Rfn F. Crilly et al., 2; Part 7, AI9/K/BRIT/289, Cpl J. H. Taylor, 5), but thirty was the number cited by more than one returnee (Part 3, AI9/K/BRIT/606, Gnr J. C. Dabbs, 5; Part 5, AI9/K/BRIT/306, Fus. P. Lydon, 2). Comparable lists from prisoners returning from Camp 1 suggest about ten regular attendees; Part 3, AI9/K/BRIT/907 et al., Fus. J. Aitken et al., 11; ibid. AI9/K/BRIT/690 et al., Pte L. Allen et al., 20–3; AI9/K/BRIT/423 et al., Rfn H. Burton et al., 3; ibid. AI9/K/BRIT/384, Pte T. H. Davies, 2. There were approximately 500 British other ranks at Chongson as against approximately 150 at Pyoktong.

[175] Ibid. AI9/K/BRIT/907 et al., Fus. J. Aitken et al., 10; see e.g. Part 5, AI9/K/BRIT/469, Pte M. Pendle, 2–3; ibid. AI9/K/BRIT/421, Cpl D. W. Hansford, 2; IWMDS, 16618/5, C. Papworth; see also Kinne, *The Wooden Boxes*, 93; Matthews in Francis S. Jones, *No Rice for Rebels*, 132–3.

[176] See NAA, Part 4, AI9/K/BRIT/160, Sgmn H. Jennings, 2; see also Part 3, AI9/K/BRIT/246 et al., Pte A. J. Allum et al., 6, interrogator's comment *re* L/Cpl Goldsmith; Part 5, AI9/K/BRIT/421, Cpl D. W. Hansford *re* threatening letter to Pte A. Savage, 2. One source suggests that while there were twenty to thirty attendees at first, this gradually shrank to no more than four (ibid. AI9/K/BRIT/469, Pte M. Pendle, 2).

[177] On the initial resistance to including propaganda in letters see Hunter, *Brainwashing*, 147–8; IWMDS, 21729/7, F. Cottam. On holding out see e.g. ibid. 15338/5, B. Murphy. On the importance of letters to morale see e.g. Large, *One Man's War in Korea*, 105; IWMDD, F. Carter, 53. On the Chinese recognizing this and using it see e.g. IWMDS, 12783/5, A. Eagles.

1952 meant aiding enemy propaganda efforts.[178] Men might outwardly reject the Chinese contention in 1952–3 that the Americans were dropping germ bombs; but in the wake of in-person confessions by various USAF officers, they might harbour private doubts, thereby justifying the enemy's extensive propaganda campaign on the subject. According to Marine S. D. Hicks, who accepted the idea despite being a reactionary in other respects, '99 per cent of all PW also believed it'.[179] An unknown but significant number of outwardly trustworthy men proved willing to act as informers for the Chinese, making it very difficult to conceal escape preparations. 'Room searches are periodically carried out,' as Captain R. L. Brignall of AI9 wrote after interviewing five repatriates in depth, 'but the CPV usually know what they are looking for and go straight for it.'[180]

Nevertheless the contrast with Camp 5 was striking, AI9 making calculations that suggested the peak level of overt collaboration was roughly twelve times higher among the British ranks at Pyoktong than among those at Chongson.[181] After the exchange of sick and wounded took place in April–May 1953, of the eighteen men sent from Chongson, AI9 considered all but five completely unaffected by captivity in terms of politics and only one a real security risk.[182] Several months later, when the armistice was announced, the inmates refused to form a jubilant throng that could be photographed for propaganda purposes. There was no cheering or shouting when the smiling commandant let them know—in fact there was absolute silence. 'We were bursting, overflowing with excitement,' wrote R. F. Matthews, 'but we were determined not to show any sign of this whilst this gang of enamelled cutthroats held the stage.'[183] In addition, all five of the ordinary soldiers later awarded the Medal of the British Empire for distinguished conduct in enemy hands came from Camp 1, as did the single ranker to win the George Cross for bravery while a captive in North Korea.[184]

Nonetheless it was not considered necessary to fence in the inhabitants of Camp 1 any more than those at Camp 5. That privilege would be reserved for those considered almost beyond redemption by the Chinese; that is to say, those reactionaries whose influence was considered so malign that they were segregated from their fellow students entirely by being sent to special high-security camps.

---

[178] See e.g. Green, *Captured at the Imjin River*, 156–60. On the propaganda features of the inter-camp Olympic Games see NAM 1989-05-163-1, R. Bruford-Davies; Farrar-Hockley, *The Edge of the Sword*, 246–7; '*United Nations' P.O. W.'s in Korea* (Beijing, 1953), 73 ff.; film clips in *They Chose China* (National Film Board of Canada, 2005).

[179] NAA, Part 4, AI9/K/BRIT/482, Mne S. D. Hicks, 3; see Part 3, AI9/K/BRIT/907 et al., Fus. J. Aitken et al., 12; ibid. AI9/K/BRIT/846, Mne P. H. Banfield, 3; O'Kane, *O'Kane's Korea*, 110–11; see also NARA, RG 319, entry 85, Phase III summaries, box 1035, Emanuel W. Pantazis, 2.

[180] NAA, Part 4, AI9/K/BRIT/14 et al., Pte A. E. Hunt, 7; see also Cunningham, *No Mercy, No Leniency*, 97.

[181] See Cunningham, *No Mercy, No Leniency*, 74, 105.

[182] NAA, Part 1, App. A to AI9(a)/S/150/87, 8 May 1953; ibid. App. A to AI9(a)/S/150/87, 12 May 1953.

[183] Matthews in Francis S. Jones, *No Rice for Rebels*, 247; see Kinne, *The Wooden Boxes*, 113; IWMDS, 18262/8, F. Carter; 16337/2, J. Grosvenor; 17468/3, D. Kaye; 16618/5, C. Papworth.

[184] Peter Gaston, *Thirty-Eighth Parallel* (Glasgow, 1976), 81–2, 137. The winner of the George Cross was Fus. Derek Kinne, who despite enormous physical pressure refused to bend to the will of the Chinese. See Kinne, *The Wooden Boxes*, 166 ff.; Michael Ashcroft, *George Cross Heroes* (London, 2010), 243–7.

6

Officers at Pinchon-ni and NCOs at Kuuptong

The Chinese had no doubt...they had no doubt whatever that that these indoctrination sessions would undermine our previous convictions, and would convert us to the principles of Marxism-Leninism. As they often said to us, under the terms of their famous lenient policy—their phrase, not mine—'we could liquidate you immediately as war criminals who've come here to wage this bloody war in Korea for world capitalism against the peace-loving peoples of the world: we have the right to liquidate you, but we know that you are just little pawns in the great capitalist game; you are tools in the hands of your capitalist masters, and therefore we are going to give you the chance of being reeducated.'

Padre Sam Davies[1]

By the latter months of 1951 it had become clear to the Chinese authorities that officer prisoners, not least among the British, were by and large impeding their efforts to impart 'truth' to the broad mass of captured personnel. In late October, therefore, a new camp was opened for the several hundred UN officers—about one-tenth of them British—hitherto held at Chongson, Pyoktong, and elsewhere.[2]

Camp 2 (Branch 1) was located on the outskirts of the village of Pinchon-ni, in a valley between steep hills more than 10 miles to the north-east of the nearest main camp and a few miles south of the Yalu. The central feature of the new camp was a long schoolhouse built during the Japanese occupation on an east–west axis. Most of the classrooms were partitioned into sleeping quarters, the remaining two being combined into a learning space. Behind and slightly above the school

---

[1] Sam Davies in *Korea: The Unknown War* (Thames Television, 1988).

[2] The 10 per cent estimate comes from a US prisoner, Conley Clarke, in his memoir *Journey Through Shadow* (Charlotte, NC, 1988), 235. The US Army estimated that about three-quarters of the population of Camp 2 were Americans: see Department of the Army, *U.S. Prisoners of War in the Korean Operation* (Fort Meade, Md., 1954), 119. Estimates as to the number of officers held here—American, British, Commonwealth, and Turkish—vary, but collectively suggest roughly 300 once everyone had arrived: see S. J. Davies, *In Spite of Dungeons* (London, 1954), 58; Anthony Farrar-Hockley, *The Edge of the Sword* (London, 1954), 212; Clarke, *Journey Through Shadow*; Frederick Pelser and Marcia E. Pelser, *Freedom Bridge* (Fairfield, Cal., 1984), 43; NARA, RG 319, entry 85, Phase II Questionnaire summaries, box 1034, Walter L. Mayo, 4. Captured ROK officers remained the responsibility of the North Koreans.

building were several houses once used by the school staff, which soon served as premises for a barbershop and also accommodation as the number of prisoners swelled. The dirt playground south and below the schoolhouse formed the centre of a compound measuring roughly 110 by 70 yards, bracketed on the east side by the newly constructed cookhouse and later a bathhouse oriented on a north–south axis. There was also a rather small and primitive lean-to latrine in the south-east corner of the compound.[3]

Nobody was going to try and get away in the depths of winter, but in February 1952, in preparation for the coming spring, the Chinese enclosed the compound with a barbed-wire fence somewhere between 8 and 10 feet in height that consisted of seven strands strung horizontally between wooden posts firmly implanted in the ground. Saplings were then woven vertically through the wire to make climbing more difficult and provide aural warning of anyone trying; and in the autumn of 1952 a second, stockade-type wooden fence was built eighteen inches beyond the initial barrier. All this, the inhabitants were disingenuously informed, was to keep wild animals out rather than men in.[4]

Living conditions at Pinchon-ni were in some ways an improvement on those at other camps. There was a wooden floor to the main building, there were small stoves and a low-wattage electric light for each room, and enough scissors and razors were provided for barbering to become a once-a-month affair. On the other hand, all that the officers had to sleep on, literally shoulder to shoulder over many months, were rice-straw mats occupying a personal space measuring 2 feet by 6 feet at best, while even with the addition of a thin quilt blanket the stoves proved inadequate in the depths of winter when the temperature at night was thought to dip to 40 degrees below zero.[5] Having to visit the latrine on the other side of the compound in such circumstances was described as 'harrowing' and 'excruciating'.[6]

Most importantly, the rations were still inadequate in quantity and quality right through to the end of the year and beyond. The mainstay of the twice-daily meals remained a small bowl of boiled sorghum, still 'nasty and very unpalatable', as Lieutenant Robin Bruford-Davies of the Ulster Rifles put it,[7] the only vegetable supplement coming in the form of Asian radishes or more occasionally seaweed and even tree fungus in the form of a weak soup.[8] Hunger remained a constant in

---

[3] Clarke, *Journey Through Shadow*, 228–31; Davies, *In Spite of Dungeons*, 57–8, 64; Farrar-Hockley, *The Edge of the Sword*, 208–10; William H. Funchess, *Korea POW* (Clemson, SC, 1997), 89–90, 99; John W. Thornton Jr, *Believed to be Alive* (Middelbury, Vt., 1981), 188–90; Colin C. King and Ronald D. Guthrie, *Escape from North Korea* (Riverwood, NSW, 2002), 95–9; NAA, Part 1, AI9/K/US/1, Capt. Zach W. Dean, 8.

[4] NAA, Part 1, AI9/K/US/1, Capt. Zach W. Dean, 8; Part 4, AI9/K/BRIT/958, 2/Lt D. J. English, 5; Funchess, *Korea POW*, 89.

[5] King and Guthrie, *Escape from North Korea*, 107; Clarke, *Journey Through Shadow*, 232; Davies, *In Spite of Dungeons*, 58; Funchess, *Korea POW*, 90; Thornton, *Believed to be Alive*, 188.

[6] King and Guthrie, *Escape from North Korea* ('excruciating'); Davies, *In Spite of Dungeons*. 57 ('harrowing').

[7] NAM 1989-05-163-1, R. Bruford-Davies; see also e.g. Funchess, *Korea POW*, 102.

[8] See e.g. IWMDS, 19664/3, V. Whitamore. On seaweed see Pelser, *Freedom Bridge*, 45. On tree fungus see IWMDS, 16759/3, D. Patchett.

Chinese hands, prisoners going so far as to pick and boil edible weeds during the growing season to supplement their extremely meagre diet.[9]

Under such circumstances men inevitably fell sick. Nutritional deficiencies produced everything from beriberi to night blindness, while in winter weakened immune systems and cramped quarters allowed respiratory diseases such as pneumonia to take hold and rapidly spread. Both in terms of diagnosis and treatment the Chinese medical response was, for many months, totally inadequate.[10]

It was apparent once again, though, that the British seemed to cope better than the Americans. As a number of concerned US officers observed, deaths from a combination of privation, disease, and despair were 'disturbingly frequent' within the American contingent.[11] In marked contrast there were no deaths at all among the British, evenly distributed among the Americans in the schoolhouse rooms—something that was put down among their many American admirers to greater self-reliance and resilience and much better collective discipline. John W. Thornton Jr, a US Navy helicopter pilot who was himself a hard-core resister, wrote of the 'dauntless spirits' of the British. 'We were very poor POWs', he later commented, 'we envied the British regimental tradition. The attitude among most of our men was "hooray for me. Screw you." '[12] It was certainly true that the senior British officers insisted on 'a very tight discipline', as the MO of the 8th Hussars put it, adding, 'you had to behave yourself'. Dr Patchett was struck by the contrast with the weaker Americans, who in some cases neglected their personal hygiene and in other instances simply refused to eat what was put in front of them: 'I suppose it was their higher standard of living and so on and so forth', he later reflected.[13]

The view that some of the Americans were simply weak-willed, an attitude perhaps exacerbated by their tendency to emote in an un-British fashion,[14] led at least some of the British to assume that all spies in Camp 2 were from the United States. According to Lieutenant S. W. Cooper (attached Royal Northumberland Fusiliers) 'all the British Officers and WOs were 100 per cent steadfast and loyal'; but 'although there were many Americans who were trusted, there were several informers among the American Officers'.[15] That there were spies among the American

[9] On boiling weeds see e.g. Thornton, *Believed to be Alive*, 202; IWMDS, 16061/2, R. Hickey. On hunger see e.g. Funchess, *Korea POW*, 105; Pelser, *Freedom Bridge*.

[10] On pneumonia see e.g. King and Guthrie, *Escape from North Korea*, 107; Thornton, *Believed to be Alive*, 190–1. On night blindness, see e.g. Clarke, *Journey Through Shadow*, 331–3; IWMDS, 1557/4, G. Temple. On beriberi see e.g. H. Osborne in Harry Spiller (ed.), *American POWs in Korea* (Jefferson, NC, 1998), 69. On the inept Chinese response to e.g. beriberi, see IWMDS, 16061/2, R. Hickey. On the inadequacies of initial Chinese medical care see also e.g. ibid. 15475/3, S. Davies; Farrar-Hockley, *The Edge of the Sword*, 220.

[11] Thornton, *Believed to be Alive*, 191; see also e.g. Clarke, *Journey Through Shadow*, 251.

[12] Thornton in Max Hastings, *The Korean War* (London, 1987), 347; Thornton, *Believed to be Alive*, 197; see Clarke, *Journey Through Shadow*, 267–8, 277–8, 347–8, 396; Pelser, *Freedom Bridge*, 51–2, 57; S. Foss in Raymond B. Lech, *Broken Soldiers* (Urbana, Il., 2000), 96.

[13] IWMDS, 16759/2–3, D. Patchett; see e.g. ibid. 19664/3, V. Whitamore; ibid. 12664/2, P. Weller; Cyril Cunningham, *No Mercy, No Leniency: Communist Mistreatment of British Prisoners of War in Korea* (Barnsley, 2000), 108.

[14] See Hastings, *The Korean War*, 347.

[15] NAA, Part 3, AI9/K/BRIT/955, Lt S. W. Cooper, 3; see NARA, RG 38, entry 1015 (a), box 4, Emanuel R. Amann, Phase II Questionnaire, question 30 response; box 7, Byron H. Beswick, Jesse V. Booker; box 27, John. N. McGlauchlin.

contingent was undoubtedly true; but it is worth noting that even after the British created their own escape committee in early 1952 because of suspicions about leaks from the previously multinational committee this did not seem to stop the Chinese from knowing all about breakout plans.[16]

Meanwhile the move to Pinchon-ni had not diminished the Chinese appetite for details on matters both professional and, above all, personal. Captives would find themselves having to fill in detailed questionnaires yet again or hauled out, often in the middle of the night, for lengthy Q&A sessions. 'Officers were continually taken for interrogation and discussion' the Reverend Sam Davies, the Church of England padre attached to the Glosters, later wrote, also noting the amount of personal detail required by the Chinese:

What property do you own?
What is your father's income?
What is your wife's political affiliation?
Where were you educated?
What is your religious affiliation?
What were your grand parents' occupations?
Name three intimate friends.[17]

Interrogation sessions were often not just about the person being questioned. 'Everything that was written was read, they wanted to know what people said, they wanted to know what they discussed, they wanted to know what their politics were, they wanted to know what their finances were, they wanted to know what their education was, they wanted to know everything about them', Lieutenant Peter Whitamore of the Ulsters recalled, 'everything.'[18]

The main goal seems to have been to build up an intimate portrait of each prisoner as an aid in the process of getting prisoners to see the error of their ways and use them as tools in the propaganda war.[19] Despite the fact that it had been considered necessary not just to separate the officers from the men but to physically segregate them in their own camp, the Chinese at Pinchon-ni—under the command of a fastidiously groomed but 'fanatical communist' by the name of Ding Fang[20]—still seemed determined to try and re-educate the inhabitants of Camp 2.[21]

Part of this effort involved trying to convince prisoners that religion really was the opiate of the masses and worthy only of ridicule, not least because of the

[16] See NAA, Part 4, AI9/K/BRIT/38 Part II, Capt. A. H. Farrar-Hockley, 1–3; Clarke, *Journey Through Shadow*, 303. News of what the British escape committee was planning may, on the other hand, have leaked from an American source because of the habit of secret committees at Camp 2 to liaise with one another. See NARA, RG 319, entry 85, Phase III Questionnaire summaries, box 1034, Walter L. Mayo, 4.

[17] Davies, *In Spite of Dungeons*, 63; see e.g. Hastings, *The Korean War*, 339.

[18] IWMDS, 19964/3, V. Whitamore.

[19] It was easier for those being questioned to spot questions of a military nature and either refuse to answer or, as in the case of an officer who had once served in the Royal Navy, pull the wool over the enemy's eyes by making up something which superficially seemed plausible but on elaboration was clearly a joke at Chinese expense. Thornton, *Believed to be Alive*, 197–8.

[20] Farrar-Hockley, *The Edge of the Sword*, 212; see Davies, *In Spite of Dungeons*, 59; Funchess, *Korea POW*, 93.

[21] Sam Davies in *Korea: The Unknown War* (Thames Television, 1988).

countervailing presence of Padre Davies, greatly admired by his fellow captives for his refusal to be intimidated by the enemy or allow fellow prisoners to forget their duty to God. 'Padre Davies gave us something rarely to be found', wrote John Thornton, '—a living example of how solid Christian faith could sustain courage, sanity and hope while at the mercy of a cruel enemy.'[22] For propaganda purposes the Chinese were forced to allow him to hold Sunday prayers and full services at Christmas and Easter, but they did everything in their power to drag their feet and diminish the impact of organized worship. 'Let me tell you that I had to go through a tremendous censorship before any religious service', Davies exclaimed in a later interview. Every word to be spoken or sung had to be written out well ahead of time, scrutinized, and was sometimes rejected: the carol *Good King Wenceslas*, for instance, was banned on the grounds that it glorified the feudal ruling class.[23] Such 'harassment' was common. On some days, as USAF navigator Fred Pelser later related, the camp authorities 'would turn up the volume of the courtyard loud-speaker, playing Chinese music which overpowered the church services. Some-times they would interrogate Sam during the week, accusing him of subversive activities against them. Sometimes they would threaten him with physical abuse or solitary confinement.'[24] Throughout all this the padre did his best, as he advised others during one particularly irritating confrontation, to 'ignore the bastards'. As a churchman he quickly regretted the profanity, but resolutely stood by the sentiment.[25]

In the course of 1952 the number and scope of the services Davies was allowed to offer were progressively whittled down, and in August he was arrested on charges of 'lying, subversive activities, slandering the Chinese policy of religious freedom, breaking the rules and regulations' and generally inciting anti-CPV sentiment. After a lot of acrimonious debate Davies was released, even though he completely refused to admit that religious worship had been used as a cover for political activity: he continued to be a thorn in the side of the camp authorities for another year.[26] In retrospect the padre thought his work helped keep up both faith and morale, Colonel J. P. 'Fred' Carne adding to the sense that worship in Church of England fashion was part of the duty of a British Officer even in captivity by using a nail to patiently carve a stone cross for the padre to use as an altarpiece.[27] 'Faith in God', an American observer concluded with regard to the otherwise 'hard-bitten' British Officer, '... stood him in as good stead as faith in regiment.'[28]

While unsuccessfully attempting to limit the influence of religious belief on the outlook and attitudes of prisoners, through the winter of 1951–2 the camp author-ities had also tried vigorously to promote faith in their own political creed. For

[22] Thornton, *Believed to be Alive*, 200; see also e.g. Clarke, *Journey Through Shadow*, 243–4.

[23] IWMDS, 15475/5, S. Davies; see also Davies, *In Spite of Dungeons*, 80, 82.

[24] Pelser, *Freedom Bridge*, 57; see also, on Chinese attitudes to worship among the prisoners, Tim Carew, *Korea* (London, 1967), 170.

[25] Thornton, *Believed to be Alive*, 201.

[26] NAA, Part 3, AI9/K/BRIT/64, Rev. S. J. Davies, 4–9; see TNA, WO 373/119, f. 186.

[27] Clarke, *Journey Through Shadow*, 255; Pelser, *Freedom Bridge*, 59. On the padre's view that faith kept up morale see IWMDS, 15475/4–5, S. Davies.

[28] William Lindsay White, *The Captives of Korea* (New York, 1957), 96.

'students', most of each day—from dawn to dusk, six days a week—was filled with lectures or readings followed by group study in the evenings coupled with occasional written examinations.[29] Comrade Sun, a small, almost girlish commissar with a high-pitched voice who was both a sincere communist and a competent English speaker, took the lead in this educational drive.[30] Unfortunately, like most of his fellows, he viewed the West in general and Britain in particular in Dickensian terms, and was prone to presenting the Marxist-Leninist viewpoint on issues either unintelligibly or in ways that left them open to ridicule.[31] Having individual prisoners read aloud from selected texts did not improve matters, as those chosen, according to Lieutenant Arthur Peal, recited 'at great speed and in an inaudible fashion'.[32] Prisoners often gave 'pointedly tactless answers'[33] on their exams, or greeted statements made during lectures with laughter and hoots of derision, reducing a furious Sun to screaming out: 'Keep silent! You do not want to hear the truth!'[34]

Efforts were made to tighten class discipline, the Chinese attitude being, as the adjutant of the Glosters put it, 'that we were naughty children, and nanny was going to punish us until we fell into line and admitted our mistakes'.[35] Those who persisted in their bad behaviour might not receive any mail. Letters, as one officer put it, 'were used as a means of persuasion'; or as another officer argued, 'as punishment and reward.'[36] They might also be sent to the headmaster-commandant—that is, Ding Fang—for a lengthy harangue or simply flung into pits for a period of solitary reflection by his big, threatening enforcer, D. P. Wong.[37] Comrade Sun, meanwhile, enlisted other Chinese staff members to monitor who was dozing off or otherwise obviously not paying attention. The padre, for example, was once caught napping

---

[29] On the daily routine see e.g. Davies, *In Spite of Dungeons*, 60; Farrar-Hockley, *The Edge of the Sword*, 211; NAM 1989-05-163-1, R. Bruford-Davies.

[30] On Sun see NAA, Part 3, AI9/K/BRIT/42, Lt J. M. C. Nicholls, 3; ibid. AI9/K/BRIT/64, Rev. S. J. Davies, 12; Davies, *In Spite of Dungeons*, 60; Farrar-Hockley, *The Edge of the Sword*, 213.

[31] On unintelligibility see e.g. IWMDS, 19664/3, V. Whitamore. On crudeness see e.g. NAA, Part 3, AI9/K/BRIT/42, Lt J. M. C. Nicholls, 2; IWMDS, 16061/3, R. Hickey; Farrar-Hockley, *The Edge of the Sword*, 213. On Sun and a Dickensian view of the West see IWMDS, 15475/5, S. Davies. As a US Army first lieutenant put it, the Chinese version of events in lectures 'was so distorted and biased it was difficult to take them seriously'. Wadie J. Rountree in Richard Peters and X. Li, *Voices from the Korean War* (Lexington, Ky., 2004), 230.

[32] NAA, Part 6, AI9/K/BRIT/977, Lt A. Peal, 2; see also Part 4, AI9/K/BRIT/38, Capt. A. H. Farrar-Hockley, 37.

[33] NAA, Part 3, AI9/K/BRIT/64, Rev. D. J. Davies, 12

[34] Farrar-Hockley, *The Edge of the Sword*, 213, 221; see e.g. IWMDS, 12664/3, P. Weller.

[35] A. Farrar-Hockley in *Korea: The Unknown War* (Thames Television, 1988).

[36] King and Guthrie, *Escape from North Korea*, 126; IWMDS, 19664/3, V. Whitamore; see also e.g. Funchess, *Korea POW*, 101. Two-way letter communication also offered the possibility of coded, secret communication with the War Office. Unfortunately those who had been taught codes during the Second World War had largely forgotten them, there existed a good deal of bureaucratic confusion among the branches concerned in London, and very little information was gleaned at either end through this means. TNA, AIR 40/2622, Code communication with British PW located in Camps in North Korea, n/d [1953].

[37] On haranguing by Ding see NAA, Part 3, AI9/K/BRIT/64, Rev. S. J. Davies, 12; Davies, *In Spite of Dungeons*, 61. On punishments see e.g. ibid.; Farrar-Hockley, *The Edge of the Sword*, 221. On D. P. Wong, the initials standing for 'Dirty Pictures' in reference to his collection of pornographic pin-ups confiscated from US personnel, see ibid. 212; Davies, *In Spite of Dungeons*, 59; Thornton, *Believed to be Alive*, 206.

during a discussion of *Outline Political History of the Americas* written by the US communist leader William Z. Foster:

Sun: 'Davies, stand up...What is your opinion of the chapter we have just read?'
           [Long Pause]
Davies: 'I'm afraid I was not listening.'
Sun: 'Why not?'
Davies: 'Well, I'm a British P.O.W. and I have other interests than American history.'
           [Silence]
Sun: 'You must correct your attitude.'
Davies: [Ponderously] 'I confess my crime.'
Sun: 'Sit down.'[38]

As this vignette indicates, even resisters such as the padre had decided that it was better to say one thing and believe another than risk a harangue or worse. As his partial namesake Robin Bruford-Davies put it, 'we let them get on with it'.[39]

This did not mean by any stretch of the imagination, however, that the British officers were being converted. Coercion was hardly likely to win hearts and minds, and quite apart from the poor standard of the instruction, there was the simple fact that the quality of life in mid-century Britain was clearly superior to that described in such glowing terms within the People's Republic of China—'there was no way that that a Chinese could ever convince me that his world would be better for *me*', as Captain James Majury of the Ulster Rifles explained[40]—allied with simple, uncomplicated patriotism: 'we just knew that Britain was right, and Britain was the best,' as Lieutenant Guy Temple of the Glosters reflected in an interview, 'and that was that, really'.[41] When a newly arrived senior US Marine officer, the redoubtable Lieutenant Colonel William G. Thrash, successfully suggested to the senior American officers from the other services as well as the British that everyone engage in a sit-down strike in protest at compulsory political indoctrination, he was eventually arrested; but the indoctrination policy was nonetheless abandoned in the late spring of 1952.[42] Nobody thought the Chinese had made any headway with the British by this point.[43]

---

[38] Davies, *In Spite of Dungeons*, 61.
[39] NAM 1989-05-163-1, R. Bruford-Davies; see also e.g. TNA, WO 208/4021, Encl. 1B, Verbatim Transcription of the Re-Interrogation of Lt Col. J. P. Carne, f. 7.
[40] Majury in Hastings, *The Korean War*, 349. This was true even though in the opinion of one US officer the British officers displayed 'socialist leanings'. NARA, RG 38, entry 1015(a1), box 42, Phase II Questionnaire, John W. Thornton, response to question 46a.
[41] IWMDS, 15557/5, G. Temple.
[42] W. Thrash in Henry Berry, *Hey, Mac, Where Ya Been?* (New York, 1988), 196. On Thrash as a 'reactionary' leader see James Angus MacDonald Jr, *The Problems of U.S. Marine Corps Prisoners of War in Korea* (Washington, DC, 1988), 165–6; Funchess, *Korea POW*, 129.
[43] See e.g. Farrar-Hockley, *The Edge of the Sword*, 221; NAA, Part 4, AI9/K/BRIT/980, Capt. A. M. Ferrie, 3; IWMDS, 22347/6, E. R. Bruford Davies; see also Ministry of Defence, *Treatment of British Prisoners of War in Korea* (London, 1955), 34. For rare evidence of the Chinese having some success see NAA, Part 4, AI9/K/BRIT/958, 2/Lt D. J. English, 3. Several officers thought that the camp staff knew they were making no headway: see Part 3, AI9/K/BRIT/955, Lt S. W. Cooper, 4; Part 6, AI9/K/BRIT/977, Lt A. Peal, 3; J. Majury in Hastings, *The Korean War*, 349.

Indicative of the situation among the officers was the way in which Western visitors steered clear of them. Wilfred Burchett passed through Pinchon-ni on his 'fact-finding' tour of the camps along the Yalu, but deliberately avoided all contact with the prisoners.[44] While covering the inter-camp Olympics (see below) Alan Winnington was approached by an officer and agreed to visit Camp 2, but—doubtless knowing what kind of reception he would face—failed to do so.[45]

Only in one subject area did the authorities at Pinchon-ni make any headway. As in other camps, the claims about germ warfare that began to be put forward later in the year were not always dismissed out of hand. The early evidence seemed to be rigged, but the broadcasting of recorded confessions caused even some of the American officers to wonder if biological warfare was in fact being waged, and it was noticed that the Chinese took great trouble to inoculate everyone against plague and cholera.[46] Others, however, seized the opportunity to play on Chinese fears about germ-laden objects falling from the sky;[47] and Padre Davies, pressed to publicly concur with the published opinion of the fellow-travelling Dean of Canterbury—a member of the supposedly neutral but in fact pro-communist international panel sent to investigate the claims—that the United States was dropping germ bombs, 'remained resolutely non-committal'.[48]

Despite the setbacks they were experiencing in terms of winning hearts and minds, the Chinese continued to try and use their charges for propaganda purposes. This campaign, which lasted down through to the end of the war, only met with marginally greater success.

It had been made clear from the start that letters promoting peace and/or praising the Lenient Policy would be sent home. While refusing to go as far as to write to their MPs, as the camp authorities desired, it was not uncommon for British officers to phrase their letters in order to maximize the odds that they would get through. This was an especially important factor early on, as the names of other prisoners could be mentioned in passing in such letters, thereby making it clear that they were still alive rather than 'missing, presumed killed'.[49]

This type of trade-off between an officer's duty and Chinese propaganda requirements, however, was by no means automatic, as the Chinese discovered when they tried to exploit traditional holidays. About a month after the camp was opened the authorities endeavoured to make use of US Thanksgiving by staging a 'feast' that would be photographed and used to show how well UN prisoners were being treated. The extra food was welcome, but it quickly became clear that the officers

---

[44] See Funchess, *Korea POW*, 116–17. Burchett was kept sufficiently cloistered from the officers that nobody else recalled a visit. See e.g. IWMDS, 16759/3, D. Patchett.

[45] Farrar-Hockley, *The Edge of the Sword*, 247–8.

[46] Davies, *In Spite of Dungeons*, 130–3; see Cunningham, *No Mercy, No Leniency*, 114. On the inoculations see NAA, Part 4, AI9/K/BRIT/981, Capt. A. H. Hickey, 2.

[47] See Funchess, *Korea POW*, 114–15; Pelser, *Freedom Bridge*, 93; G. Own in Ted Barris, *Deadlock in Korea* (Toronto, 1993), 272.

[48] Davies, *In Spite of Dungeons*, 132.

[49] See e.g. IWMDS, 16759/2, D. Patchett. On the Chinese wanting officers to write to MPs, etc., see NAA, Part I, AI9/K/US/1, Capt. Zach W. Dean, 15. On inserting the names of as many other prisoners as possible into a letter see e.g. NAM 1989-05-163-1, R. Bruford-Davies.

were neither grateful enough to allow their photographs to be taken in appropriate poses with happy expressions nor willing to pen testimonials as to the excellent treatment they were receiving at the hands of the CPV.[50]

At this point the junior officers were taking their lead from those of higher rank, and when the camp authorities insisted on the election of a Daily Life Committee the vote was carefully organized so that selected senior officers were unanimously elected. Lieutenant Colonel Gerald Brown of the USAF was made chairman, while the US Army and USMC were each represented by a major, as was the British Army in the person of Denis Harding. The camp authorities knew through informers what had happened, but for the moment tolerated the committee and the irritating way in which its members sought to sabotage Chinese aims by, for instance, quietly letting prisoners know the kinds of leading questions prisoners should resist answering during interrogations.[51]

That there were limits to Chinese patience became apparent in the wake of problems surrounding the exploitation of Christmas celebrations for propaganda purposes. Special extras such as the first communion service and a serving of rice wine and peanuts were provided in the expectation that the recipients of this largesse would thereafter be more amenable to aligning themselves with Chinese propaganda aims. A day or so after Christmas, the camp inmates were assembled in the morning and addressed by D. P. Wong, who invited prisoners to put their names to a giant greeting card that would be sent to the commander of CPV forces, General Peng. 'We all sat there absolutely dumbfounded and silent', Sam Davies recalled.[52] As covertly as they could the two most senior men in the audience, Lieutenant Colonel Fred Carne for the British and Lieutenant Colonel Gerald Brown for the Americans, made it clear that officers should not sign. 'Nobody moved', Davies related. Wong, clearly surprised, gave them five minutes to change their minds, but 'we all sat there'. After thirty minutes had passed, Wong lost his temper. 'Everyone will come forward and sign this card and march out of the room!' he raved, 'everybody! There's no excuse for anybody not to do it, you must do this! The right thing to do: and if you do not do this you will be kept in here without food until you die! There will be no chow call tonight!'[53] Perhaps guessing that with the armistice talks underway—a piece of news the Chinese had shared earlier in the year—Wong was no longer in a position to argue as he once had in another camp that 'no one knows that you are here ... [the] world will forget you' and that therefore anything at all could be done to UN prisoners who resisted,[54] the assembled men decided to call his bluff. By the early evening Wong had backpeddled and allowed the prisoners to return to their quarters and consume their evening meal.[55] He apparently saved face through a counter-proposal generated by

---

[50] Farrar-Hockley, *The Edge of the Sword*, 214.

[51] Cunningham, *No Mercy, No Leniency*, 111; Farrar-Hockley, *The Edge of the Sword*, 214–15; TNA, WO 208/4021, Encl. 1B, Verbatim Transcription of Re-Interrogation of Lt Col. J. P. Carne, ff. 8, 12.

[52] IWMDS, 15475/5, S. Davies; see Davies, *In Spite of Dungeons*, 66–8; Farrar-Hockley, *The Edge of the Sword*, 214.

[53] IWMDS, 15475/5, S. Davies.

[54] Farrar-Hockley, *The Edge of the Sword*, 213.   [55] IWMDS, 1547/5, S. Davies.

the senior officers whereby prisoners would agree to sign a card which wished Peng 'an early peace and a speedy return to China!'—a double-entendre that Wong and the other English speakers were rather slow to spot.[56]

In the third week of February 1952 the camp authorities struck back. One by one senior officers, including Major Harding and Colonel Carne (who, recognizing that he was already a troublemaker in enemy eyes, thought it best to work behind the scenes rather than serve on the Daily Life Committee), were arrested on charges of subversion.[57] Over the next two weeks a great deal of physical pressure was exerted to extract confessions concerning plots to undermine Chinese authority. The Americans seem to have been the first to buckle, but Ding soon got what he wanted—or so it seemed at first—from the British as well. Carne verbally agreed to confess after being tied up and left outside in arctic temperatures for several hours without a coat.[58] Harding only conceded after it was put to him that by doing so he could ameliorate the pressure being exerted on Carne, and thereafter resolutely refused to sign a certificate agreeing to pass on military information. Tony Farrar-Hockley related what Harding told him he had had to endure in consequence:

> As Ding never personally supervised physical pressure on prisoners, it was Sun who took Denis to an out-house and had him strung up to a beam, arranging it so that Denis's hands were secured so far up behind his back that he had to stand on tip-toe. Every hour, for four hours, Sun returned to ask if Denis had changed his mind: Denis had not. Sun left him until morning, when he was cut down. The next night began with another refusal to sign the certificate, after which Sun left Denis, stripped to the waist, outside Ding's house until he was blue with cold and too chilled to speak. After being taken back to a warm room for a time, he was sufficiently revived to utter another refusal. Sun took him to a cell down in the centre of the village and tied him again to a beam in the same way as the previous night.

Harding still refused to agree, and the next day was cut down and returned to imprisonment, unable to use his wrists at all.[59]

On 8 February the rest of the camp was assembled in the camp library to hear the plotters confess their crimes. The Americans were too much in shock, but both Harding and Carne departed from the script that had been prepared for them. According to Padre Davies, without elaboration the CO of the Glosters:

> confessed to all the things we'd expect him to do as a commanding officer... confessing he'd done his best to influence the junior and younger officers in his command against the indoctrination lectures, he confessed to forbidding his officers to sign the

---

[56] Cunningham, *No Mercy, No Leniency*, 111.

[57] NAA, Part 6, AI9/K/BRIT/69, Maj. M. D. G. C. Ryan, 4; TNA, WO 208/4021, Encl. 1B, Verbatim Transcription of Re-Interrogation of Lt Col. J. P. Carne, f. 8.

[58] TNA, WO 208/4021, Encl. 1B, Verbatim Transcription of Re-Interrogation of Lt Col. J. P. Carne, ff. 10–11. On evidence that Brown was tortured until his will was broken see Clarke, *Journey Through Shadow*, 268.

[59] Farrar-Hockley, *The Edge of the Sword*, 216–17; see Cunningham, *No Mercy, No Leniency*, 112; TNA, WO 373/119, citation for Maj. E. D. Harding, ff. 243–5. Carne, given the cold treatment again, eventually signed the certificate. TNA, WO 208/4021, Encl. 1B, Verbatim Transcription of the Re-Interrogation of Lt Col. J. P. Carne, ff. 12–13.

greeting card to General Peng...he confessed to not co-operating with the Chinese.[60]

According to an American observer, Lieutenant Conley Clarke, US Army, Carne did not even go this far:

> Colonel Carne got slowly to his feet. He moved to the front [and] center of the seated prisoners [cross-legged on the floor], a sheaf of papers in his hand. He faced the POWs and came to a position of rigid attention. White hair, broad shoulders, slender hips, heels tight together, and piercing eyes combined to give the officer a most distinguished appearance. Neither the shabby prison uniform nor the distractions of the total environment could alter the dignity of the man as he squared his shoulders and began speaking... 'I have committed no crime. I have nothing to confess.' The Colonel stopped talking. He looked squarely at the assembled POWs for perhaps thirty seconds. There was complete silence, a stillness that had to be a salute to the man's composure and words. Then the Colonel did a sharp military facing movement and returned to his seat.[61]

This, combined with the obvious physical distress of Brown and Harding, undermined whatever chance the camp authorities had of passing their actions off as just. When, after each man had—or had not—confessed in front of his peers, Comrade Sun announced that Carne and Harding were being sentenced to six months of imprisonment, he was booed.[62]

Ding and his associates nevertheless believed that getting rid of 'plotters' would make the remaining inhabitants of Camp 2 more malleable. The purging process was apparently completed through a new series of arrests a few months later. After it became clear that the prisoners were looking to Major Joe Ryan of the Ulster Rifles for leadership rather than the US Army officer whom the Chinese had tortured into becoming a collaborator while at Pyoktong, Ryan was taken out of the compound to begin a lengthy stint of interrogation at the hands of the North Koreans.[63] Shortly thereafter Ding made a speech to the assembled inmates in which he stated that he was so sure that escape from North Korea was impossible that he would offer anyone who wanted to try rations and a liberal head start if they put their names on a list. Not realizing that the commandant was baiting a trap, many did so, allowing Ding to take into custody two-dozen troublemakers.[64]

A more cooperative attitude also appeared likely from the Chinese perspective due to improvements in living conditions that occurred in 1952. The food was getting better, with rice replacing sorghum and the appearance of steamed bread and the occasional bit of pork.[65] As for medical care, prisoners learnt to secretly

[60] IWMDS, 15475/5, S. Davies; see Cunningham, *No Mercy, No Leniency*.

[61] Clarke, *Journey Through Shadow*, 207–8. Carne's own memories of the event were hazy: see TNA, WO 208/4021, Encl. 1B, Verbatim Transcription of the Re-Interrogation of Lt Col. J. P. Carne, f. 13.

[62] Farrar-Hockley, *The Edge of the Sword*, 217.

[63] NAA, Part 6, AI9/K/BRIT/69, Maj M. D. G. C. Ryan, 4–5, 12–13, 16; Cunningham, *No Mercy, No Leniency*, 68–9, 113.

[64] Philip D. Chinnery, *Korean Atrocity!* (Annapolis, Md., 2000), 166; Funchess, *Korea POW*, 94.

[65] See e.g. Davies, *In Spite of Dungeons*, 62; Farrar-Hockley, *The Edge of the Sword*, 211; Clarke, *Journey Through Shadow*, 242–3, 253; Pelser, *Freedom Bridge*, 65; IWMDS, 16759/3, D. Patchett.

consult one of the British or American doctors before and after approaching the camp medical staff, thereby helping them determine whether or not the treatment prescribed was legitimate. More importantly, the quality of Chinese medical assistance was slowly being enhanced.[66]

In April compulsory classes, already diminishing, were quietly dropped, and the British were allowed to stage a pantomime (albeit only after intense scrutiny by the censor) for Easter.[67] A good deal of effort was put into finding ways to fill the suddenly much expanded free time at men's disposal. Crude chess pieces and decks of cards were manufactured from whatever was at hand, though Carne before his arrest had made it clear that there were rigid limits to the amounts in IOU money that British officers could gamble away playing bridge.[68] There were only six novels in the camp library, and these nineteenth-century classics were in such demand that Guy Temple recalled having to read *War and Peace* in under thirty-six hours so the volume could get to the next man as quickly as possible.[69] Political education having fallen by the wayside—no voluntary study group appears to have emerged at Pinchon-ni, though officers might still read the communist pamphlets available in the library as a way of passing the time[70]—the prisoners themselves organized lecture series and classes in everything from foreign languages to mathematics.[71]

There were also less high-minded ways to divert attention from the boredom of camp life, such as contests to see, with the aid of a lighted candle for ignition purposes, who could deliver the most spectacular flame when breaking wind. Before the Chinese found out, senior officers banned the practice on the grounds that it was not behaviour becoming officers and gentlemen; but not before one British officer had scorched himself, and another had emerged the overall winner ('*I've* got the *quality!*').[72] More constructive outdoor forms of competition emerged as spring gave way to summer. With a limited amount of help from the Chinese, the prisoners created the equipment necessary to play games such as cricket, football, softball and baseball, netball, volleyball, and basketball.[73]

Despite everything, the officer prisoners made it clear in the spring of 1952 that they were still not prepared to act in accordance with the Chinese idea of how persons 'liberated' by the CPV ought to behave. The wake-up call, the first interaction of the day between guards and prisoners, offered plenty of scope for mischief. Members of a squad might refuse to get up, or alternatively could rouse themselves early, hide, and give the sentry sent to wake them the alarming impression that

[66] NAA, Part 1, AI9/K/US/1, Capt. Zach W. Dean, 15; Part 3, AI9/K/BRIT/955, Lt S. W. Cooper, 4; Part 4, AI9/K/BRIT/980, Capt. A. M. Ferrie, 2; ibid. AI9/K/BRIT/981, Capt. R. P. Hickey, 2; see also, regarding dentistry, Clarke, *Journey Through Shadow*, 261–2, 285–6.

[67] Farrar-Hockley, *The Edge of the Sword*, 221, 223–4.

[68] IWMDS, 16061/3, R. Hickey; Davies, *In Spite of Dungeons*, 64.

[69] IWMDS, 15557/5, G. Temple; Davies, *In Spite of Dungeons*.

[70] Dr Patchett later commented that 'I got quite interested reading those [pamphlets]' (IWMDS, 16759/2, D. Patchett).

[71] Ibid. 16759/3, D. Patchett; see Davies, *In Spite of Dungeons*, 64.

[72] Thornton, *Believed to be Alive*, 215–21; see Clarke, *Journey Through Shadow*, 301.

[73] See Davies, *In Spite of Dungeons*, 64; Farrar-Hockley, *The Edge of the Sword*, 241; Pelser, *Freedom Bridge*, 63; NAM 1989-05-163-1, R. Bruford-Davies; NAA, Part 4, AI9/K/BRIT/958, 2/Lt D. J. English, 5.

they had all escaped during the night.[74] The next order of business, mustering on parade to be counted, also offered opportunities for causing irritation. Squads might at unpredictable times arrive on parade so late that some of the early arrivals drifted away before the delayed count was completed, everyone generally making as much of a nuisance of themselves as they could.[75] When an attempt was made to have squad leaders salute the Chinese platoon commander and have each man come to attention when his name was called the prisoners flatly refused, only relenting when it was made clear that if they did not do so the American officer chosen by the camp authorities as their representative would be tortured again. Nevertheless the roll-call continued to be, in the words of an Australian pilot, 'a farce'.[76] Not everyone was keen on this sort of troublemaking, since apart from anything else such reactionary behaviour meant 'you were a marked man', making it that much harder, as Guy Temple observed, to unobtrusively prepare for an escape bid; but there were plenty of officers 'who thought it their duty to cause the Chinese as much trouble as they possibly could so that they would have to bring in more guards'.[77]

Then in the summer of 1952 came Crazy Week. The aim was not to bring in more guards or indeed irritate the Chinese, but rather to baffle them and create uncertainty, thereby boosting prisoner morale. The idea of behaving in a manner such that guards coming from a different culture and speaking a foreign language could not decide if the captives had gone mad or were sending them up had been used during the Second World War, and Crazy Week arose out of the experiences of Regimental Sergeant Major Jack Hobbs of the Glosters, who had spent much of the previous conflict as a guest of the Germans.[78]

The Americans took up the concept with enthusiasm. F-86 fighter pilots took to running around the compound with their arms swept back, engaging in mock dog-fights and formation-flying displays. Others would point at nothing in the sky. Invisible creatures and machines offered great scope for personal preference, as a number of Americans demonstrated. Ralph Nardella took to walking an imaginary canine; Bill Funchess started operating a plough pulled by a recalcitrant mule; and most notoriously, John 'Rotorhead' Thornton, the US Navy helicopter pilot, began to ride an invisible motorcycle around, complete with a full range of sound effects.[79]

The British seem to have taken a more collectivist approach to Crazy Week. They would play bridge games with invisible cards; they might gather in circles to

[74] Thornton, *Believed to be Alive*, 201, 204–5.

[75] See IWMDS, 16759/3, D. Patchett; Rountree in Peters and Li, *Voices from the Korean War*, 230.

[76] NAA, Part 7, AI9/K/AUST/1016, P/O B. L. Thompson, 5.

[77] IWMDS, 15557/5, G. Temple.

[78] Edward Hunter, *Brainwashing* (New York, 1956), 185. On Hobbs as a German POW see Clarke, *Journey Through Shadow*, 347–8. On British POWs going 'crazy' to baffle the Germans in the Second World War see S. P. MacKenzie, *The Colditz Myth* (Oxford, 2004), 204–7.

[79] Thornton, *Believed to be Alive*, 207 ff. (also NARA, RG 38, entry 1015(a1), box 42, Phase III Questionnaire, John W. Thornton, 24); Funchess, *Korea POW*, 115–16; Pelser, *Freedom Bridge*, 67; Rountree in Peters and Li, *Voices from the Korean War*, 230–1; Davies, *In Spite of Dungeons*, 77; see Hunter, *Brainwashing*, 149 ff.

stare fixedly at a point on the ground; and on one memorable occasion, in the wake of a saki issue in honour of a Chinese festival and the unauthorized singing of, among other things, *God Save the Queen*, they took their lead from the senior South African in the camp and, followed by the Americans, formed a conga line and snaked around the compound while pretending to do a Zulu war dance.[80]

The initial reaction of the camp authorities was one of satisfying gullibility followed by uncertainty as to whether men were going insane or pulling their legs in some manner they could not quite understand. Seeing groups of men pointing at the sky, guards would strain to see what was never there in the first place. Drawn to the prisoners gathered together and staring at something on the ground, an unsuspecting member of the Chinese People's Volunteers, his curiosity piqued, would walk up to see what was going on; at which point the prisoners would drift away and he would see...absolutely nothing. Passing sentries did not seem to realize, despite Nardella's profuse apologies, that his invisible dog was using them as lamp-posts. By his own account Rotorhead did such a realistic job with his motorbike that the Chinese came to think he really did believe the invisible machine was real and insisted on confiscating it; at which point his squad mates insisted that they return it. As for the conga line, the company commander was sufficiently worried that this was the start of a riot to appeal to the padre to intercede before things got out of hand.[81] A US Army report concluded that the Chinese were 'thoroughly confused' by Crazy Week, while Major 'Sam' Weller happily recalled that 'we drove the Chinese almost mad'.[82]

Inevitably, however, the staff worked out that they were being made fools of. 'We had to be careful playing games of nerves with the Chinese', Funchess wrote. 'If we needled them in a controlled fashion we could get away with a lot [but if] we went too far with the goading, they would start handing out punishment.' Arrests were made and the camp inhabitants told in no uncertain terms that Crazy Week had to stop.[83]

The most blatant indication that improving conditions were only strengthening the will of the officer-reactionaries was the ongoing interest in getting away. It was known that there were informers in the camp—the British blamed the Americans for leaks while all and sundry viewed those who had been at the Peace Fighters' Camp with particular suspicion[84]—so the British contingent formed a small escape committee of their own early in 1952 headed, after the removal of Major Ryan, by Captain Tony Farrar-Hockley.[85] Efforts were made to create non-perishable and portable rations by drying small strips of pork, and the blue uniforms issued by the

[80] Farrar-Hockley, *The Edge of the Sword*, 239–40; Funchess, *Korea POW*, 115; Davies, *In Spite of Dungeons*, 77–8; IWMDS, 12664/3, P. Weller.

[81] Farrar-Hockley, *The Edge of the Sword*, 230; Thornton, *Believed to be Alive*, 213–14; Davies, *In Spite of Dungeons*, 77–8; Funchess, *Korea POW*, 116.

[82] IWMDS, 12664/3, P. Weller; Department of the Army, *U.S. Prisoners of War*, 385.

[83] Funchess, *Korea POW*, 115; see Davies, *In Spite of Dungeons*, 78; NAA, Part 4, AI9/K/BRIT/38, Capt. A. H. Farrar-Hockley, 29.

[84] Lech, *Broken Soldiers*, 147. On the British assuming all informers were American see e.g. NAA, Part 3, AI9/K/BRIT/955, Lt S. W. Cooper, 3; NAM, 1989-05-163-1, R. Bruford-Davies.

[85] NAA, Part 4, AI9/K/BRIT/38, Pat II, Capt. A. H. Farrar-Hockley, 1.

Chinese were re-dyed and re-made into something resembling Korean peasant garb.[86] Keeping everything secret proved next to impossible, though; so that, for example, at the start of August 1952 a well-planned break involving a pre-positioned cache of escaping kit that was led by Farrar-Hockley himself was over almost before it began due to the fact that the Chinese had obviously been tipped off by an informer and simply lay in wait.[87] Officers nonetheless kept trying, a total of forty-one making attempts that year alone, twelve of that number being British: hence the need for the improved fence.[88]

* * *

To a certain extent the Chinese had a little less difficulty with the thirty-eight British sergeants concentrated with the rest of the senior NCOs in August 1952 at Camp 4, on the Wiwon River. Located on the edge of the village of Kuuptong and made up of wooden huts and other buildings divided into two compounds surrounded by wire fencing, Camp 4 held approximately 600 men in total. Living conditions were soon comparatively good, what with electric light in the huts, a library with a few novels as well as the usual political material, and, latterly, planks with which to build shelf beds. The food, which also improved with time, was sufficient to make men 'fit and healthy', in the words of one British sergeant from the Glosters, and there was plenty of sporting activity and little or no indoctrination.[89] There seems to have been no compunction about sending a British football team to the inter-camp Olympics in November, at least one British NCO remained openly progressive along with couple of other suspected cases, and less initiative than among the officers seems to have been slow on the escaping front.[90]

Yet while less troublesome than the officers at Camp 2, the NCOs at Camp 4 were far from being model prisoners from the Chinese perspective. The vast majority were loyal men who, while less aggressive than the officers, made it clear that there were real limits to the extent to which they would work with their captors. For example, when, after serving as sanitary representative, Sergeant P. J. Hoper of the Glosters was asked to read a speech praising the camp authorities for the fine way in which they were treating prisoners in early September 1952, he bluntly

---

[86] On escape clothing see IWMDS, 22347/6, E. R. Bruford-Davies. On escape rations see ibid. 16759/2, D. Patchett.

[87] Farrar-Hockley, *The Edge of the Sword*, 228 ff.; NAA, Part 4, AI9/K/BRIT/38 Part II, Capt. A. H. Farrar-Hockley, 28; Clarke, *Journey Through Shadow*, 303; NARA, RG 319, entry 85, Phase III summaries, box 1025, Shelton H. Foss, 5–6; see also, on the Chinese knowing about escape bids ahead of time, IWMDS, 19664/3–4, V. Whitamore. Another officer thought that this sort of thing occurred because Farrar-Hockley was insufficiently security-conscious (IWMDS, 22347/6, E. R. Bruford-Davies).

[88] Cunningham, *No Mercy, No Leniency*, 116.

[89] NAA, Part 6, AI9/K/BRIT/2, Sgt S. Robinson, 5 et al.; see e.g. Part 3, AI9/K/BRIT/971 et al., Sgt P. C. Crompton et al., 3–4; IWMDS, 21729/7, F. Cottam; see also Department of the Army, *U.S. Prisoners of War*, 120.

[90] NAA, Part 3, AI9/K/BRIT/971 et al., Sgt P. C. Crompton et al., 3–4. On the known progressives see also Part 6, AI9/K/BRIT/852, Sgt P. V. Petherick, 2. On the Olympic football team see also Part 7, AI9/K/BRIT/965, Sgt W. H. Tuggey, 3. On escaping see Part 6, AI9/K/BRIT/2 Part II, Sjt S. Robinson, 1–2.

refused. As a result he was arrested and thrown into jail for seventy days, only being released after the senior British NCO ordered him to write a self-criticism on humanitarian grounds.[91] Then there was the Chinese insistence that a wall be built to prevent the British and American sergeants from talking, something that Sergeant H. J. Peglet of the Glosters, among others, objected to on the grounds that the Chinese were always talking about prisoners only working for their own benefit and he could see no advantage at all in being cut off like this. He and two others were arrested, with Pegler himself flung into a cellar with eighteen inches of water on the floor for ten days until he agreed to reconsider his position.[92] The influence of the couple of British progressives, meanwhile, was more than counter-balanced by the position of the likes of Sergeant W. P. O'Hara of the Ulster Rifles, who, as an AI9 interrogator put it, 'continued to exert a great anti-Communist influence over his fellow PW'.[93]

* * *

Nonetheless the officers at Camp 2 generated more of a headache for the Chinese than the NCOs at Camp 4. There were fewer of them, but their numbers, along with their willingness to cause trouble, were slowly expanding.

Starting in March 1952, most newly captured aircrew, then individual officers whom the Chinese wished to keep a particularly close eye on, and, latterly, those for whom there was no room elsewhere, could be sent to a new branch of Camp 2 located in the village of Chang-ni on the south bank of the Yalu about a dozen miles north-east of the original camp. Here in Branch 3, prisoners were distributed amongst at least seventeen village buildings—some still occupied by their Korean inhabitants—in groups ranging from a few dozen down to single pairs. Fences round certain buildings and close supervision by the Chinese everywhere preventing much contact between the different groups who in aggregate numbered as many as 200 men. The vast majority of the inhabitants were American, but alongside a small number of captured South African and Australian pilots were a handful of British officers.[94] Several of the latter made life difficult for the camp authorities, the indefatigable Major Joe Ryan lodging complaints, refusing until pushed very hard to confess to supposed crimes, and making every effort to escape.

[91] Ibid. Part 4, AI9/K/BRIT/1001, Sgt P. J. Hoper, 4.

[92] Ibid. Part 6, AI9/K/BRIT/877, Sgt H. J. Pegler, 2; see Part 3, AI9/K/BRIT/971 et al., Sgt P. C. Crompton et al., 3.

[93] Ibid. Part 5, AI9/K/BRIT/999, Sgt W. P. O'Hara, 5.

[94] The RAF was represented by F/O M. O. Bergh, who had ejected over enemy territory in August 1952 while attached to 77 Squadron RAAF. Aside from a couple of officers captured in the spring of 1953, the British Army presence at Chang-ni consisted of Maj. Joe Ryan, sent there in July 1952, and 2/Lt L. S. Adams-Acton, a Royal Northumberland Fusiliers officer who had been captured while working with partisans on a coastal island in December 1951. On various parts and aspects of Camp 2 (Branch 3), in effect a conglomeration of mostly small and isolated compounds, see e.g. NAA, Part 4, AI9/K/SAAF/2, 2/Lt R. E. Gasson, 7 ff.; Part 3, AI9/K/BRIT/956, 2/Lt N. F. Deaville, 3 ff.; Part 4, AI9/K/AUST/959, Capt. P. J. Greville, 3 ff.; Duane Thorin, *A Ride to Panmunjom* (Chicago, 1956); D. Thorin memoir, <http://www.usgennet.org/usa/topic/preservation/journals/pegasus/peg-p-1.htm> (accessed 14 January 2011).

He himself made an unsuccessful bid as late as mid-July 1953, as did Second Lieutenant Leo Adams-Acton, who was shot and killed.[95]

A far larger number of British officers from the original Camp 2 compound had found themselves relocated in October 1952. That month around 150 of the UN officers were formed into a second company and sent without warning to a compound in a narrow valley over a mile away. The likely reason for this was a desire, largely for propaganda reasons, to ease the crowding in what was known as Camp 2 (Branch 1). This Annexe to Camp 2—not to be confused with either Branch 3 mentioned above or Branch 2, covered in the next chapter—consisted of an multiroom barracks building of traditional Korean construction and a thatched roof situated on a north–south axis, with two similar buildings on the opposite axis to the west comprising, respectively, a library plus barber shop on the one hand and a kitchen plus a few more sleeping quarters on the other. The area between the three main buildings served as a parade ground, and the resulting square compound was soon enclosed by a barbed wire fence into which saplings were diligently woven. The move eased crowding somewhat in the main camp;[96] but prisoners sent to the smaller Annexe, including fifteen of the British officers, were jammed in to the point where personal sleeping space was little more than that of a coffin, and found that the traditional Korean heating arrangements meant some men were too hot while others froze at night during the winter of 1952–3.[97]

The staff member with whom the Annexe population most often came into contact was Comrade Chang, who seems to have been both the most amicable and the most dangerous of the English-speaking Chinese the officers encountered. An expert linguist, he was, as Farrar-Hockley remembered, 'an unprincipled opportunist' who at the same time was 'the only Chinese in the Camp with sufficient intelligence to see that the best approach to us as a group was with politeness, and amity'. Chang's charm and skill eased relations with the rest of the Chinese staff and perhaps led some to forget that his aims and outlook were exactly the same as the rest of the CPV, however well disguised.[98]

It may have been Chang who tipped the scales in convincing the officers to send a contingent to the inter-camp Olympics to be held at Pyoktong starting in the middle of November. It was recognized that this was a propaganda stunt, and according to Farrar-Hockley 'there was considerable doubt amongst ourselves as to whether we should participate or not'.[99] Those left behind in the schoolhouse seem

[95] On the death of Adams-Acton see Anthony Perrins (ed.), *'A Pretty Rough Do Altogether': The Fifth Fusiliers in Korea, 1950–1951* (Alnwick, 2004), 342; NARA, RG 38, entry 1015 (a), box 42, Phase II Questionnaire, John W. Thornton, 24. On Ryan and Weller at Branch 3 see NAA, Part 6, AI9/K/BRIT/69, Maj. M. D. G. C. Ryan, 7–9. On the mixed views of among the Americans about how to respond to the Chinese at Branch 3 see Thorin, *A Ride to Panmunjom*.

[96] NAA, Part 3, AI9/K/AUST/58, F/O R. D. Guthrie, 9.

[97] Ibid. Part 1, AI9/K/US/1, Capt. Zach W. Dean, 9; Part 3, AI9/K/BRIT/70 et al., Capt. T. R. Littlewood et al., 2, Appendix B; Farrar-Hockley, *The Edge of the Sword*, 245; Clarke, *Journey Through Shadow*, 322–5; Pelser, *Freedom Bridge*, 69–70; King and Guthrie, *Escape from North Korea*, 123–4.

[98] Farrar-Hockley, *The Edge of the Sword*, 245–6. On underestimating Chang see e.g. NAA, Part 4, AI9/K/BRIT/958, 2/Lt D. J. English, 5.

[99] Farrar-Hockley, *The Edge of the Sword*, 247.

to have been inclined to reject the idea of sending a team, but in the Annexe it was eventually decided that it would be worthwhile to go in order to make contact again with the other ranks and find out how they had been faring—a position that tipped the scales overall in favour of participation.[100] Unfortunately the Chinese kept the officers segregated from the other ranks at the inter-camp Olympics, and though the participants were not asked to engage in any kind of blatant 'peace' campaign activity, the authorities at Pyoktong staged the event in such as way as to be able to photograph and film men for the purposes of producing a pamphlet and documentary showing healthy men getting plenty to eat. This was not entirely unexpected, but it was still galling to see later in the pages of the *Daily Worker*.[101]

The decision to participate may nonetheless have had a positive effect from the officers' perspective in that during the following spring prisoners from Branch 2, the camp to which reactionaries from Pyoktong and Chongson had been sent (see chapter 7), were allowed to visit the officers for a sporting tournament. This seems to have done both groups a lot of good, as Farrar-Hockley related in his memoir of captivity:

> I had often been told by the Chinese and the North Koreans how bitterly the men hated their officers; how we despised them. This was a remark which hurt, but I had never foreseen an opportunity to refute it such as occurred when we saw the men who were our comrades from our own units. Riflemen [A.] McNab and [T.] Agnew could not stop shaking hands with [Captain] James [Majury]. And from my own Battalion there was [Privates T. P.] Nugent and [R. L.] English of [Major] Sam [Weller]'s Support Company Headquarters, Sergeant [B. M.] Smith of C Company, and Corporal [C. A.] Bailey of the Anti-Tank Platoon. There were two gunners, and two Royal Marines from the Commando besides. We stood on our square after prolonged hand-shakes, quite unable to express fully our great joy at meeting again.

Indeed, some time passed 'before we could even begin to exchange news'.[102] Farrar-Hockley took the opportunity to pass on some potentially useful information concerning escape planning and the need to keep up appearances in front of the Chinese.[103]

Allowing inter-company sporting events was part of wider set of improvements that occurred in the spring and summer of 1953. Stalin had died in March, opening the way for real progress in the armistice talks at Panmunjom such as an exchange of sick and wounded that took place the following month. (A trio of American officers from Camp 2 were allowed to depart, though none of the British whom it was thought by their fellows ought to go; but unlike in the case of

---

[100] NAA, Part 4, AI9/K/BRIT/958, 2/Lt D. J. English, 5; Farrar-Hockley, *The Edge of the Sword*. A baser motive for participating in the inter-camp Olympics was, as a USMC pilot put it, 'to get away from camp for a while'. NARA, RG 38, entry 1051 (a), Phase II Questionnaire, Jesse V. Booker, response to question 8.

[101] See Department of the Army, *U.S. Prisoners of War*, 374–5. On the propaganda generated and reactions to it see also e.g. NAM 1989-05-163-1, R. Bruford-Davies; Farrar-Hockley, *The Edge of the Sword*, 247–8.

[102] Farrar-Hockley, *The Edge of the Sword*, 260.

[103] NAA, Part 6, AI9/K/BRIT/548, Rfn H. Smith, 4; Part 7, AI9/K/BRIT/157 Part II, Cpl W. K. Westwood, 1.

many of other ranks sent home through Operation Little Switch there seems to have been no suggestion that those officers allowed to go were progressives.[104]) With the prospect of the war coming to an end soon rather than sometime in the indefinite future, the Chinese did their best to put the best possible face on life for UN captives. Officers noted that the quality and even, to a degree, the quantity of the food and tobacco rations provided improved significantly as the armistice talks progressed. As the padre wrote, 'the summer diet of 1953 contained tomatoes, greens, a few eggs and canned meat sometimes as often as three times a week'.[105] Wooden tables, chairs, and bunks were installed, new washbowls issued, and each man presented with an individual razor, nail-clippers, and a toilet bag.[106] For those who played football the Chinese went to the trouble of finding sets of uniforms; those interested in theatre were allowed to stage *Pygmalion* on the basis of what Davies recalled of the play's script and what the camp authorities could provide in the way of costume material; and for readers, the number and variety of novels increased.[107]

All this largesse did not, however, make the inhabitants of Camp 2 (Branch 1) or its Annexe more docile and amenable to Chinese authority. It was true enough that both the British and the Americans had agreed to send a representative to a show conference on camp conditions held at Pyoktong in May 1953, but this was only because, in the case of the former, the senior British officer not under arrest at the time, Major Denis Harding, wanted to try once more to make contact with the Other Ranks.[108] In a number of other respects the officers proved as difficult as ever from the Chinese perspective, not least the British.

Prior to Easter 1953, which fell on 5 April, the authorities had agreed to allow prisoners from both Branch 1 and the Annexe to attend a joint celebration. Their only condition, after scrutinizing every word to be said or sung, was that the song *You'll Never Walk Alone* be dropped. The significance of the lyrics to the Chinese remained a mystery to the prisoners, but the Americans were willing to accept this one restriction. The British, on the other hand, refused to concede on principle; so the Americans, to avoid a split, then reversed themselves and no joint event took place. The Chinese, according to Tony Farrar-Hockley, were 'very much put out'.[109]

Then there was the ongoing propensity of some of the officers to try and flee the lenient embrace of the CPV. Though once again a carefully laid escape plan had

---

[104] See Farrar-Hockley, *The Edge of the Sword*, 261; see also A. M. Harris, *Only One More River to Cross* (Canberra, 2004), 94.

[105] Davies, *In Spite of Dungeons*, 63; see also e.g. IWMDS, 12664/3, P. Weller; NAA, Part 3, AI9/K/BRIT/955, Lt S. W. Cooper, 3; Farrar-Hockley, *The Edge of the Sword*, 269.

[106] Farrar-Hockley, *The Edge of the Sword*; Davies, *In Spite of Dungeons*, 142; IWMDS, 21729/7, F. Cottam.

[107] On *Pygmalion* see Davies, *In Spite of Dungeons*, 136–7; NAM 1989-05-163-1, R. Bruford-Davies; IWMDS, 22347/6, E. R. Bruford-Davies. On the novels see Davies, *In Spite of Dungeons*, 145; Farrar-Hockley, *The Edge of the Sword*, 248. On the football kit see Davies, *In Spite of Dungeons*, 142.

[108] NAA, Part 4, AI9/K/BRIT/981, Capt. R. P. Hickey, 3. The date is listed in this report as May 1952, but this is a typo. See MacDonald, *The Problems of U.S. Marine Corps Prisoners*, 217.

[109] MacDonald, *The Problems of U.S. Marine Corps Prisoners*, 218.

been betrayed by persons unknown and the participants arrested, the fact remained that no less than half-a-dozen British and American prisoners had been preparing a break from the Annexe even before the spring thaw.[110] As the weather improved the camp authorities, despite—or perhaps because of—what they were being told by informers, continued to worry that groups of officers were either planning escapes or otherwise engaging in 'plots' again the CPV.[111] This state of mind was what produced, apparently because it was feared that the prisoners were preparing some sort of insurrection, a sudden spate of trench-digging and heightened security in Branch 1 in the spring.[112] It also helps explain why, after a disgruntled or simply insane North Korean peasant tried to assassinate Ding Fang in June—and was immediately gunned down after he missed—the camp authorities immediately suspected that various British prisoners had somehow orchestrated this random act of violence.[113]

On the other hand information passed by informers sometimes led the camp authorities to more concrete instances of what from their perspective amounted to planned insubordination. As it became clear that an armistice was looming, the senior UN officers devoted some thought to maintaining discipline among the prisoners when the war ended, the worry being that spontaneous displays of anti-Chinese sentiment by hotheads—setting fire to the buildings, for instance—might give the enemy an excuse to hold people back and sentence them to jail time as 'criminals'. Thus in June word was passed down through Lieutenant Colonel Alarich L. E. Zacherle to the Americans and Major Weller to the British that when the armistice was announced everyone should remain calm and act responsibly. This was also what the Chinese wanted, but it did not take them long to decide that the undermining of a principle—that prisoner rank did not count and only they issued orders—outweighed the content of what was conveyed.[114]

They were also unhappy with the idea of the British celebrating the forthcoming coronation of Queen Elizabeth II. The camp authorities undoubtedly knew that secret preparations involving such things as the baking of a cake were underway, and tried to prevent anything happening on June 1—Coronation Day—by refusing a request by Padre Davies to hold a commemoration service in Branch 1 and issuing dire warnings against any celebrations in the Annexe. Plans for a coronation

---

[110] Farrar-Hockley, *The Edge of the Sword*, 251–2; IWMDS, 19664/3, V. Whitamore; Clarke, *Journey Through Shadow*, 335; NAA, Part 4, AI9/K/BRIT/38, Capt. A. H. Farrar-Hockley, 31–2.

[111] Farrar-Hockley, *The Edge of the Sword*, 265–6. On further escape planning see e.g. NAA, Part 4, AI9/K/BRIT/38, Capt. A. H. Farrar-Hockley, 32.

[112] See NAA, Part 6, AI9/K/BRIT/977, Lt A. Peal, 3.

[113] Ibid. Part 4, AI9/K/BRIT/38, Capt. A. H. Farrar-Hockley, 33. On the shooting see also Funchess, *Korea POW*, 108–9. Fred Carne was probably not the only officer to have thought about bumping off Ding Fang but had second thoughts about the consequences for the general inmate population. See TNA, WO 208/4021, Encl. 1B, Verbatim Transcription of the Re-Interrogation of Lt Col. J. P. Carne, f. 48. In fact the only plot really being hatched was on the other side of UN lines, where information passed by Little Switch returnees led to the formulation in the summer of 1953 of a scheme, eventually abandoned, to drop a special operations group by parachute in order to rescue Carne. Harris, *Only One More River to Cross*, 94–100.

[114] Farrar-Hockley, *The Edge of the Sword*, 264; Clarke, *Journey Through Shadow*, 385, 395–6, 390; IWMDS, 19387/6, A. Perrins.

meal nevertheless went ahead in both locations. In the Annexe, Comrade Chang decided to look the other way once it was discovered that a picture of the Queen taken from a newspaper had been put up, and the National Anthem was sung. In Branch 1, on the other hand, Comrade Sun refused to turn a blind eye when he personally observed the celebratory cake, saw a picture of the Queen clipped from the *Daily Worker*, and heard officers singing *God Save the Queen*. He led a guard detachment into the room where the event was being held, trying to seize as much offending evidence as possible. Those present, however, quickly concealed, ate, or drank what remained, and the commotion quickly drew a crowd of sympathetic Americans onlookers willing to boo and swear at the Chinese. The entire guard was turned out as Davies and Sun, both enraged, confronted each other:

Davies: 'Sun, you have offered the British people tonight an insult we shall not forget!'

Sun: 'You call yourselves The People!…You are not The People!…You are the enemies of The People!'[115]

All this only confirmed the Chinese sense that they were being conspired against, and retaliation soon followed.

Major Weller was arrested, as was Colonel Zacherle, on charges of undermining CPV authority. Both were put under a lot of pressure to admit to the error of their ways by, among other things, being made to stand rigidly at attention for anything from six to twenty-four hours, and while Zacherle eventually wrote a short, bare-bones confession that ended with a curt admission of having acted 'rashly', Weller would not even go this far. This 'capitalistic warmonger', as D. P. Wong termed him, 'adamantly refused to criticize himself or write any kind of confession'. Towards the end of July, Zacherle and Weller were sentenced to at least six months of hard labour.[116]

Once again this act of retribution, along with further arrests, failed to cure the remaining officers of their reactionary habits. Escape plans were being prepared right down to the day the armistice was announced.[117] On that day, 27 July 1953, moreover, the junior officers stood by the expectations of their seniors concerning appropriate behaviour. In Branch 1, the prisoners were assembled to listen to D. P. Wong translate Ding Fang's proclamation that a cease-fire had been agreed. 'The Chinese cameramen were poised ready for snaps of the "joyful prisoners hailing the great victory of the peace-loving peoples at Panmunjom"', as Padre Davies recalled. But nobody moved, cheered, or spoke. 'We did not want to give the Chinese the satisfaction', as US Army Lieutenant William H. Funchess put it.[118] In the Annexe the cat had already been let out of the bag by an overly garrulous guard

---

[115] King and Guthrie, *Escape from North Korea*, 131–2; see Farrar-Hockley, *The Edge of the Sword*, 263; Davies, *In Spite of Dungeons*, 138–9; NAM 1989-05-163-1, R. Bruford-Davies.

[116] Clarke, *Journey Through Shadow*, 396; TNA, WO 373/119, citation for Maj. P. W. Weller, f. 188; see Cunningham, *No Mercy, No Leniency*, 115–16.

[117] See NAA, Part 4, AI9/K/BRIT/980, Capt. A. M. Ferrie, 3; Part 3, AI9/K/BRIT/42, Lt J. M. C. Nicholls, 3; IWMDS, 15557/5, G. Temple.

[118] Funchess, *Korea POW*, 130; Davies, *In Spite of Dungeons*, 146; see IWMDS, 19664/4, V. Whitamore.

several weeks earlier; but Ding, the staff having vehemently denied in the mean-time the veracity of the guard's information, paid an afternoon visit accompanied by an entourage of photographers to try and elicit a positive response. Again, how-ever, his announcement was met only by silence. 'Without a picture taken, without a sound of thankfulness, without a smile from captives or captors', wrote Captain Conley Clarke, US Army, 'the interpreter stated, "You are dismissed."'[119]

Despite their lack of public reaction, the British residents at Pinchon-ni in par-ticular were emboldened by the news of the armistice and their imminent depar-ture. Davies, for example, became more confrontational in his dealings with the Chinese, demanding the release of Major Weller and dismissing the argument that he would be held back to complete his sentence.[120] He was not alone, as became clear on the day the prisoners were due to be transferred southward for repatria-tion. The Chinese suddenly confiscated, among other items, the stone cross Colo-nel Carne had carved. The Americans did not see this as something worth arguing over, but the senior British officer present at the time, Major Denis Harding, made it clear that no British officer would leave Pinchon-ni unless the cross was returned. Once more the Americans agreed to follow the British lead in stubbornness, and the camp authorities, eager to bring matters to a final close, capitulated on this matter.[121]

It was not just the officers, however, who caused headaches for the enemy. In hiving off those soldiers who made trouble at Pyoktong and then at Chongson the Chinese planned to concentrate their bad apples in a way that negated their influ-ence on the general rank and file and—or so it seemed in 1951–2—offered the chance for a more intensive attempt at converting the hard cases to the cause of the peace-loving peoples of the world. The first aim was achievable; the second, it eventually became clear, was not.

[119] Clarke, *Journey Through Shadow*, 392; see ibid. 390–1, 381–2. The sergeants at Camp 4 seem to have been taken by surprise, but seem to have done little other than to listen closely. IWMDS, 21729/7, F. Cottam.
[120] Davies, *In Spite of Dungeons*, 148. Weller was indeed released as a result of the armistice, though among the last to cross over at Panmunjom. Cunningham, *No Mercy, No Leniency*, 116.
[121] MacDonald, *The Problems of U.S. Marine Corps Prisoners*, 218–19.

7

The Reactionaries at Changson and Sonyi

They kept trying to teach us about communism, and to get us to say and write peace letters and things like that. And we just wouldn't do it, because we knew half of what they said was an absolute lie and the other half was fantasy. They couldn't see we would just tell lies for now, and say that we agreed with them. They just didn't understand this. [But] we had to be very careful what we did so it couldn't be construed as helping the enemy...

RM Corporal J. W. Peskett[1]

In the late summer and autumn of 1951 the Chinese POW administration at Pyoktong tried to solve the problem of reactionary influence by shipping some of the worst cases from Camp 5 south-westward some 35 miles down the Yalu to Changson (not to be confused with Chongson, roughly 12 miles further south) where they would meet batches of prisoners recently handed over by the North Koreans. Of the over 150 men involved, twenty-one were either British soldiers from Pyoktong or Royal Marines sent from the Pyongyang area. This was yet another camp on the edge of a village, the prisoners inhabiting huts in two compounds, one on either side of a creek, thirteen of the British being on the south side and the other eight on the north side.[2]

For the riflemen from Pyoktong, Camp 3—a second branch of which would be opened in August of the following year to accommodate recently captured UN soldiers[3]—was a retrograde step. 'Conditions were not good', one of them reported after his release. 'Food and accommodation were bad, and there were several cases of men being refused medical treatment because the Chinese said there was nothing wrong with them, and then the men died.'[4] The guards brought in were not above using their rifle butts and bayonets, and prisoners had to be cautious in their dealings with them.[5] For the Royal Marines and others coming directly from North Korean custody, on the other hand, Changson was a step up from what they had

[1] IWMDS, 14025/4, J. Peskett; see NAA, Part 6, AI9/K/BRIT/479, Cpl J. W. Peskett, 4.
[2] NAA, Part 3, AI9/K/BRIT/153, Rfn T. Agnew, 2; Part 6, AI9/K/BRIT/548, Rfn H. Smith, 3. On the Americans see e.g. Lloyd W. Pate as told to B. J. Cutler, *Reactionary!* (New York, 1956), 76–7.
[3] Ministry of Defence, *Treatment of British Prisoners of War in Korea* (London, 1955), 37.
[4] NAA, Part 6, AI9/K/BRIT/548, Rfn H. Smith, 3.
[5] See e.g. ibid. Part 3, AI9/K/BRIT/481, 817, Rfn F. Brodie and Rfn R. Traynor, 2; Part 6, AI9/K/BRIT/479, Cpl J. W. Peskett, 5; IWMDS, 14025/4, J. Peskett.

thus far experienced, especially with regard to food and even with respect to medical treatment.[6]

It was clear to everyone, though, that the Chinese were still intent on trying to enlighten men they regarded as wayward pawns of imperialism. There was to be compulsory political indoctrination in Camp 3, complete with mass lectures and group study sessions.[7] Among the British the Chinese often got the answers they wanted but were oblivious to the fact that that they were being outwitted by men used to saying one thing while thinking another. Corporal John Peskett of the Royal Marines was fairly typical in later reporting that while 'not influenced in any way by the indoctrination process' he 'attended lectures when he could not avoid it, and answered questions etc in the manner in which he knew the Chinese wanted them answered'.[8] This led some of the Americans to believe that the British were sympathetic to communism and favoured by the enemy.[9] That their allies were not really pro-communist was demonstrated by the fact that, when compulsory indoctrination was phased out in 1952, the British displayed a complete lack of interest in voluntary study.[10] Further proof came when Alan Winnington visited Camp 3 later that year. 'He lectured on the Korean Peace Talks and severely criticized the U.S. and Great Britain', US Army corporal Victor J. Newbury reported shortly after his release. 'When he was booed by his audience, he said he had been invited by the prisoners and would continue. Someone asked him to name the prisoners who had invited him and he refused.'[11]

While Marxism-Leninism generated no genuine enthusiasm in men's minds, escaping often occupied the thoughts of both the marines and soldiers at Changson. Despite the lack of a fence round the camp, the difficulties involved in getting out of North Korea were formidable. Yet this did not stop men from trying once the winter was over. A pair of marines, S. D. Hicks and P. H. Banfield, began hoarding food in the spring of 1952 in preparation for a westward trek to the coast. In late May, the haversack in which they had stored their escape rations was discovered by an American and, under suspicious circumstances, passed over to the Chinese. Despite the fact that the Chinese undoubtedly knew that an escape was being planned, the two marines decided to try again, Hicks asking his hutmates to contribute food for a new bid for freedom in early June. When they

---

[6] See NAA, Part 3, AI9/K/BRIT/934, Cpl F. Beadle, 5. On those who had come from North Korean hands finding Changson an improvement see e.g. Part 4, AI9/K/BRIT/1019, Pilot 3 R. H. Johnson, 6; Part 7, AI9/K/BRIT/895, Pte A. G. W. Tremlett, 5.

[7] There is some uncertainty about when compulsory indoctrination started and was discontinued at Camp 3. One source indicates it started at once and was given up in February 1953 (see ibid.). Another source states that it did not begin until January 1952 and was still going on when the British left in August 1953 (see ibid. Part 3, AI9/K/BRIT/934, Cpl F. Beadle, 5).

[8] Ibid. Part 6, AI9/K/BRIT/479, Cpl J. W. Peskett, 4.

[9] See e.g. NARA, RG 319, entry 85, Phase III summaries, box 1025, Nicholas J. Aramino; box 1035, Richard Perez, 4. The same sentiments were present in Camp 3 Branch 2: see ibid. RG 38, entry 1015(a1), Phase II questionnaire, question 46a, box 36, Louis Romero Jr, Lance G. Ricker; box 38, Sidney Oehl; box 43, James E. Tuscano; box 45, Michaux L. Williams, Preston D. Woodard.

[10] See NAA, Part 6, AI9/K/BRIT/548, Rfn H. Smith, 2; Part 7, AI9/K/BRIT/895, Pte A. G. W. Tremlett, 3.

[11] NARA, RG 319, entry 1015 (a), Phase III summaries, box 1034, Victor J. Newbury, 3.

tried to sneak away under cover of darkness, however, they were spotted by a sentry with a torch who, luckily, could not identify or apprehend them before they were able to scramble back to their billets. That they had been informed on became clear the next day when the escape rations they had hastily re-concealed were discovered and handed over to the camp authorities. This failure, however, did not deter others from trying—albeit with no greater success.[12]

Members of the British contingent at Camp 3 (Branch 1) were also not above playing tricks on their more obnoxious captors. Thus a guard who annoyed sleeping men by waking them with his torch during head counts found himself one night staring at an apparently dead man hanging from a noose attached to the rafters of a hut. He shrieked, dropped his torch, and ran out to wake the camp authorities. Meanwhile, as the staff was woken and the guard company turned out, the men involved, including the 'corpse,' hid their props and took up sleeping positions. When the staff rushed in and saw nothing amiss the guard was severely reprimanded. Through informants the camp authorities eventually discovered what had happened and warned the prisoners not to try this stunt again, but enemy ascendancy was nonetheless compromised. 'We had a wonderful time in that camp', John Peskett later commented.[13]

These men, however, were by no means the only rank-and-file British reactionaries with whom the Chinese had to contend in 1951–2. As had become dismayingly apparent, there were even more such wayward types at Chongson. In August of 1952 the British were removed from Camp 3 and sent to Camp 1. From there hard-core reactionaries from both camps, numbering as many as 200 men in all, about thirty of them British, were sent to a new location, Camp 2 (Branch 2) in the village of Sonyi. This turned out to be the usual collection of huts and other buildings, this time dotted on either side of a road that ran parallel to a tributary of the Yalu River in a valley about 30 miles north-east of Chongson. In all there were three compounds, including a separate area for NCOs not sent to Camp 4 and a facility for those under arrest. The main compound was already surrounded by wire when the men arrived, along with five sentry boxes mounted 6 feet off the ground. By the spring of 1953 the original barrier had been replaced by a formidable 10-foot-tall bamboo fence—'so thickly interwoven', R. F. Matthews recalled, 'that a cat couldn't get though'—while the other two compounds were enclosed by wire.[14]

Officially, as one former inmate explained, the prisoners were being sent to this new camp so that they could 'intensify their studies'.[15] In practice, though, the authorities had abandoned all hope of getting such dyed-in-the-wool reactionaries

---

[12] NAA, Part 4, AI9/K/BRIT/482 Part II, Mne S. D. Hicks, 1–2; Part 3, AI9/K/BRIT/846, Mne P. H. Banfield, 3. On escape attempts see also IWMDS, 14025/4, J. Peskett; Pate in Cutler, *Reactionary!*, 93–4.
     [13] IWMDS, 14025/4, J. Peskett.
     [14] R. F. Matthews as told to Francis S. Jones, *No Rice for Rebels* (London, 1956), 235; see Derek Kinne, *The Wooden Boxes* (London, 1955), 170–3, 176–7; NAA, Part 3, AI9/K/BRIT/13, Pte M. L. Bounden, 3–4, 6.
     [15] NAA, Part 3, AI9/K/BRIT/153, Rfn T. Agnew, 2.

to change their minds about communism. 'You've been sent here because you don't want to learn the truth', the chief instructor, Comrade Lee, announced to the new arrivals.[16] As an AI9 officer later put it:

> It seems that the Chinese realized their failure to make much impression on 'these poor unenlightened creatures,' and it was best for all concerned if they were segregated from their more fortunate and progressive comrades. They had shown that they were not interested in politics, and were incapable of absorbing the doctrine of their expert instructors, and furthermore the majority of them failed to appreciate the CCF [Chinese Communist Forces]'s efforts to make them comfortable.[17]

Aside from periodic attempts to convince prisoners that the United States was engaging in bacteriological warfare—on which the British resolutely refused to comment despite a fairly subtle approach taken by Comrade Lee[18]—the Chinese made no effort to revive compulsory study: they 'just left us alone', Corporal Bill Westwood recalled. As for voluntary classes, according to Sergeant B. M. Smith, also from the Glosters, 'nobody attended'.[19]

Even before it became evident that political education would not be high on the enemy agenda, the concentration of so many reactionaries made the odds in favour of the communists having set up the camp with the altruistic aim of improving their lot extremely slim. 'As recognized bad men', a private from the Glosters reflected, 'we did not expect much from our captors and we weren't disappointed.'[20] Living conditions, though they improved over time, were initially not very good. There was more work to do, camp rules and regulations were much more strictly enforced, and the place was better guarded than either Pyoktong or Changson. 'This was a particularly harsh camp', recalled Sergeant David Sharp of the Northumberland Fusiliers, 'discipline was strict'. Unlike other camps, Sonyi did not send teams to the inter-camp Olympics at Pyoktong in November. After all, as R. F. Matthews explained, the place was a de facto 'penal establishment for recalcitrant and uncooperative P. O.W.s'.[21]

According to one of the riflemen from Camp 3 the fact that the 'Chinese hardly bothered PWs with political instruction' worked to their advantage, since in return 'the PWs rather eased off their policy of annoying the Chinese'.[22] If so, this trend was certainly not necessarily apparent to the camp authorities.

[16] IWMDS, 19871/3, W. Westwood.
[17] NAA, Part 3, AI9/K/BRIT/13, Pte M. L. Bounden, 7; see also Matthews in Jones, *No Rice for Rebels*, 203.
[18] IWMDS, 19871/3, W. Westwood; NAA, Part 7, AI9/K/BRIT/157, Cpl W. K. Westwood, 2; Part 3, AI9/K/BRIT/13, Pte M. L. Bounden, 7.
[19] NAA, Part 6, AI9/K/BRIT/549, Sgt B. M. Smith, 4; IWMDS, 19871/3, W. Westwood.
[20] Matthews in Jones, *No Rice for Rebels*, 211; NAA, Part 3, AI9/K/BRIT/13, Pte M. L. Bounden, 3.
[21] Matthews in Jones, *No Rice for Rebels*, 202; IWMDS, 17929/6, D. Sharp. On poor initial conditions see e.g. NAA, Part 6, AI9/K/BRIT/548, Rfn H. Smith, 3; Part 3, AI9/K/BRIT/934, Cpl F. Beadle, 5; see also, with respect to food, Matthews in Jones, *No Rice for Rebels*, 211; NAA, Part 3, AI9/K/BRIT/153, Rfn T. Agnew, 2. On more manual labour see Part 6, AI9/K/BRIT/549, Sgt B. M. Smith, 4. On tighter discipline see ibid. 3; Part 3, AI9/K/BRIT/934, Cpl F. Beadle, 5; ibid. AI9/K/BRIT/13 Part II, Pte M. L. Boundin, 3. On no participation in the inter-camp Olympics see Part I, M. L. Boundin, 3.
[22] NAA, Part 6, AI9/K/BRIT/548, Rfn H. Smith, 3.

From the start the prisoners were experienced enough to recognize the dangers posed by committee elections and formed a united front against them, as Lieutenant M. G. Farmer of AI9 related after talking with Sergeant Smith:

> The Chinese tried to get the PWs to organise their own committee for running things but the PWs refused because it had been their experience that anyone singled out as a squad leader or as an organiser of anything was always the one to get into trouble if anything went wrong. Consequently they did not want to elect a dozen or so of themselves who would thereby be liable to be responsible for any misbehaviour of the other PWs alleged or otherwise.

The camp authorities had to appoint squad leaders without even the pretence of prisoner participation.[23]

Furthermore, the hard-core reactionaries by no means gave up entirely on baiting the enemy. Without classes they had an awful lot of time on their hands. 'We were bored', Private R. F. Matthews of the Glosters conceded. In the spring some men took to smoking marijuana gathered in the hills mixed with their tobacco. But as Fusilier Derek Kinne admitted, this was merely 'a novelty—a stupid novelty—by which we tried to relieve our boredom'. There was, Matthews thought, a 'danger, as most of us realized. that we might grow soft and acquiescent'. Having an occasional go at the Chinese was one way of averting this fate.[24]

In February 1953 a group celebrating someone's birthday sang a song they had recently composed which included the line 'When they hang old Mao Tse-tung.' A nearby guard overheard and rightly concluded that something derogatory was being said—or rather sung—about the Chairman. Either because of this piece of blasphemy or because the men had refused to collect wood because the Chinese were using their gatherings too (accounts differ), the commandant reduced the food and fuel rations of the men concerned. He soon had to relent after the group managed to coach one among their number to appear on the verge of death due to the poor living conditions. It was correctly surmised that the authorities would not want to risk further prisoner casualties in light of the embarrassment caused fourteen months earlier when prisoner lists were first exchanged at the armistice talks and it became clear that a huge gap existed in the number of men still alive as compared to the numbers of captives initially announced in the communist media.[25]

This was by no means the only instance when the Chinese were baited by the 'bad men' of Sonyi. Matthews remembered another incident that occurred not long afterward:

> The evening check lasted longer than usual. The guards watched as [Sung] Tsun [the unstable guard commander] lined us up and called the roll. Normally he would have counted us, and that would have been the end of it, but we answered smartly enough. Tsun's mispronunciation of names was too old a joke to wring laughs at this stage.

---

[23] Ibid. AI9/K/BRIT/549, Sgt B. M. Smith, 4.

[24] Matthews in Jones, *No Rice for Rebels*, 225; Kinne, *The Wooden Boxes*, 176.

[25] Matthews in Jones, *No Rice for Rebels*, 213–23; Kinne, *The Wooden Boxes*, pp. 175–6. On POW lists and the armistice talks see Walter G. Hermes, *Truce Tent and Fighting Front* (Washington, DC, 1966), 141 ff.

'Mass Shoes,' [Matthews] 'Makkabee' [McCabe] signalled that they were present and correct, and began walking away...Tsun called us back abruptly. He got us lined up again, glanced around to make sure the guards were watching, opened his mouth wide, and roared 'Hup! Numb-burr!!' The men on the right-hand side of the line reacted quickly. 'Ee, ur, sam, sur,' they chanted, 'wur, leo, chee...' We got as far as seven before Tsun realised we were counting in Chinese. He stopped us, shouted 'English! English!' and tried again. 'Hup! Numb-burr!!' he bellowed. It was the way he closed his eyes and stuck his chin out on the 'burr!!' that amused most of us. Frank Upjohn started correctly, and the count went to four, but by then it was a shambles. Mickey Flynn...was too convulsed to continue. He steadied his hands on his knees and laughed until tears came to his eyes. Within seconds all seventeen of us were grinning at the sight of Tsun standing outraged and infuriated in front of us.

The guard commander exacted his revenge by making the hated sorghum the standard ration once more.[26]

The ability and willingness of the Chinese to retaliate did mean there were limits as to how far most men were willing to go. When Fusilier Derek Kinne, who had been so badly beaten by the Chinese that he sustained a double hernia and held a special grudge, added DDT to the dough being used to make bread for the staff, there were no objections. However, when this failed to have a satisfactory effect and he started grinding up bits of glass he had collected for the same purpose, his friends forcibly restrained him on the reasonable premise that killing a staff member or two in a way that could be traced, as opposed to trying to make them ill in a more-or-less undetectable fashion, would produce unacceptably harsh counter-measures.[27]

Moreover by the spring of 1953, as the likelihood of an armistice in the near future increased and living standards—everything from food and tobacco to sports and letter-writing—improved, some men tacitly accepted the Chinese view that there was no point in trying to get away. 'We weren't interested in escape', Matthews admitted. 'Conditions were good, the war was ending, and incentive was missing.'[28]

On the other hand many of the British continued to engage in what was, from the Chinese perspective, antisocial behaviour through into the summer. Prodded by Farrar-Hockley during the football-match visit, Bill Westwood had, despite being a bit dubious about escaping at this stage, set up a cell that collected kit and developed plans that would have gone into operation if the war had not ended when it did.[29] A sense that improving conditions meant that the Chinese wanted prisoners to look as healthy as possible because an exchange was indeed in the offing may have dampened most men's ardour for escape but at the same

---

[26] Matthews in Jones, *No Rice for Rebels*, 223–4.

[27] Ibid. 226; Kinne, *The Wooden Boxes*, 179.

[28] Matthews in Jones, *No Rice for Rebels*, 236. On improving conditions see e.g. IWMDS, 1987/3, W. Westwood; NAA, Part 6, AI9/K/BRIT/548, Rfn H. Smith, 3.

[29] NAA, Part 7, AI9/K/BRIT/157 Part II, Cpl W. K. Westwood, 1–2; IWMDS, 19871/3, W. Westwood.

time given them a sense that the camp authorities could be pushed farther than in the past. Thus when one of the hard cases was arrested for supposedly threatening a guard with one the axes used for chopping wood, his friends announced that if he was not released they would 'refuse to co-operate with the Chinese People's Volunteers'. What this would have amounted to in practice was not put to the test since the authorities did indeed back down and release the man in question.[30]

Then there was the matter of the coronation of Queen Elizabeth II, which the *Daily Worker* and incoming letters indicated was due to take place at the beginning of June. The Chinese had denied a British request that they be allowed to celebrate, but this order was simply ignored. Corporal Bill Westwood of the Royal Marines managed to make a Union Jack and, at the request of the Americans, a Stars and Stripes for the occasion. Comrade Lee got wind of this, then arrested the two men and warned the British that they would never be seen again unless the flags were handed over. Under these circumstances Westwood felt he had no choice but to confess. Lee wanted the flags ceremoniously burned in front of the paraded prisoners, but Westwood convinced him to allow them to be disposed of in the cookhouse fire. Through sleight of hand he was able to retrieve a few bits before the fire consumed everything, and these were then secretly interred in a special pot for use during the coronation day service that the authorities had banned. Meanwhile, and unknown to the Chinese, Corporal Charlie Bailey had been making red, white and blue paper rosettes. On the day in question Bailey distributed the rosettes and led a secret service of thanksgiving that ended with the singing of *God Save the Queen*. This was overheard by the guards who rushed in with bayonets atop their rifles and arrested Bailey. On evening roll call the British all appeared wearing the rosettes, which Lee ordered removed. This was met with outright refusal, and the guard was called out again and more arrests were made as the Chinese struggled to confiscate the rosettes from men determined not to hand them over. Most men simply tore the rosettes up rather than allow them to fall into enemy hands, while Frank Upjohn held his within a clenched fist that the guards could not pry open. 'If I give this up', Kinne remembered him shouting while struggling valiantly with comrade Lee and his minions, 'I shall be giving up our flag.' Replacement rosettes were smuggled into the jail with the food from the cookhouse.[31]

All this was too much for the Chinese to ignore. Sorghum once more became the ration staple, and a warning was issued—and believed—to the effect that if anything like this riotous assembly happened again, Bailey would disappear for good.[32] Within a matter of days of the coronation episode, Camp 2 (Branch 2) was broken up, its inmates dispersed between the main camps.[33] This act of closure

[30] Matthews in Jones, *No Rice for Rebels*, 232–3.

[31] Kinne, *The Wooden Boxes*, 183; see ibid. 180–2; NAA, Part 6, AI9/K/BRIT/548, Rfn H. Smith, 4; Part 7, AI9/K/BRIT/157, Cpl W. K. Westwood, 4; IWMDS, 19871/3, W. Westwood; Edward Hunter, *Brainwashing* (New York, 1956), 191–2.

[32] IWMDS, 19871/3, W. Westwood; Kinne, *The Wooden Boxes*, 183.

[33] NAA, Part 6, AI9/K/BRIT/548, Rfn H. Smith, 4.

may simply have been in order to concentrate prisoners in anticipation of their repatriation as the armistice negotiations drew towards their end the following month. On the other hand it may have been out of recognition that what had originally seemed 'the easy way out'—a special camp for what Lee dubbed 'the dregs' among the Anglo-Americans—was in fact more trouble than it was worth.[34]

---

[34] IWMDS, 19871/3, W. Westwood ('dregs'); Matthews in Jones, *No Rice for Rebels*, 203 ('easy way out').

Conclusion

*I made my decision and stuck to it ... when the war ended I was face-to-face with
a Chinese general, telling him I wished to go to China.*

Marine Andrew Condron[1]

Since the end of 1951 the issue of whether or not military prisoners should be auto-
matically repatriated had resulted in a deadlock in the armistice negotiations at Panmunjom. The communists insisted on compulsory and complete repatriation while
their adversaries proved unwilling to push those who had been forced into enemy service to return to the communist fold, and there appeared no room for compromise.[2]

Yet in the first quarter of 1953, despite a great deal of mutual suspicion, an
agreement was reached on a partial exchange of sick and badly wounded prisoners.
In order to wrest the initiative from the International Red Cross and the General
Assembly of the United Nations where support for a resolution was building, the
US State Department and the Joint Chiefs of Staff had agreed to allow the United
Nations Command in Korea to issue an invitation for such an exchange in February. The expectation was that the communists would reject the offer, thereby cast-
ing them in an unfavourable light on the international stage.[3] This was something
that Mao was now keen to avoid, however, and for the sake of world opinion he let
it be known in March that China would welcome a resumption of negotiations at
Panmunjom and an agreement on the swapping of seriously ill and injured
captives.[4] The result was what on the UN side was known as Operation Little
Switch, whereby between 20 April and 3 May 1953, 6,224 sick and wounded captives were sent northward and 684 prisoners were sent southward through Panmunjom.[5] The thirty-two British soldiers involved in the exchange were first flown

---

[1] *Daily Express*, 15 October 1962, 7.

[2] Many South Koreans had been forcibly conscripted in to the North Korean People's Army and
later captured, while among the CPV prisoners there were many former Nationalists who preferred
rejoining Chiang Kai-shek on Taiwan over returning to the mainland. In the end, and sometimes
under pressure, 14,235 Chinese and approximately 32,500 Koreans chose not to return to the people's
democracies, while 325 Koreans, 22 Americans, and 1 Briton decided against returning (respectively)
to South Korea, the United States, and Great Britain. See Walter G. Hermes, *Truce Tent and Fighting
Front* (Washington, DC, 1966), 451, 515.

[3] Ibid. 411.

[4] Shu Guang Zhang, *Mao's Military Romanticism* (Lawrence, Kan., 1995), 239.

[5] Hermes, *Truce Tent and Fighting Front*, 514. A total of 446 civilian internees were also sent
northward.

to Japan in two batches, where a British nurse noted curiously that 'on the whole, most of this first convoy of POWs were in relatively good shape'.[6] They were then flown home by stages to RAF Lyneham, where they were met by relatives and spoke to the press. 'First reports indicate that they have all been treated better than was feared', a British Pathé newsreel narrator concluded on 4 May.[7] As officers from AI9 quickly discovered over the next few days as they interviewed the men in Tidworth hospital, the surprisingly benign picture being painted of Chinese captivity was due in large part to the fact that roughly one-third of the returnees had been chosen because of their progressive attitude rather the extent to which they were truly in bad health.[8]

A much more substantial breakthrough in the Panmunjom armistice negotiations came after 25 May when the United States made a number of procedural concessions on the prisoner repatriation issue which the Chinese found broadly acceptable. Further progress was delayed due to opposition from President Syngman Rhee and subsequent Chinese efforts to expose the military weakness of the Republic of Korea through offensive action. Nevertheless a final agreement was eventually reached whereby in the wake of a ceasefire any prisoners who did not wish to be repatriated would be held under Indian supervision for a period of three months at Panmunjom to reflect on their decision, during which time representatives of the states concerned would be given a chance to make a case for a change of heart. On 27 July 1953 the armistice was signed.[9]

This paved the way for what the UN side called Operation Big Switch, the more-or-less simultaneous exchange of the bulk of the prisoners held by each side in batches during August and early September. Once the armistice was announced in the Yalu camps everyone was very keen for this process to begin. Expectation, though, was tempered by the nagging fear that something might go wrong and, among the reactionaries, worry that the enemy would make good on earlier threats not to release convicted 'criminals'.[10] With the possible exception of a number of American aircrew survivors[11] this proved not to be the case, though the Chinese

---

[6] E. J. McNair, *A British Nurse in the Korean War* (Stroud, 2007), 152. On the journey through Panmunjom see Lofty Large, *One Man's War in Korea* (London, 1988), 141–5; IWMDS, 24610/12-13, B. Guess; 12605/6, S. Mercer.

[7] POWs Home (aka Korea POW's Return to Lyneham), <http://www.britishpathe.com/record. php?id=30966> (accessed 15 November 2010). Most of the British repatriates had refused to talk to the press at Panmunjom, one exception 'saying as little as possible.' Large, *One Man's War in Korea*, 144–5.

[8] Cyril Cunningham, *No Mercy, No Leniency: Communist Mistreatment of British Prisoners of War in Korea* (Barnsley, 2000), 155–6; see NAA, Part 1, Encl. 2A, Preliminary Interrogation Report on British Ex POW Released in Korea, 8 May 1953; ibid. Encl. 2B, Interrogation Report on British Ex POW Released in Korea (Batch No. 2), 12 May 1953. The progressives, not surprisingly, gave the communist press a positive picture of captivity: see *Daily Worker*, 2 May 1953, 1; 3, 8 May 1953, 1; 9 March 1953, 2; 11 May 1953, 1; 16 May 1953, 2.

[9] Hermes, *Truce Tent and Fighting Front*, 429 ff.; Shu, *Mao's Military Romanticism*, 242 ff.

[10] See e.g. Anthony Farrar-Hockley, *The Edge of the Sword* (London, 1954), 268; Dennis Lankford, *I Defy! The Story of Lieutenant Dennis Lankford* (London, 1954), 153.

[11] It is possible that a number of USAF personnel shot down over North Korea or Manchuria were transported to the Soviet Union for further interrogation and never returned. See Laurence Jolidon, *Last Seen Alive* (Austin, Tex., 1995).

did nothing to allay fears and in fact played on them by apparently arranging the journey southward and the actual release date according to how cooperative or otherwise a man had been. Thus while most of the prisoners set off in the first two weeks of August some of the hard-core rank-and-file types were held back for a week or more and the officers were not sent on their way until the third week of August.[12]

The trek southward was circuitous, initially involving for most a hair-raising trip north-eastward in trucks inching their way along mountainside tracks to the railhead at Manpo. From there prisoners were loaded aboard stinking cattle trucks for a stop-start, rickety journey spanning several days through the countryside and devastated towns and cities of North Korea to a point where they could be trucked to a transit camp the Chinese had set up at Kaesong.[13]

Though conditions here were good—'we received everything you could think of', remembered Marine Edward Curd, '...anything that [would show] the Chinese were treating you well'[14]—men were often on edge due to fear that the exchange might still not take place. After all, there had been several occasions over the past couple of years when the Chinese had hinted that an armistice was in the offing, only for hopes to be dashed when they announced that the Americans were making further negotiation impossible. Corporal Ronald Norley recalled that among his party in the transit camp 'everyone was agreed that if it fell through again we weren't going back to the camp [at Chongson], we were going to make a break for it'.[15] Each evening starting on 4 August an English-speaking Chinese staff member would call out a list of up to fifty names for exchange the following day. 'The fortunate ones would be showered with congratulations', Lieutenant Dennis Lankford related, adding that for those such as himself whose name was not called as days stretched into weeks anxiety grew. 'Those left behind grew restive and sleepless', Padre Sam Davies wrote some months later. 'Boredom and uneasy surmise took their toll.'[16]

It was true enough that the Chinese were passing over the progressives first for propaganda purposes, and did not start returning officers until 28 August.[17] In

[12] On the dates see Farrar-Hockley, *The Edge of the Sword*, 269; S. J. Davies, *In Spite of Dungeons* (London, 1954), 148; David Green, *Captured at the Imjin River* (Barnsley, 2003), 164. On holding back reactionaries see e.g. Derek Kinne, *The Wooden Boxes* (London, 1955), 188.

[13] On the journey see Davies, *In Spite of Dungeons*, 148–9; Farrar-Hockley, *The Edge of the Sword*, 271; Green, *Captured at the Imjin River*, 165–8; Lankford, *I Defy!*, 154–7; D. G. Mather in John R. P. Landsdown, *With the Carriers in Korea* (Southside, 1997), 391; IWMDS, 19047/4, F. Brodie; 16850/10, W. Gibson; 17283/6, A. Eagles; 16850/9, W. Gibson; 19387/5, A. Perrins; 18439/4, A. Tyas; 13711/2, J. Underwood; 19664/4, V. Whitamore.

[14] IWMDS, 10250/4, E. Curd; see also e.g. ibid. 20299/3, J. Shaw; Henry O'Kane, *O'Kane's Korea* (Kenilworth, 1988), 114. Alan Winnington reported favourably for the communist press on the transit camp after visiting the first—and thus progressive—group of British prisoners to arrive at Kaesong. *Daily Worker*, 5 August 1953, 1.

[15] IWMDS, 15539/4, R. Norley.

[16] Davies, *In Spite of Dungeons*, 149; Lankford, *I Defy!*, 157–8; see Green, *Captured at the Imjin River*, 168; IWMDS, 22347/6, E. Bruford-Davies; 15338/6, B. Murphy.

[17] On starting to return officers on 28 August, see *Daily Telegraph*, 29 August 1953, 1. On the propaganda value of the initial returnees see names and stories in *Daily Worker*, 6–8 August 1953, and compare with AI9 conclusions for these individuals in NAA, Parts 1–7.

the end, however, during the first week of September even the troublemakers were taken by Chinese trucks to the demarcation line and then escorted aboard American vehicles to what was labelled Freedom Village.[18] Often there was a senior figure at the doorway of this marquee-tent facility to greet them. In the case of the British it might be one of the brigade commanders or perhaps the Commonwealth Division supremo himself, Major General Sir Mike West. 'He shook me by the hand, and he welcomed me back, and gave me a packet of twenty players, and he told be the test score', Private David Kaye recalled of his own encounter, 'and I knew I was back.'[19]

The sense of relief among the men they were greeting could sometimes get the better of them. As he got off the truck, Lance Corporal R. F. Matthews of the Glosters was slapped from behind on the shoulder and heard an American voice boom 'Welcome back to Liberty!'

> I turned, beaming, gloriously happy, thumped the smiling American in return, and finally embraced him. 'You ugly old coot,' I crowed deliriously. 'Am I glad to see you!' Four little stars on the fatigue jacket winked as the American detached himself to greet the next man. One of our redcaps [military policemen], standing a few paces behind, stared at me in what seemed horrified disapproval. The Yank next to him was grinning broadly. I went up to them. 'What's wrong!' I asked, 'Who's that chap?' The G.I.'s smile threatened to split his face. 'Boy, can that guy take it,' he said admiringly. He turned his grin to me. 'You goddam Limeys've been beatin' the hell outa him all day, and he still comes up smilin'. Son, that's General Maxwell D. Taylor [commanding all UN forces in Korea].[20]

Men might be so deliriously happy, indeed, that the redcaps themselves found themselves hugged and kissed on occasion.[21] Inside Freedom Village they were cleaned up, questioned, given a quick medical check, and issued with either American clothing or British jungle uniforms. There were swarms of newspapermen eager to interview the ex-prisoners, but British Army intelligence officers kept them at arm's length, advising early arrivals not to speak to the press in case something they said about what they had undergone jeopardized the return of the remaining prisoners and later organizing press conferences in which certain questions were ignored.[22]

'My first impression was that everyone seemed to look so big, strong, fit and healthy', Rifleman Henry O'Kane recalled years later.[23] Attention quickly refocused,

---

[18] The very last Briton across was Sergeant David Sharp, Royal Northumberland Fusiliers, a confirmed reactionary. *Daily Telegraph*, 7 September 1953, 9.

[19] IWMDS, 17468/3, D. Kaye; see also e.g. ibid. 17929/6, D. Sharp; O'Kane, *O'Kane's Korea*, 115. At least one Ulster rifleman felt that the divisional commander devoted too much attention to the 'Glorious Glosters' compared to other units (ibid. 18439/4, A. Tyas) while one of the Glosters noted that while British returnees got a single packet of cigarettes the Yanks got a whole carton (ibid. 18459/2, W. Clark).

[20] R. F. Matthews as told to Francis S. Jones, *No Rice For Rebels* (London, 1956), 256.

[21] G. Costello in *Forgotten Heroes* (BBC, 2001).

[22] See e.g. IWMDS, 17929/6, D. Sharp; 16850/10, W. Gibson; see also TNA, AIR 40/2640, Encl. 8A, I. F. Valentine letter, 12 August 1953.

[23] O'Kane, *O'Kane's Korea*.

though, on the consumable feast laid out by US Army cooks. As Rifleman Bill Gibson remembered in an interview many years later, 'there was every known food you could wish to eat. Lines upon lines, beautifully laid-out.'[24] The British return-ees were then ferried to Britannia Camp, the Commonwealth forces base outside Seoul. Here they were welcomed by members of the Women's Voluntary Service, handed some pay, allowed to send a telegram home, given a more thorough medi-cal exam, briefed on current events and allowed 'food, anything you wanted, twenty-four hours a day', Rifleman John Shaw recalled, adding: 'it was just heaven'.[25]

After several days the returnees were transported by mostly Australian transport aircraft from Kimpo airfield to Osaka, from whence they were ferried to the Aus-tralian-run British Commonwealth Forces base at Kure. Here, over the course of several weeks, they were issued uniforms with all the appropriate ribbons and badges, had their pay and records properly sorted out, and were debriefed by rep-resentatives of AI9. The atmosphere, though, was very relaxed, with the ex-prisoners allowed to visit the town at will. 'It were terrific after what we'd been through, a big holiday', Rifleman Frank Brodie recalled.[26] It was also a time of happy reunions. When the CO of the Glosters, Lieutenant Colonel J. P. 'Fred' Carne, released on 1 September, arrived two days later at Kure, he was mobbed by his men and carried around on their shoulders.[27]

Finally the British ex-prisoners were shipped homeward aboard the troopships *Asturias* and *Empire Orwell*, stopping at the usual ports of call on the way during the six weeks at sea. On arrival in Southampton in mid-September and mid-October they were greeted as returning heroes, HM Customs officers turning a blind eye to what they had acquired in the way of presents, the admiring press in attendance en masse, and relatives and other well-wishers cheering them from the quayside: all 'very enjoyable', as Bill Gibson put it.[28]

Not all was sweetness and light in the aftermath of Operation Big Switch, how-ever. For one thing, not everyone crossed the demarcation line. For another, there were scores to settle on the way home for those who did, and issues for the authori-ties to grapple with concerning what to do about collaborators.

Having given way on the issue of voluntary repatriation, the Chinese knew that the world would take note that some CPV personnel would refuse to return to Mao's embrace. To try and ameliorate the propaganda victory that the United

---

[24] IWMDS, 16850/10, W. Gibson; see e.g. IWMDD, F. Carter, 74; Andrew Salmon, *To the Last Round* (London, 2009), 298.

[25] IWMDS, 20299/3, J. Shaw; see e.g. ibid. 17929/6, D. Sharp; Green, *Captured at the Imjin River*, 169–70.

[26] IWMDS, 19047/5, F. Brodie; see O'Kane, *O'Kane's Korea*, 115; IWMDS, 10749/8, R. Erricker; 16850/10, W Gibson; 17929/6, D. Sharp; IWMDD, F. Carter, 74; Green, *Captured at the Imjin River*, 171 ff. On the relaxed approach—which some in authority thought excessive in light of the way in which some ex-prisoners took advantage of the situation to become drunk and disorderly—see TNA, WO 32/16231, Encl. 1A, Conduct of Returning Ex-PW, October 1953. On the repatriation plan see also AIR 40/2640, Encl. 186A, App. A.

[27] *Daily Telegraph*, 4 September 1953, 7.

[28] IWMDS, 16850/10, W. Gibson; see *The Times*, 17 September 1953, 8; 15 October 1953, 8.

States would thus achieve, efforts were made to persuade some of the American progressives to themselves refuse repatriation in order to make more of their lives in the People's Republic of China. In the end, despite efforts to dissuade them during the mandated three-month reflection period under Indian Army supervision in the neutral zone, twenty-one US Army personnel took and held this position...along with a solitary Royal Marine, Andrew Condron.[29]

The inclusion of this Scotsman among the Americans does not seem to have been part of the Chinese plan. No apparent effort had been made to persuade the British to participate, and fellow progressives at Pyoktong were quite shocked by his announcement. So too, apparently, were the Chinese themselves, who by his own account tried hard yet failed to change his mind. Having studied communism at length, Condron now wanted to see it in action.[30] During the three-month grace period in the neutral zone he bluntly rejected official British efforts to communicate with him while he still had a chance to change his mind. Major Michael McNabb, an intelligence officer, wanted to interview him, but Condron was adamant: 'Don't waste your time and the taxpayer's money.'[31] The fact that even a single British serviceman had volunteered to 'stay with the Reds', as the *Daily Express* put it, was widely reported in the press and a public embarrassment to the British authorities.[32]

Meanwhile, now that the Chinese were no longer present to protect the progressives and punish the reactionaries, the latter were keen to see the former receive their just deserts. *Daily Express* correspondent Russell Spurr interviewed sixteen men from Camp 2 (Branch 2) at Britannia Camp after their release, some of whom 'vowed vengeance' against the progressives. Cooler heads such as Sergeant Bernard Smith of the Glosters favoured official action. 'In fairness to prisoners who had a rough time', he stated, 'there should be a Government inquiry into the activities of the rats and squealers.'[33] There were plenty of men, though, who were willing to take justice into their own hands, and a few days later two suspected collaborators asked for official protection against possible action by their erstwhile campmates.[34] On the voyage home those suspected of being informants or known to be

---

[29] Virginia Pasley, *22 Stayed* (London, 1955). Two Americans decided during the three-month limbo period to change their minds and return to the USA. See Raymond B. Lech, *Broken Soldiers* (Urbana, Il., 2000), 196–9.

[30] IWMDS, 9693/7, A. Condron. On friends being taken by surprise see e.g. ibid. 10982/6, E Beckerley. The Americans, on the other hand, were courted: see e.g. Morris R. Wills as told to J. Robert Jackson, *Turncoat* (Englewood Cliffs, NJ, 1968), 60; Clarence Adams, *An American Dream*, ed. Della Adams and Lewis H. Carlson (Amherst, Mass., 2007), 64.

[31] *Daily Express*, 25 September 1953, 2; see TNA, ADM 1/27482, 170803Z, Rear 1 Comwel Div to Admiralty, Air Ministry, 17 December 1953; ibid. 240700Z, Britcom Japan to Admiralty, Air Ministry, 25 November 1953; Pasley, *22 Stayed*, 186–7, 197. For an observer's impressions of the limbo period, efforts to change men's minds, and their reactions, see S. N. Prasad, *History of the Custodian Force (India) in Korea 1953–54* (Delhi, 1976).

[32] *Daily Express*, 25 September 1953, 2; see also e.g. *Daily Telegraph*, 25 September 1953, 7; *The Times*, 25 September 1953, 6; 23 January 1954, 6; 27 January 1954, 5; 28 January 1954, 8; 25 February 1954, 5; *Daily Worker*, 25 September 1953, 4; TNA, ADM 1/24687, Non-return of Royal Marine POW from Korea: policy on publicity, 1953.

[33] *Daily Express*, 12 August 1953, 1.

[34] TNA, WO 208/4014, Encl. 18a, 'Highlights' for the week ending 16 August 1953.

progressive were heavily victimized by their peers. A corporal from the Glosters, for example, was tossed overboard into Osaka harbour and later again into Hong Kong harbour, fears for his life then forcing the authorities to send him home alone on an oil tanker.[35] Rumours aboard ship that plans were afoot to dump half-a-dozen of the progressives into the sea when the inevitable fog appeared in home waters led them to be hurriedly disembarked at Singapore. Farrar-Hockley, once again serving as de facto adjutant, had to intervene personally to stop several others being thrown overboard.[36] 'I think a few [other] retributions took place, mostly punch-ups', Bill Gibson later reflected, 'people got their own back... it did take place.' The problem was severe enough for the police to interview witnesses before the ship docked at Portsmouth out of suspicion that a soldier who slit his own throat and wrists had in fact been murdered.[37]

Taking the evidence of Little Switch a little too prophetically, there were those in Whitehall who feared that perhaps as many as half those returned through Big Switch would have been successfully indoctrinated by the communists. The press got wind of this as well as talk within AI9 concerning the possibility of a possible counter-indoctrination programme to be run by the Royal Army Educational Corps. 'There remains the fear that the returned converts are bearing a doctrinal poison which may be exploited in many ways by Communists at home', *The Times* reported. 'This, some feel, should be eradicated by a special course of counter-education.' It was soon realized, however, that this was neither practicable nor advisable. As *The Times* leader-writer went on to comment, 'it would show little faith in the values of our own society to think that those values could not reassert themselves without aid of a professional political educator or psychiatrist'. The educational corps had neither the manpower nor a political programme to match what the Chinese had deployed, and in any event the vast majority of the returning ex-prisoners were due for release. As an AI9 officer put it, 'neither they nor their relatives would thank the authorities if they delayed their demobilization for political purposes'. The idea was shelved on orders from the Prime Minister, Winston Churchill.[38]

That still left the question of what action to take, if any, against collaborators and in relation to the potential security threat posed by men who had in fact turned communist and planned to remain with the Royal Marines or the British

---

[35] Cunningham, *No Mercy, No Leniency*, 158. At least ten men had to be segregated for their own safety at this point. TNA, WO 32/20495, Hong Kong: ORs in Protective Custody, n/d; ibid. Encl. 75A, FARELF to War Office, 14 September 1953.

[36] Salmon, *To the Last Round*, 298–9.

[37] IWMDS, 16850/10, W. Gibson. On the suicide see also O'Kane, *O'Kane's Korea*, 116; IWMDS, 19047/4, F. Brodie. Anti-progressive action may also have been spurred by resentment at speculation in the press that large numbers of returnees had been affected by communist indoctrination. See *The Times*, 17 September 1953, 8. It may also have been partly in reaction to efforts by the progressives while in Kure to terrorize those who knew of their activities into staying quiet. See NAA, Part 3, AI9/K/BRIT/317, Gnr E. Digan, 3.

[38] *The Times*, 16 September 1953, 9; see TNA, WO 32/19273, A. Head minute, 12 May 1953; ibid. AG to SofS minute, 5 June 1953; ibid. Encl. 43A, Counter-Indoctrination of Released Prisoners of War, n/d; PREM 11/871, Duff to Colville, 17 April 1953; see also Cunningham, *No Mercy, No Leniency*, 155–6.

Army. The former was the most pressing issue, not least because some of the ex-prisoners were very unwilling to forgive and forget even after they disembarked. 'The majority of the reactionaries are at a loss to understand why those whom they consider have misbehaved in the camps are being given the same treatment as themselves once they have been released', an AI9 report dated 22 October 1953 noted. 'Although it has been explained to them that they must not take the law into their own hands they still feel a certain amount of resentment as nothing has so far happened to those PW.' The fury that had caused the shipboard incidents was still there.[39]

In fact even while Big Switch was still underway, the service ministries had been assessing the possibility of courts martial. Simply becoming a communist, as the Prime Minister himself had noted at the time of Little Switch, did not constitute a military offence. As for aiding the enemy, which most certainly did, sufficient proof was going to be difficult to obtain. It could be argued, for instance, that signatures on petitions calling on soldiers to switch their allegiance were forgeries, while most of the broadcast transcripts simply praised the Chinese and condemned the Americans, which might be difficult to prove actually aided the enemy. Only after all the potential cases had been thoroughly investigated should a decision be taken about courts martial. As the Minister of Defence, Lord Alexander, put it in a memo to the Prime Minister on the day the *Asturias* docked at Southampton, the service ministers agreed that 'disciplinary action should only be taken against returned prisoners of war in really serious cases and where there was a reasonable certainty of obtaining a conviction'.[40]

Over three-dozen cases were investigated by the Special Investigation Branch over the next few months, but without useful result. The evidence simply was not sufficient to support charges of voluntarily aiding the enemy, and while charges of conduct prejudicial to good order and discipline might be laid in some cases there was no certainty of conviction. 'I have therefore decided', Alexander informed Churchill at the end of February 1954, 'to take no action against any of the 39 soldiers against whom these allegations have been made.' The Prime Minster agreed that 'no further action should be taken'.[41]

As for those whose term of service was not up, through debriefing sessions in Japan and earlier examination of the Little Switch repatriates while in military hospital in England, AI9 had built up a reasonably accurate picture of which

---

[39] TNA, WO 208/4012, Report on the success of Communist indoctrination among British PW in North Korea, with particular reference to after effects on their return to the United Kingdom, 22 October 1953, 5–6.

[40] TNA, PREM 11/871 (also DEFE 7/1033), Alexander to Churchill, 16 September 1953; see DEFE 7/1033, SM/P(53)28, Repatriated Prisoners of War from Korea: Disciplinary Action, 3 September 1953; WO 32/20495, Disciplinary Action—PW Korea, attached Encl. 64A, 26 August 1953; DEFE 10/259, SM/P(53)12, SM/P(53)28; AIR 20/11380, *passim*. On the authorities keeping track of broadcasts, petitions, letters, etc. between 1950 and 1953 see WO 208/4014, Encls. 1A–36A; see also NAA, A2151, KB1073/12B; TNA, ADM 1/24997; WO 216/805, VCIGS to AG, 7 January 1952 (letters); TNA, FO 369/4742–4745, *passim* (broadcasts).

[41] TNA, AIR 20/1380, Hanna to Beards, 4 March 1954; DEFE 7/1033, Alexander to Churchill. 29 February 1954; see also DEFE 7/1805, The Version of the JIC Report Prepared for the Information of the Public: Draft Report of the Principal Personnel Officers' Committee, 1.

ex-prisoners due to return to units after three months of leave were likely to have developed communist sympathies, and passed their findings on to MI5. As far as can be ascertained nobody was forced out, but the likelihood is that access to sensitive material was restricted and promotion prospects thereby blighted, particularly after 1961 when SIS officer George Blake was unmasked as a double agent recruited during the Korean War (see chapter 1).[42] On the other hand the careers of known reactionaries who continued to make the British Army their profession might prosper; Lofty Large, for instance, was able to join the Special Air Service while Tony Farrar-Hockley eventually rose to the rank of lieutenant general.[43]

There were those in Whitehall who were keen to highlight in a more official manner in the public arena not only what British servicemen had gone through at the hands of their captors but also the extent to which communists hailing from Britain were implicated in the propaganda effort. It turned out that nothing much could be done through the courts on the latter issue, largely because a charge of treason would likely not stick in light of the fact that Britain had not declared war on China during the conflict in Korea.[44] This was no bar, however, to publicly naming and shaming those involved while highlighting the trials and tribulations of the prisoners themselves. Hence at the end of May 1954 the three service ministers agreed that an internal report for the Joint Intelligence Committee based on AI9 evaluations dealing with the treatment of British prisoners in the Korean War should be reworked by the Information Research Department of the Foreign Office into 'a form suitable for public release'. This would then be forwarded to the Minister of Defence for submission to the Cabinet with a view to publication by Her Majesty's Stationary Office as a purchasable pamphlet.[45]

A draft was compiled with the help of AI9 and, with modifications, vetted by the Cabinet in December 1954. 'White Papers are usually objective', as the Lord Privy Seal, Henry Crookshank, commented, '—this isn't.' While the identities of ex-prisoners who had endured a great deal at enemy hands were concealed in order to protect their privacy, those party members and fellow travellers who had visited the camps were publicly identified and their activities individually chron-

[42] Cunningham, *No Mercy, No Leniency*, 156, 158–9; see TNA, WO 32/20495, Army Personnel who have been in Communist Hands 1951–61, memo attached Encl. 144A, DMI to DUS(A), 6 June 1961.

[43] On Farrar-Hockley's post-1953 career see e.g. obituary in *Guardian*, 15 March 2006. On Large's post-1953 career see Lofty Large, *Soldier Against the Odds* (Edinburgh, 1999). See also TNA, WO 32/20495, Encls. 150A, 153A, Ex-Korean Prisoners of War, 9 May, 24 May 1953.

[44] On Monica Felton, Jack Gaster, Michael Shapiro, and Alan Winnington see TNA, DPP 2/2423–24325, *passim*; LCO 2/5755, *passim*; LO 2/227, *passim*; LO2/235, *passim*; PREM 8/1525, CP(51)157, 19 June 1951; see also KV 2/2/1559. Given the ongoing controversy surrounding the supposed persecution of Wilfred Burchett by the Australian government from 1955 through 1972 (see Jamie Miller, 'The Forgotten History War: Wilfred Burchett, Australia and the Cold War', *The Asia-Pacific Journal: Japan Focus*, 30 September 2008, <http://www.japanfocus.org/-Jamie-Miller/2912> (accessed 5 December 2010)), the decision by the British not to take action was a wise one.

[45] See TNA, DEFE 7/1805, The Version of the JIC Report Prepared for the Information of the Public: Draft Report to the Principal Personnel Officers' Committee, 2, attached PWP/P(54)7, 21 October 1954; see DEFE 13/220, Brook to Macmillan, 8 March 1955; AIR 8/2473, Extract from Minutes of CC(54)87, 16 December 1954; DEFE 10/127, Communist Treatment of British Prisoners of War in Korea, revised October 1954; CAB 159/15, JIC(54)31, 7 April 1954.

icled, as was the campaign by the CPGB through front organizations to exploit relatives for propaganda and political purposes through the party's unique access to information about those held captive in North Korea. Yet despite some concern expressed by Churchill and the Attorney General, Sir Reginald Manningham-Buller, that the government might be vulnerable to charges of libel, pressure from Anthony Eden (Foreign Secretary), Anthony Head (War Minister), and Sir Walter Monckton (Minister of Labour and National Service) produced a consensus whereby it was agreed that the Cabinet should 'accept the risk' and give a green light to publication.[46]

After some delay due to a desire to try and minimize the offence the Chinese would take while various negotiations were proceeding, the forty-one-page pamphlet *Treatment of British Prisoners of War in Korea*, identified as having been compiled by the Ministry of Defence on the blue paper cover and on the title page, appeared at the end of February 1955, costing one shilling to purchase. Sales through the subsequent two weeks were considerable, as was the public reaction.[47]

As some in Whitehall had foreseen, the evidence in the Blue Book of collusion with the Chinese by British subjects Alan Winnington, Michael Shapiro, Jack Gaster, and Monica Felton under the guise of fact-finding and journalism led to calls from a half-dozen patriotic MPs for legal proceedings to be taken against them on the grounds of treason. Some of the Tories even wanted a Bill of Attainder—effectively the withdrawal of the rights of citizenship—to be made out against them. The Prime Minister was very much against this, and as the Attorney General pointed out in the House of Commons on 7 March, Winnington and Shapiro were both out of the country while in the cases of both Gaster and Felton the evidence did not suffice to justify a prosecution.[48]

---

[46] TNA, CAB 195/13, Sir Norman Brook's notes on cabinet meeting C87(54), 15 December 1954, 38–9; see CAB129/72, C(54)383, Publicity for the Treatment of British Prisoners-of-War in Korea., note by the Minister of Defence, 7 December 1954; see DEFE 13/220, Brook to Macmillan, 8 March 1955. On protecting the privacy of ex-prisoners see Harold Macmillan written answer to Woodrow Wyatt, *Parliamentary Debates, House of Commons, Fifth Series*, vol. 537, 3 March 1955, col. 308.

[47] Ministry of Defence, *Treatment of British Prisoners of War in Korea* (London, 1955); see TNA, ADM 1/25760, Head of NL note, 24 February 1955. On the cost and sales see *Parliamentary Debates, House of Commons, Fifth Series*, vol. 538 (written answers), Macmillan to Gough, 18 March 1955, col. 145; TNA, DEFE 7/1805, Encl. 107, minute to private secretary, 4 March 1955. On dissemination plans for the Blue Book see TNA, INF 12/767. The contents were widely reported and commented on in the national press. See e.g. *The Times*, 28 February 1955, 7; *Daily Telegraph*, 28 February 1955, 6; *Manchester Guardian*, 28 February 1955, 9; *Daily Express*, 28 February 1955, 4; *Daily Herald*, 28 February 1955, 2.

[48] *Parliamentary Debates, Fifth Series, House of Commons*, vol. 538 (oral answers), 7 March 1955, cols. 31–2; see TNA, CAB 195/13, Norman Brook notes on C20955, 3 March 1955, 124–5; *Daily Telegraph*, 28 February 1955, 9. Though he appeared in the Blue Book, Wilfred Burchett was not the subject of accusation in Parliament, presumably because he was an Australian rather than a British subject. No action was taken by the Australian government in his case beyond a refusal to issue him with a new passport in 1955 after the one he had been travelling on was stolen. For a largely sympathetic account of Burchett's career and the controversies surrounding it see Miller, 'The Forgotten History War'.

This did not satisfy the patriots, who were in a state of high dudgeon and responded accordingly. Phrases such as 'behaved in a thoroughly traitorous manner' (Brigadier Terence Clarke, Tory MP for Portsmouth West) and 'at the end of the last war people were hanged for lesser crimes than these people have committed' (Mr Percy Daines, Labour and Co-op MP, East Ham North) were thrown out with abandon. Manningham-Buller found himself in the position of having to defend due process and then explain, mostly to members of his own party, with reference to former progressives being trotted out by the *Daily Worker* contradicting the claims made in the Blue Book, that the right to privacy of the individuals whose mistreatment had been chronicled therein had to be respected.[49]

Knowing that the People's Republic of China would not be happy with how its treatment of prisoners was portrayed in the pamphlet, the Foreign Office delayed its release until after Dag Hammarskjöld, Secretary-General of the United Nations, had returned from talks in Beijing about the release of twelve US airmen still held by the Chinese.[50] Zhou Enlai, the Chinese premier, was angered when it came out, though it is worth noting that the People's Republic had itself published a rather rosy English-language compilation of pieces edited by some of the ex-prisoners who had gone to China, including Condron, under the title *Thinking Soldiers* the previous month.[51]

Predictably the CPGB expressed outrage at the Blue Book. Frank Gullett, the news editor of the *Daily Worker*, implied that it was a fabrication because no names of the supposed victims were given. Alan Winnington repeated the view he heard in Beijing that it was simply 'a hastily concocted effort to confuse the British public, who want friendship and don't want war with the Chinese people', and an editorial dismissed it as 'an example of the Big Lie'.[52] Perhaps pressured by some of his left-wing constituents, Willie Hamilton, who had succeeded the Communist MP Willie Gallacher in Fife West as a Labour candidate five years before, rose in the House of Commons on 10 March to ask the Lord Privy Seal, Harry Crookshank:

> whether the Government intend to give any time for discussion of the Ministry of Defence pamphlet on the treatment of prisoners of war in Korea? Is he aware that

---

[49] *Parliamentary Debates, House of Commons, Fifth Series*, vol. 538 (oral answers), 7 March 1955, cols 31–5.

[50] See TNA, ADM 1/25760, note to Beck, 30 December 1954. The Prime Minister also effectively banned a BBC programme on the subject of Chinese mistreatment due to be broadcast on 2 January 1955 as 'contrary to the public interest as calculated to perpetuate or revive hatred and bitterness between peoples'. CAB 21/4020, Prime Minister to Postmaster General, 17 December 1954; CAB 195/13, Brook notes on C87(54), 15 December 1954, 37; see also WO 32/20495, Encl. 103A, BBC Broadcast—Ex-PW from Korea memo, 11 March 1954. Britain had only recently established formal diplomatic relations with the People's Republic of China: see James Tuck-Hong Tang, *Britain's Encounter with Revolutionary China, 1949–54* (Basingstoke, 1992), ch. 4.

[51] Andrew M. Condron, Richard G. Corden, Larance V. Sullivan (eds), *Thinking Soldiers* (Beijing, 1955); TNA, CAB 195/13, Sir Norman Brook notes on C19(1955), 2 March 1955, 118; DEFE 7/1805, Encl. 99, Peking Legation to Foreign Office, 28 February 1955; see also DO 35/5862, New China News Agency, Daily Bulletin No. 1251, 1 March 1955.

[52] *Daily Worker*, 28 February 1955, 1, 4; see also e.g. J. Gaster letter in *Manchester Guardian*, 1 March 1955, 9.

there are damaging statements in that pamphlet, damaging either to the Ministry of Defence if they are not true, or damaging to the individuals concerned if they are? Is he also aware that the matter cannot be left where it is?

Having witnessed how the Attorney General had been roughed up in the House by the backbench Tories three days before, the government was not keen to oblige Hamilton and set the stage for an assault by left-wing backbenchers across the floor.[53]

Luckily for the ministers concerned, the right-wing storm of indignation blew itself out after the parliamentary fracas on 7 March. As for the far left, the gamble that the 'visitors' named in the Blue Book would not be in a position to go to court turned out to be correct. When Hamilton asked the Minister of Defence a couple of weeks later 'what legal actions against his Department are now pending consequent on the publication of the pamphlet on the treatment of British prisoners of war in Korea', Harold Macmillan was able simply to write 'None.' Efforts by Hamilton to imply that the stories related in the Blue Book had been coerced went nowhere, Macmillan explaining that this was not the case—'men were encouraged to tell their stories in their own way and the whole procedure was informal'—and that the publication of the pamphlet was entirely in the service of truth. 'When the reports of what our men had to say became fully available', he wrote in reply to one of several leading questions put by Hamilton, 'it was thought that they revealed a situation about which the British public was entitled to be informed.'[54]

The communist case against anonymous sources also lost steam because memoirs of harrowing captivity in which the author's name was prominently displayed on the cover and title page had begun to appear in bookshops. After being serialized in *John Bull* magazine, *The Edge of the Sword*, by Anthony Farrar-Hockley, had appeared in the autumn of 1954 under the Muller imprint, around the same time as the story of Dennis Lankford's trials and tribulations entitled *I Defy!* came out with Alan Wingate. These were followed by *In Spite of Dungeons*, the memoir of Chaplain Davies that Hodder and Stoughton published in November of the same year. It might have been argued that these were all accounts by officers, that is to say ipso facto Establishment types; but then in the autumn of 1955 came the memoir of the maverick Derek Kinne, *The Wooden Boxes*, also published by Muller, and then in 1956 the account of another reactionary member of the rank and file, R. F. Matthews, entitled *No Rice for Rebels*, which came out through Bodley Head. All went through more than one print run, in the case of *The Edge of the Sword*, penned as it was by a serving officer and the most successful of all, no doubt with the blessing of the military authorities.[55]

It was these memoirs, in combination with the popular Blue Book, that would form the basis of the contention, oft-repeated in popular histories over the years,

[53] *Parliamentary Debates, House of Commons, Fifth Series*, vol. 538, 10 March 1955, col. 623.

[54] Ibid., 23 March 1955 (written answers), cols 187–8.

[55] Matthews in Jones, *No Rice For Rebels*; Kinne, *The Wooden Boxes*; Davies, *In Spite of Dungeons*; Farrar-Hockley, *The Edge of the Sword*; Lankford, *I Defy!*. On subsequent printings see British Library catalogue.

that, to quote a distinguished journalist writing a few years ago, enemy efforts at subversion were 'remarkably ineffective'.[56] Such summary conclusions, however, conceal as much as they reveal about what happened to British prisoners in North Korea between 1950 and 1953.

To be sure, as reported in the Blue Book, only about forty of the returnees—a mere 4 per cent of the total—were identified as true converts by AI9, and some of them had possessed communist links before they even set sail for Korea. Of the remaining one-third of the rank and file thought to have been affected to some degree, they were judged to have 'most likely responded to the influence of normal home life' and become progressively less radical.[57] This would certainly explain why Chinese hopes for a strong 'ex-prisoners of war for peace' front organization which key progressives would secretly control for political ends never materialized in the United Kingdom.[58]

As for the national party to which some of the converts and fellow travellers intended to attach themselves on their return to the United Kingdom,[59] it was a far cry from the dynamic and triumphant mass movement that instructors had represented the Communist Party of China to be. The CPGB was in 1953–4 very much on the fringe of British politics, possessing as it did only about 34,000 members and having lost its two briefly held parliamentary seats back in 1950.[60] Hence, while individual returnees might be very keen at first to join the Party, the small-minded petty bureaucracy and suspicion encountered at the national and local level could swiftly lead to disillusionement.[61] Things would only get worse for the CPGB in the coming years, the party losing a third of its membership between February 1956 and February 1958 in the wake of revelations about Stalin and the Soviet invasion of Hungary.[62] To judge by available MI5 records, no ex-prisoner of the Chinese who associated himself with the party directly or indirectly became sufficiently prominent to justify the opening of a file.[63]

---

[56] Andrew Marr, *A History of Modern Britain* (London, 2007), 103; see also, e.g. Salmon, *To the Last Round*, 282; Richard Garrett, *P. O.W.* (Newton Abbot, 1981), 205–16.

[57] Ministry of Defence, *Treatment of British Prisoners of War in Korea*, v, 34–5; see e.g. NAA, Part 3, AI9/K/BRIT/165 et al., Gnr D. Boulton et al., 3; Part 4, AI9/K/BRIT/292, Rfn W. Heaney, 3.

[58] On Chinese hopes see Lech, *Broken Soldiers*, 188–9. In the UK the CPGB had already set up the Ex-Services Movement for Peace as a front organization, and though a few progressives did join up after repatriation the organization was only a fiftieth of the size of the mainstream British Legion and of marginal significance at best. See TNA, WO 32/20495, Encl. 74A, Elliot to Rumbold, 9 September 1953; Encl. 94A, Foreign Office to War Office, 14 October 1953; LHASC, CP/CENT/EC/02/06, memo on Ex-Service Work by L. Golhard, 18 February 1952. On the later trajectory of Korea veteran organizations in the UK see <http://www.bkva.co.uk/membership.htm> (accessed 27 April 2011).

[59] See e.g. NAA, Part 3, AI9/K/BRIT/317, Gnr E. Digan, 2.

[60] Henry Pelling, *The British Communist Party* (London, 1958), 163, 192–3.

[61] Cunningham, *No Mercy, No Leniency*, 158–9. On initial enthusiasm at the idea of joining the CPGB see e.g. *Daily Worker*, 24 October 1953, 3; NAA, Part 3, AI9/K/BRIT/293, Rfn K. Clarke, 3.

[62] James Eaden and David Renton, *The Communist Party of Great Britain since 1920* (Basingstoke, 2002), 120.

[63] Compare those listed as 'black' in NAA, Parts 1–7 with TNA, with KV 2 files. It should be stressed that both sets of data are incomplete: but it is also worth noting that the official history of MI5, while detailing the extent to which the CPGB was closely scrutinized by the security service in the 1950s, makes no mention of ex-prisoner involvement. See Christopher Andrew, *Defend the Realm* (London, 2009), ch. 5.

The passage of the years tended to soften or overturn the stances of those who had once been overtly progressive in the Yalu camps. 'You agreed with it at the time,' Edward Curd, formerly of the Royal Marines, reflected decades later, 'but when you look back now, [you have] nothing at all in common with them [communists], really.'[64] Drummer Tony Eagles, by the time he went home, had 'developed an interest in Communism as a result of indoctrination', according to AI9, and 'intends to maintain his interest in progressive politics' even though he had 'not yet decided to become a Communist'. Nearly forty years later he was stressing that 'I'm very anti-socialist, I'm afraid.'[65] In 1953, Gunner Jack Arnall was 'convinced that the Communists were right' according to AI9; yet thirty-four years later, he was at pains to stress that, while still a socialist as he had been before capture, 'I'm not a Communist now, don't get me wrong.'[66] Even the one British serviceman who had refused repatriation in 1953, Andrew Condron, eventually grew disillusioned with communism. He returned to the UK from China in 1962, readapted himself to capitalist society, and became successful enough in publishing to send his son to a private school and eventually Cambridge. 'If you can't beat'em,' he explained by way of justification, 'join'em.'[67]

Even George Blake, the SIS man who became a dedicated and effective double agent for the Russians until exposed in 1961, eventually found himself forced to reassess his convictions. Having escaped from imprisonment in Wormwood Scrubs in 1966 and fled to Moscow, he was an on-hand witness to the implosion of Soviet communism twenty-five years later. Though never publicly regretting his actions, Blake did admit in a 1997 interview that 'obviously it [communism] has failed ... no question about it'.[68]

However, the fact that there were no effective long-term converts among those who returned from Korea—Blake was already a leftist when he volunteered his services to the Russians and did so without benefit of anything approaching 'brainwashing'[69]—should not obscure the extent to which groups of British prisoners when held in North Korea *did* serve the interests of their captors. While the war was on there was a genuine sense of 'outrage' in the War Office, as an AI9 official put it, at the way in which significant numbers of prisoners were publicly 'condemning the United Nations aggression and demanding peace on Communist terms!'[70] Most men involved did not, to be sure, believe in the causes they were espousing; yet this cannot obscure the reality that by taking part in rallies, signing

---

[64] IWMDS, 10250/2, E. Curd; compare with NAA, Part 3, AI9/K/BRIT/309 et al., Mne G. F. Balchin et al., 5.

[65] IWMDS, 17283/5, A. Eagles; NAA, Part 4, AI9/K/BRIT/391, Dmr A. Eagles, 3.

[66] IWMDS, 09972/4, J. Arnall; NAA, Part 3, AI9/K/BRIT/86, Gnr J. Arnall, 2.

[67] A. Condron in Max Hastings, *The Korean War* (London, 1987), 407; see S. P. MacKenzie, 'The Individualist Collaborator: Andy Condron in Korea and China, 1950–1962', *War & Society*, 30 (2011), 147–65.

[68] Blake interview, <http://www.pbs.org/redfiles/kgb/deep/interv/k_int_goerge_blake.htm> (accessed 18 October 2011).

[69] See Andrew, *Defend the Realm*, 488–9, 944, n. 25; Blake interview, <http://www.pbs.org/redfiles/kgb/deep/interv/k_int_george_blake.htm> (accessed 18 October 2011), 4.

[70] Cunningham, *No Mercy, No Leniency*, xiii; see also Leslie Wayper, *Mars and Minerva* (Winchester, 2004), 275; David Rose, *Off the Record* (Staplehurst, 1996), 173.

petitions, making broadcasts, writing letters, and even participating in apparently innocuous events like the inter-camp Olympics, prisoners were contributing to enemy propaganda efforts designed to convince the world that captives were being treated well and that they agreed with the party line on international affairs.[71] Moreover, within the camps a network of informers helped the Chinese authorities constantly disrupt British efforts at maintaining their own chain of command and establishing secure escape organizations.[72]

To say one thing while thinking another during the period of compulsory indoctrination—'we weren't so stupid as to make that obvious to them', as a private in the Glosters later commented[73]—was a practice that even most officers accepted as a legitimate way of avoiding protracted and fruitless arguments and missed meals. 'There was never any point' in engaging the instructors in debate, a junior officer from the Ulsters later argued, since 'there was no rational discussion with the Chinese'.[74] Furthermore, it rapidly became apparent that anyone who continued to try and dodge lessons or, more seriously, openly question the party line was liable to go missing. 'Prisoners did disappear in North Korea', Rifleman Henry O'Kane remembered thinking in reference to the risk involved in arguing too long and too hard with the instructors.[75] It was known that some were transferred to mysterious unknown destinations while others remained in the vicinity of the main camps for indefinite periods in cells, holes, or tiny wooden hutches; and those who were eventually released confirmed that conditions for those arrested were, to say the least, unpleasant. 'The camp jail was a place to be avoided if possible', Lofty Large stated in reference to Camp 1.[76] In any event, given that there was no external audience and that fellow prisoners could easily see when someone was consciously spouting what Private Bill Clark labelled 'a load of rubbish which they [the instructors] would think was good' was not something to which the British authorities in the UK took exception when they learned about it.[77]

Appeals and petitions, on the other hand, like personal letters containing 'peace' propaganda, were meant for external consumption and those who signed therefore garnered far less sympathy in official circles.[78] There were, however, some mitigating circumstances.

---

[71] See e.g. activities listed in Intreps on returnees, TNA, WO 208/4014; *Daily Worker*, 31 January 1951, 3; 22 March 1951, 3; 16 April 1951, 1; 7 January 1952, 1; 15 January 1952, 3; 1 July 1953, 1.

[72] NAA, Second Cover, Communist Treatment of British Prisoners of War in Korea, 4.

[73] Green, *Captured at the Imjin River*, 120.

[74] IWMDS, 19964/3, V. Whitamore; see NAA, Part 1, App D to AI9(a)/S/150/87, Political Indoctrination, 8 May 1953, 1; see also e.g. Davies, *In Spite of Dungeons*, 62; Matthews in Jones, *No Rice For Rebels*, 63.

[75] O'Kane, *O'Kane's Korea*, 91.

[76] Large, *One Man's War in Korea*, 125. On knowledge of men being sent to unspecified locations elsewhere for arguing during indoctrination see e.g. NAA, Part 3, AI9/K/BRIT/293, Rfn K. Clarke, 3. On dodging lessons and the consequences see e.g. Part 3, AI9/K/BRIT/95 et al., Rfn R. Cartlidge et al., 4, 7; Davies, *In Spite of Dungeons*, 62. On being arrested for being argumentative see e.g. J. King in Tony Strachen (ed.), *In the Clutch of Circumstance* (Victoria, BC, 1985), 103; Davies, *In Spite of Dungeons*, 61; see also K. Godwin on Chongson commandant's speech in *The Back Badge*, 4 (1953), 231.

[77] IWMDS, 18459/2, W. Clark. On AI9 accepting such subterfuge see NAA, Part 1, App D to AI9(a)/S/150/87, Political Indoctrination, 1. On tolerance see e.g. Rose, *Off the Record*.

[78] Cunningham, *No Mercy, No Leniency*, xiii.

In certain instances prisoners had been instructed by officers to play along with the enemy. Lieutenant Terry Waters, while refusing to go himself at the cost of his life had, in order to preserve the lives of others, instructed the British being held in the Caves (Camp 9) to agree to go to Camp 12 despite correctly guessing that this was a North Korean propaganda factory.[79] Once in the Peace Fighters' Camp, captives were told by the senior officer, Lieutenant Colonel Paul Liles of the US Army, who was determined to get everyone out alive, to cooperate and assured that he would personally assume postwar responsibility for what they had done in the way of propaganda activities.[80] In the case of Chinese camps, Major John N. McLaughlin, USMC, was reported to have advised prisoners to sign a Peace Appeal at Kanggye in February 1951 in order to get their names out to the Free World;[81] and while some men ended up concocting a much more liberal interpretation of what was meant than he ever imagined, Major Joe Ryan had apparently issued instructions that prisoners 'string along' the Chinese just before his removal from Pyoktong in October of the same year.[82]

Given that the enemy did not recognize the Geneva Conventions and it was only eighteen months into the war that prisoner lists began to be exchanged, it was understandable that many captives should conclude that adding a few words praising their treatment and perhaps calling for an end to hostilities in personal letters was a reasonable price to pay for reassuring loved ones. The cleverest might even include something to indicate the propaganda content without alerting Chinese censors, such as the British soldier who wrote in a letter to his parents: 'Tell the family we are being well fed and well treated. Don't forget to tell this to all my pals in the Dog and Duck and most of all don't forget to tell it to the Marines.'[83]

In other cases men might find their names on petitions due to deception on the part of the Chinese. Captives might sign one document that they considered innocuous, such as an autobiographical outline or a blank sheet of paper, and eventually discover that a facsimile had been appended to an appeal that they had never seen. They also might be quoted in the communist press as saying things they did not recognize. Even officers might occasionally fall prey to ruses, as when Lieutenant Robin Bruford-Davies of the Ulsters discovered that he had put his name to a peace petition while so ill with dysentery at Camp 5 that he 'did not know what he was signing'.[84]

[79] NAA, Part 4, AI9/K/BRIT/1001, Sgt P. J. Hoper, 3–4.

[80] See e.g. ibid. Part 3, AI9/K/BRIT/287, Tpr S. Carr, 4; Part 5, AI9/K/BRIT/308, Rfn F. Moore, 3; Part 6, AI9/K/BRIT/3, Rfn E. F. Spencer, 3; Part 7, AI9/K/BRIT/289, Cpl J. H. Taylor, 4. On Liles's motivation see Lech, *Broken Soldiers, passim.*

[81] NAA, Part 3, AI9/K/BRIT/61, Mne B. Martin, 3.

[82] Ibid. AI9/K/BRIT/89, L/Cpl A. W. Buxton, 2; Part 1, Interrogation Report on British Ex-PW Released in Korea: Batch 2 (supplementary), 28 June 1953, Rfn. E. F. Spencer, 7.

[83] Cunningham, *No Mercy, No Leniency,* 163. On including propaganda to get the word out see e.g. NAA, Part 3, AI9/K/BRIT/313, Pte S. W. Slimm, 2.

[84] Ibid. AI9/K/BRIT/72, Lt E. R. Bruford-Davies, 2; see TNA, WO 208/4012, Report on the success of Communist indoctrination among British PW in North Korea, 22 October 1953, 3; see also e.g. NAA, Part 3, AI9/K/BRIT/824, Pte R. B. Allum, 2; Part 5, AI9/K/BRIT/306, Fus. P. Lyndon, 3; Part 6, AI9/K/BRIT/307, Rfn J. Stevenson, 2.

There was also a coercive aspect to the business of signing documents. Veiled hints of retribution if the camp authorities were not accommodated might be dropped—e.g. 'It would be better for you if you do this'[85]—as well as on occasion the prospect of increased or decreased rations depending on what happened.[86] Those individuals who resisted might be made an example of. As Rifleman J. T. Alexander explained, 'the men [at Pyoktong] soon realized that although no immediate punishment ensued for those who refused to sign they were ear-marked and later arrested and punished on false charges'.[87]

Finally there was the simple fact that British servicemen captured in Korea in 1950–1 had never been instructed about what to do under the circumstances they found themselves in. This unfortunate state of affairs was mainly because nothing quite like the Lenient Policy had been encountered before; but, even after it became clear that the Chinese were using captives as propaganda tools, unit commanders proved highly resistant to allowing AI9 briefings on the grounds that talk of capture would undermine morale, which in turn meant that the dozens of men taken prisoner in the static phase of the war between 1951 and 1953 also had little against which to measure their behaviour in enemy hands.[88] British officers in captivity quickly understood what was happening and refused to go along willingly with enemy aims. The rank and file, however, many of whom had only a limited education and possessed no understanding of either political economy or international affairs, might not be able to distinguish harmless from harmful acts. Thus petitions calling for a negotiated settlement might seem quite innocuous to those who thought peace a good idea and who failed to see to what use such documents could be put.[89]

Yet in spite of all this, the fact remains that some men behaved worse than others with respect to becoming propaganda tools for the enemy. In certain cases individuals from the start cooperated enthusiastically with the Chinese: in a few instances because they were already associated with the CPGB; in others because they anticipated and were given privileges.[90] In other cases fear of what the camp authorities would do subsequent to a refusal produced results. As an ex-prisoner

---

[85] Ibid. Part 5, AI9/K/BRIT/4, Sgt W. A. Lucas, 5; see e.g. ibid. AI9/K/BRIT/98, L/Cpl W. Massey, 3; AI9/K/BRIT/106 et al., Rfn B. C. Canavan, 2.

[86] See e.g. ibid. Part 3, AI9/K/BRIT/131 et al., Rfn R. Dodd et al., 3; Part 7, AI9/K/BRIT/289, Cpl J. H. Taylor, 3.

[87] Ibid. Part 3, AI9/K/BRIT/658, Rfn J. T. Alexander, 3; see e.g. ibid. AI9/K/BRIT/246 et al., Pte A. J. Allum et al., 3.

[88] In 1952–3 the Royal Army Educational Corps got involved in radio broadcasts and discussion pamphlets discussing, among other subjects, the reasons for the British presence in Korea (Wayper, *Mars and Minerva*, 275); but in Korea itself COs were often resistant to attempts by AI9 representatives to brief men on what to do after capture on the grounds that this undermined the idea of fighting to the last man and last round (Cunningham, *No Mercy, No Leniency*, 162; Rose, *Off the Record*).

[89] See e.g. NAA, Part 4, AI9/K/BRIT/530, Mne J. E. Goodman, 6; ibid. AI9/K/BRIT/512, Rfn R. Green, 3; ibid., AI9/K/BRIT/300, Tpr C. H. Holland, 3; Part 5, AI9/K/BRIT/318, Pte K. Millward, 3.

[90] See e.g., with reference to a group of Black Watch soldiers captured in November 1952, ibid. Part 3, AI9/K/BRIT/991 et al., Pte G. J. Bailey, 2–3 (on Sgt J. McPherson); ibid. AI9/K/BRIT/88, Pte R. Brand, 2 (on whose activities see TNA, WO 208/4014, Encl. 3A, A2583, Air Ministry to BRPWIU Bricosat Japan, 6 August 1953).

from the Ulsters put it with respect to peace appeals, 'it was better to sign them than to antagonise the Chinese'.[91]

The service departments did understand that it was too much to expect ordinary men to emulate the actions of extraordinary figures such as Lieutenant Terry Waters or Fusilier Derek Kinne in refusing to cooperate with the enemy even in the face of certain death or after sustaining major injuries. The award of the George Cross to both men—the former posthumously—was a symbol of the extent to which they had gone far beyond the call of duty through undertaking 'acts of the greatest heroism or of the most conspicuous courage in circumstances of extreme danger'.[92] It was tacitly understood and accepted that in the face of serious threats to life and limb captives might be coerced into actions they abhorred. Thus, for example, nobody at the Ministry of Defence thought any the less of Lieutenant Colonel J. P. 'Fred' Carne of the Glosters for having agreed to write a 'confession' on a couple of occasions after what amounted to bouts of torture.[93]

What bothered the authorities was when British captives started collaborating without even the pretense of initial resistance, notably in Camp 5. At Chongson it was discovered that if men maintained a more-or-less united front in the face of nebulous Chinese threats, then the enemy might be faced down over issues such the insistence that prisoners include calls for peace in their outgoing letters.[94] As for informers, the reactionaries had their suspicions and did their best to isolate them.[95] Yet at Pyoktong, as an AI9 officer noted with reference to the large number of broadcasts and propaganda documents emanating from Camp 5, almost everyone concerned admitted that 'there was no compulsion to do these things'. Even in the case of informers, the bane of all camps, the inmates 'do not appear to have over excited themselves in their efforts to pin-point them'.[96]

---

[91] NAA, Part 6, AI9/K/BRIT/307, Rfn J. Stevenson, 3; see also e.g. ibid. AI9/K/BRIT/489, Pte M. Pendle, 2, 3; Part 4, AI9/K/BRIT/843, Rfn S. H. Greer, 3; Part 5, AI9/K/BRIT/301, Rfn P. Morgan, 2; Part 3, AI9/K/BRIT/1000, Sgt S. F. Baxter, 2.

[92] On the award of the George Cross to Kinne and Waters see Ministry of Defence, *Treatment of British Prisoners of War in Korea*, 38–41. On e.g. Kinne as exceptional see Green, *Captured at the Imjin River*, 141.

[93] TNA, WO 208/4021, Encl. 1B, Verbatim Transcription of the Re-Interrogation of Lt Col. J. P. Carne, ff. 11–13. Carne was treated so badly overall that he seems to have experienced something akin to hallucinations towards the end of his captivity. See ibid. Encl. 1A, Preliminary Appreciation of the Chinese Interrogation of Lt Col. J. P. Carne by C. Cunningham, AI9, 21 December 1953; DO 35/5822, Statement made by Lt Col. J. P. Carne, 7 September 1953; FO 371/105529, FK1076/287. If there had been any doubt about the ethical behaviour of Carne while a prisoner it is highly unlikely that he would have been awarded the Victoria Cross for his valorous leadership during the Battle of the Imjin.

[94] NAA, Part 5, AI9/K/BRIT/4, Sgt W. A. Lucas, 5. While it was in consequence not made compulsory, men rightly guessed that inserting the odd propaganda phrase increased the chances of a letter getting through.

[95] IWMDS, 30075/2, J. Wiseman. The tendency was to equate informers with the overt progressives, which may have been an error. See NAA, Part 3, AI9/K/BRIT/690 et al., Pte L. Allen et al., 20; AI9/K/BRIT/363 et al., Pte N. Batts et al., 2; AI9/K/BRIT/811 et al., Bdr L. Bristow, 3; AI9/K/BRIT/365 et al., Pte J. W. C. Collins et al., 2; AI9/K/BRIT/606, Gnr J. C. Dabbs, 5.

[96] NAA, Part 4, AI9/K/BRIT/96, Rfn F. Harper, 2–3, comments by Capt. R. B. Trant. As elsewhere, the tendency at Camp 5 was for reactionaries to equate informing with overt progressivism, which may have been an error. See e.g. ibid. Part 5, AI9/K/BRIT/321, Rfn P. Neeson, 2.

It could be argued that the greater success of political indoctrination at Pyoktong as compared to Chongson and the other camps induced lessened resistance to engaging in propaganda activities. After all, AI9 produced figures that indicated the number of men identified as having engaged in significant political collaboration was 70 per cent higher in Camp 5 as compared to Camp 1.[97] But since, according to an AI9 interrogating officer, the 'majority of men [from Pyoktong] tackled with their contaminated letters or broadcasts, which in many cases are only just short of being subversive, readily agreed that they did not believe that which they said', political indoctrination only goes so far by way of explanation.[98]

An alternate theory of the time involved failure of character or lack of moral fibre on the part of those who collaborated. Thus interrogating officers might attribute failure to resist on the part of men who did not come to believe in communism in terms of 'a weak minded attitude' or 'general "spinelessness"', and lack of determination to stand out against the enemy'.[99] It was certainly true that the Chinese were always ready to take advantage. 'If you were weak willed,' as Marine S. D. Hicks put it, 'they had you.'[100]

A more fruitful explanation, though, involves the examples set by those truly committed, either for or against, on the question of collaboration. The more malleable majority element among the prisoners was willing to follow whichever dominating lead was presented from within the prison population. Hence the rifleman who signed a petition at Pyoktong 'because most people did' and those at Chongson who found it worthwhile to alert their fellow captives to the dangers involved in collaboration. As Fusilier Derek Kinne put it:

> if the danger arose that they [the passive majority] might occasionally be led [by the Chinese] unresisting towards some dangerous act—[e.g.] participation in a march led by 'progressives' carrying banners bearing political slogans—then the danger was averted by the 'reactionaries' who, by their words and deeds—their own stout example of non-cooperation in some cases—made clear where the danger lay, what issues were at stake.[101]

What ultimately seems to have mattered most in determining the relative progressive or reactionary trajectory of particular camps was leadership, something the Chinese recognized and tried to influence by segregating and then separating officers, senior NCOs, and indeed reactionaries in general from the rank and file. As noted in chapter 5, the captured officers of the Gloucestershire Regiment, with Colonel Carne and Majors Harding and Weller in the lead, had managed before their removal from Chongson to impress upon their men the need to maintain cohesion and discipline while avoiding as far as possible becoming tools of their captors. The remaining reactionaries carried on in the same vein with respect to the uncommitted majority, helped a great deal by the lack of true commitment dis-

---

[97] Ibid. Second Cover, App. A to AI9/PW/KOREA/1004 of 22 October 1953.
[98] Ibid. Part 4, AI9/K/BRIT/96, Rfn F. Harper, 3, comment by Capt. R. B. Trant.
[99] Ibid; ibid. AI9/K/BRIT/300, Tpr C. H. Holland, 3, comment by Capt. J. P. Hayes.
[100] Ibid. AI9/K/BRIT/482, Mne S. D. Hicks, 3; see also e.g. O'Kane, *O'Kane's Korea*, 91.
[101] Kinne, *The Wooden Boxes*, 102; NAA, Part 5, AI9/K/BRIT/291, Rfn W. H. Liggett, 3.

played by opportunistic progressives. The situation at Pyoktong, as chronicled in chapter 3, was different, in so far as Major Joe Ryan had approximately a third fewer officers and senior NCOs relative to the rank-and-file population to enforce his will than did Carne. Complicating his task further was the absence of any commissioned or senior non-commissioned officers from the Royal Marines to help counter-balance the progressive leadership role being assumed by the widely admired Andrew Condron,[102] and the presence of only one rather ineffective senior NCO—'a rather weak character who could not say "NO" '[103]—to deal with what turned into a highly progressive contingent from the 8th Hussars.[104] Furthermore, he also may have inadvertently left instructions that could be deliberately misconstrued by those anxious not to cross the Chinese.[105]

However they had behaved in captivity, ex-prisoners from the summer of 1953 onward had to make the transition from captivity to a new life. At first the adjustment could be tricky, lack of practice causing some returnees difficulty in carrying out everyday tasks and conducting normal relations with those around them. Many seem to have had nightmares, and some turned to drink. Long-term health problems aside, though, most appear to have learned eventually to cope with the past and take up the threads of their lives. 'They'd given me time,' John Peskett, who stayed on in the Royal Marines, later said of his wife and a sympathetic RM officer, 'and that's all I needed.'[106]

Though in private sufficiently worried to eventually approve a programme designed to make servicemen more aware of communist designs and what was expected of them if they fell into enemy hands,[107] the service ministries were happy enough through the effect of their own Blue Book, the published memoirs of hard-core reactionaries, and then American accounts which implied or suggested that prisoners from the UK had behaved better than their counterparts from the US,[108] to see a public image develop of Britons consistently and successfully resisting their North Korean and Chinese captors. The reality, as this book has tried to indicate, was rather less clear cut. Along with hard-core reactionaries there were enthusiastic progressives, the numbers in and influence of each group over the uncommitted majority who, as R. F. Matthews put it, only 'wanted to make the best of things until the day of eventual release',[109] varying over time and from place to place.

---

[102] See Peter Thomas, *41 Independent Commando Royal Marines* (Portsmouth, 1990), 56.
[103] NAA, Part 3, AI9/K/BRIT/845, Sgt F. Andrews, 2.
[104] Peter Gaston, *Korea 1950–1953: Prisoners of War* (Eastbourne, 1976).
[105] NAA, Part 3, AI9/K/BRIT/89, L/Cpl A. W. Buxton, 2; Part 1, Interrogation Report on British Ex-PW Released in Korea: Batch 2 (supplementary), 28 June 1953, Rfn E. F. Spencer, 7.
[106] IWMDS, 14025/4, J. Peskett. On adjusting see e.g. ibid. 18459/2, W. Clark; 12783/6, A. Eagles; 24610/13, B. Guess; 16061/3, R. Hickey; 17468/3, D. Kaye; 16618/6, C. Papworth; 16759/3, D. Patchett; 18544/2, C. Sharpling; Andy McNab, *Immediate Action* (London, 1995), 141.
[107] See TNA, AIR 8/2473, Extract from SM/M(56)2, 18 January 1956.
[108] See e.g. William Lindsay White, *The Captives of Korea* (New York, 1957), 84–5; Edward Hunter, *Brainwashing* (New York, 1956), ch. 7. As noted elsewhere, in reality different circumstances help to explain different outcomes in the case of British and American prisoners. See Jeffrey Grey, 'Other Fronts: Resistance, Collaboration and Survival among United Nations Prisoners during the Korean War' in Peter Dennis and Jeffrey Grey (eds.), *The Korean War* (Canberra, 2000), 136–49.
[109] Matthews, *No Rice For Rebels*, 133.

In the end it might be said that though they did not achieve their long-term strategic goal of establishing the seeds for covert cells of influence at the heart of what was seen at the time as one of the great capitalist powers, the communists were successful in the short term, through having persuaded enough prisoners by means fair and foul to cooperate as informants or mouthpieces while the fighting continued, to thwart most escape bids and disseminate the desired propaganda to the outside world. This would not be the last time that captured British servicemen would be coerced into mouthing scripted responses for the media, as the experiences of the handfuls of aircrew, marines, and sailors taken prisoner by Iraq and Iran in the last twenty-odd years indicate. Thus far, however, the Korean War remains the last time any prisoner was officially recognized for exemplary or gallant conduct whilst in enemy hands.[110] And while the behaviour of British prisoners in North Korea as a whole may not always have been either what the military authorities at the time might have wished or what the popular image still suggests, the mixed record narrated herein only further highlights the courage and fortitude of those exceptional officers and men who understood that the fight had not ended after they had laid down their arms.[111]

---

[110] See John Peters and John Nichols, *Tornado Down* (London: Michael Joseph, 1992); <http://edinburghnews.scotsman.com/world/Iran-vows-to-release-British.2539819.jp> (accessed 10 June 2011); <http://news.bbc.co.uk/2/hi/uk_news/6509813.stm> (accessed 10 June 2011).

[111] For citations see TNA, WO 373/119.

Select Bibliography

ARCHIVAL SOURCES

Labour History Archive and Study Centre, People's History Museum, Manchester
CP/CENT/EC/02/; CP/CENT/PEA/02.

National Archives of Australia, Canberra
A2151, KB1073/11G, KB1073/12G.

National Archives, Kew
ADM 1; AIR 8, 40; CAB 21, 129, 195; DEFE 7, 10, 13; DPP 2; FO 369, 371; HO 45; INF 12; LCO 2; LO 2; PREM 8, 11; WO 32, 208.

National Archives and Records Administration, Archives II, College Park , Maryland
RG 38, 319.

UNPUBLISHED WRITINGS

Beckerley, E. (IWMDD); Condron, A. (SLV); Carter, F. (IWMDD); Kaye, D. (IWMDD); Maguire, R. (IWMDD); Shaw, J. (IWMDD).

INTERVIEWS/ADDRESSES (IWMDS UNLESS OTHERWISE NOTED)

Arnall, J.; Beckerley, E.; Blake, G. (<http://www.pbs.org/redfiles/kgb/deep/interv/k_int-george_blake.htm> (accessed 18 October 2011)); Brodie, F.; Bruford-Davies, R. (NAM; IWMDS); Carter, F.; Clark, W.; Condron, A.; Cottom, F.; Curd, E.; Davies, S.; (<http://www.thekoreanwar.co.uk/html/sound_bites.html> (accessed 12 August 2007)); DeLong, J. (<http://www.koreanwar-educator.org> (accessed 13 November 2010)); Donnelly, E. (<http://www.kmike.com/oz/kr/chapter23.htm> (accessed 18 April 2005)); Dyer, J.; Eagles, A.; Edwards, A. (<http://www.koreanwar-educator.org> (accessed 13 November 2010)); Erricker, R.; Farrar-Hockley, A. (IWMDS; <http://www.thekoreanwar.co.uk/html/sound_bites.html> (accessed 11 August 2007)); Gibson, W.; Gilder, A.; Greville, P. (<http://www.awm.gov.au/korea/faces/pow/pow.htm> (accessed 10 March 2009)); Grosvenor, J.; Guess, B.; Griffith, D. (<http://www.loc.gov/vets/stories/pow-korea.html#stories> (accessed 15 November 2010)); Hawkins, A.; Hickey, R.; Hobson, G.; Jaunal, J. (<http://www.koreanwar-educator.org/memoirs/juanal_jack/index.htm> (accessed 11 January 2011)); Kaye, D.; Kinne, D. (<http://www.thekoreanwar.co.uk/html/sound_bites.html> (accessed 11 August 2007)); Mares J. (<http://www.loc.gov/vets/stories/pow-korea.html#stories> (accessed 14 November 2010)); P. May (<http://www.thekoreanwar.co.uk/html/sound_bites.html> (accessed 12 August 2007)); Mercer, S.(IWMDS; NAM); Murphy, B.; Norley, R.; O'Brien, M.; Papworth, C.; Patchett, D.; Peskett, J.; Richards, G.; Sharp, D.; Sharpling, C.; Shaw, J.; Thorin, D. (<http://www.usgennet.org/usa/topic/preservation/journals/pegasus.html> (accessed 14 January 2011)); Tyas, A.; Underwood, J.; Weller, P.; Westwood, W.; Whitamore, V.; Wiseman, J.

NEWSPAPERS, MAGAZINES, JOURNALS

The Back Badge [Journal of the Gloucestershire Regiment]; Catholic Herald; Daily Express; Daily Herald; Daily Telegraph; Daily Worker; [Manchester] Guardian; Shanghai News, The Times.

FILM DOCUMENTARIES/NEWSREELS

They Chose China (National Film Board of Canada, 2005).
Forgotten Heroes: Korea Remembered (BBC, 2001).
Korea: The Unknown War (Thames Television, 1988).
POWs Home (British Pathé, 1953).

UNPUBLISHED THESES

McIntyre, Robert Bruce, 'The Forgotten Thirty-Three: An Examination of Canadian Prisoners of War of the Korean War' (History MA thesis, University of Waterloo, 1994).

PUBLISHED PRIMARY SOURCES

Adams, C., *An American Dream*, ed. Della Adams and Lewis H. Carlson (Amherst, Mass., 2007).
Baldovi, L. (ed.), *A Foxhole View: Personal Accounts of Hawaii's Korean War Veterans* (Honolulu, 2002).
Bassett, R. M. with L. H. Carlson, *And The Wind Blew Cold: The Story of an American POW in North Korea* (Kent, OH, 2002).
Berry, H., *Hey, Mac, Where Ya Been? Living Memories of the U.S. Marines in the Korean War* (New York, 1988).
Blake, G., *No Other Choice: An Autobiography* (New York, 1990).
Burchett, W., *This Monstrous War* (Melbourne: Joseph Waters, 1953).
——*At the Barricades: Forty Years on the Cutting Edge of History* (New York, 1981).
——*Memoirs of a Rebel Journalist*, ed. G. Burchett and N. Shimmin (Sydney, 2005).
Chinese People's Committee for World Peace, *'United Nations' P.O.W.'s in Korea* (Beijing, 1953).
Clarke, C., *Journey through Shadow: 839 Days in Hell: A POW's Survival in North Korea* (Charlotte, NC, 1988).
Condron, A. M., R. G. Cordon, and L. B. Sullivan (eds), *Thinking Soldiers: By Men Who Fought in Korea* (Beijing, 1955).
Crosbie, P., *Three Winters Cold* (Dublin, 1955).
Culbertson, R. E., 'The Korean War—a Former POW's Story', *Ex-POW Bulletin*, 14(3) (1993), 20–30.
Davies, N., *Red Winds From the North* (Knebworth, 1999).
Davies, S. J., *In Spite of Dungeons: The Experiences as a Prisoner-of-War in North Korea of the Chaplain to the First Battalion, the Gloucestershire Regiment* (London, 1954).
Dean, W. F. as told to W. L. Worden, *General Dean's Story* (New York, 1954).
Deane, P., *I Was a Captive in Korea* (New York, 1953).
——[Philippe Deane Gigantes], *I Should Have Died* (New York, 1977).
Esensten, S., 'Memories of Life as a POW 35 Years Later', Part I, *The Greybeards*, 11(4) (1997), 6–8.

—— 'Memories of Life as a POW 35 Years Later', Part II, *The Greybeards*, 11(6) (1997), 6–9.

—— 'Memories of Life as a POW 35 Years Later', Part III, *The Greybeards*, 12(1) (1998), 34–8.

Farrar-Hockley, A., *The Edge of the Sword* (London, 1954).

Funchess, W. H., *Korea POW: A Thousand Days of Torment, November 4, 1950—September 6, 1953* (Clemson, SC, 1997).

Goodman, A. E. (ed.), *Negotiating While Fighting: The Diary of Admiral C. Turner Joy at the Korean Armistice Conference* (Stanford, 1978).

Green, D., *Captured at the Imjin River: The Korean War Memoirs of a Gloster, 1950–1953* (Barnsley, 2003).

Harris, A. M., *Only One River to Cross: An Australian Soldier Behind Enemy Lines in Korea* (Canberra, 2004).

King, J., 'Korea' in Tony Strachen (ed.), *In the Clutch of Circumstance: Reminiscences of the Canadian National Prisoners of War Association* (Victoria, BC, 1985), 97–104.

Kinne, D., *The Wooden Boxes* (London, 1955).

Knox, D., *The Korean War: Pusan to Chosin: An Oral History* (San Diego, 1985).

—— *The Korean War: Uncertain Victory: An Oral History* (San Diego, 1988).

Lankford, D., *I Defy! The Story of Lieutenant Dennis Lankford* (London, 1954).

Large, L., *One Man's War in Korea* (London, 1988).

McNab, A., *Immediate Action* (London, 1995).

McNair, E. J., *A British Nurse in the Korean War: Shadows of the Far Forgotten* (Stroud, 2007).

Mahurin, W. M., *Honest John: The Autobiography of Walker M. Mahurin* (New York, 1962).

Matthews, R. F., as told to F. S. Jones *No Rice for Rebels: A Story of the Korean War* (London, 1956).

Méray, T., *On Burchett*, trans. Mátyás Sárközi (Kallista, Vic., 2008).

Ministry of Defence, *Treatment of British Prisoners of War in Korea* (London, 1955).

O'Kane, H., *O'Kane's Korea: A Soldier's Tale of Three Years of Combat and Captivity in Korea, 1950–53* (Kenilworth, 1988).

Pate, L. W. as told to B. J. Cutler, *Reactionary!* (New York, 1955).

Pelser, F. and M. E. Pelser, *Freedom Bridge* (Fairfield, Cal., 1984).

Perrins, A. (ed.), *'A Pretty Rough Do Altogether': The Fifth Fusiliers in Korea, 1950–1951* (Alnwick, 2004).

Peters, R. and X. Li, *Voices from the Korean War: Personal Stories of American, Korean, and Chinese Soldiers* (Lexington, Ky., 2004).

Petredis, P. G., *Escape from North Korea* (Victoria, BC, 2005).

Prasad, S. N., *History of the Custodian Force (India) in Korea 1953–54* (Delhi, 1976).

Rose, D., *Off the Record: The Life and Letters of a Black Watch Officer* (Staplehurst, 1996).

Rowley, Arden Allen *Korea-POW: A Thousand Days With Life on Hold*, 3rd edn, rev. (Mesa, Ariz., 2003).

Thompson, J., *True Colors: 1004 Days as a Prisoner of War* (Port Washington, NY, 1989).

Thorin, D., *A Ride to Panmunjom* (Chicago, 1956).

Thornton, J. W., *Believed to Be Alive* (Middlebury, Vt., 1981).

Tomedi, R., *No Bugles, No Drums: An Oral History of the Korean War* (New York, 1993).

United States Senate, Committee on Government Operations, *Korean War Atrocities* (Washington, DC, 1953).

Wills, M. R. as told to J. R. Moskin, *Turncoat: An American's 12 Years in Communist China* (Englewood Cliffs, NJ, 1966).
Winnington, A., *Breakfast with Mao: Memoirs of a Foreign Correspondent* (London, 1986).
Winnington, A. and W. Burchett, *Plain Perfidy* (Beijing, 1954).
Zellers, L., *In Enemy Hands: A Prisoner in North Korea* (Lexington, Ky., 1991).

PUBLISHED SECONDARY SOURCES

Andrew, C., *Defend the Realm: The Authorized History of MI5* (London, 2009).
Andrew, C. and O. Gordievsky, *KGB: The Inside Story of Its Foreign Operations from Lenin to Gorbachev* (New York, 1990).
Avery, P. M., *They Came Home: Korean POWs Tell Their Stories* (Kimberley City, Mo., 2004).
Avery, P. M. and J. Faulkner, *Sunchon Tunnel Massacre Survivors* (Branson, Mo., 2008).
Barclay, C. N., *The First Commonwealth Division: The Story of the British Commonwealth Land Forces in Korea, 1950–1953* (Aldershot, 1954).
Biderman, A. D., *March to Calumny: The Story of American POWs in the Korean War* (New York, 1963).
Blair, C., Jr, *Beyond Courage* (New York, 1955).
Carew, T., *Korea: The Commonwealth at War* (London, 1967).
Carlson, L., *Remembered Prisoners of a Forgotten War: An Oral History of Korean War POWs* (New York, 2002).
Catchpole, B., *The Korean War* (London, 2000).
Chen Zhiyong, 'The Doctor and the Prisoner' *China Pictorial*, October 2003, <http://www.china-pictorial.com/chpic/htdocs/English/content/200310/3-2.htm> (accessed 19 April 2005).
Chinnery, P. D., *Korean Atrocity! Forgotten War Crimes, 1950–1953* (Annapolis, Md., 2000).
Cookridge, E. H., *Shadow of a Spy: The Complete Dossier on George Blake* (London, 1967).
Cooper, G., *Fight, Dig and Live: The Story of the Royal Engineers in the Korean War* (Barnsley, 2011).
Cunningham, C., *No Mercy, No Leniency: Communist Mistreatment of British Prisoners of War in Korea* (Barnsley, 2000).
Davis, R. E., *Ex-POWs of Alabama*, ed. A. S. Cooper (Montgomery, Ala., 1984).
Doherty, R., *The Sons of Ulster: Ulstermen at War from the Somme to Korea* (Belfast, 1992).
Doyle, R. C., *Voices from Captivity: Interpreting the American POW Narrative* (Lawrence, Kan., 1994).
Dvorchak, R. J., *Battle for Korea: A History of the Korean Conflict* (Cambridge, Mass., 2003).
Farrar-Hockley, A., *The British Part in the Korean War*, 2 vols (London, 1990, 1995).
Gaston, P., *Korea 1950–1953: Prisoners of War: The British Army* (Eastbourne, 1976).
—— *Thirty-Eighth Parallel: The British in Korea* (Glasgow, 1976).
Grey, J., 'Other Fronts: Resistance, Collaboration and Survival among United Nations Prisoners during the Korean War' in P. Dennis and J. Grey (eds), *The Korean War: A 50 Year Retrospective* (Canberra, 2000), 136–49.
Hanson, T. E., *Combat Ready? The Eighth Army on the Eve of the Korean War* (College Station, Tex., 2010).
Harding, E. D., *The Imjin Roll* (Gloucester, 1981).
Hastings, M., *The Korean War* (London, 1987).

Hayhurst, F., *Green Berets in Korea: The Story of 41 Independent Commando Royal Marines* (Cambridge, 2001).

Hermes, W. G., *United States Army in the Korean War: Truce Tent and Fighting Front* (Washington, DC, 1966).

Hickey, M., *The Korean War: The West Confronts Communism* (New York, 2000).

Hickman, T., *The Call-Up: A History of National Service* (London, 2004).

Jolidon, L., *Last Seen Alive: The Search for Missing POWs from the Korean War* (Austin, Tex., 1995).

Kenyon, A., *Valiant Dust: Graphic Stories from the Life of Herbert A. Lord* (London, 1966).

King, C. G. and R. D. Guthrie, *Escape from North Korea: The Ron Guthrie Story* (Riverwood, NSW, 2002).

Landsdown, J. R. P., *With the Carriers in Korea: The Fleet Air Arm Story, 1950–1953* (Southside, 1997).

Lane, R. A., *Ambassador in Chains: The Life of Bishop Patrick James Byrne* (New York, 1955).

Laybourn, K., *Marxism in Britain: Dissent, Decline and Re-emergence, 1945–c.2000* (London, 2006).

Lech, R. B., *Broken Soldiers* (Urbana, Il., 2000).

MacDonald, J. A., Jr, *The Problems of U.S. Marine Corps Prisoners of War in Korea* (Washington, DC, 1988).

Maher, W. L., *A Shepherd in Combat Boots: Chaplain Emil Kapaun of the 1st Cavalry Division* (Shippensburg, Penn., 1997).

Marr, A., *A History of Modern Britain* (London, 2007).

Martin, M. J., *The Korean War: Life as a POW* (Farmington Hills, Mich., 2004).

Miller, J., 'The Forgotten History War: Wilfred Burchett, Australia and the Cold War', *The Asia-Pacific Journal: Japan Focus*, 30 September 2008, <http://www.japanfocus.org/-Jamie-Miller/2912> (accessed 5 December 2010).

Millett, A. R., *The Korean War* (Washington, DC, 2007).

—— *The War For Korea, 1950–1951: They Came from the North* (Lawrence, Kan., 2010).

Moorehead, C., *Dunant's Dream: War, Switzerland, and the History of the Red Cross* (New York, 1999).

Paisley, V., *22 Stayed* (London, 1955).

Pelling, H., *The British Communist Party: A Historical Profile* (London, 1958).

Salmon, A., *To the Last Round: The Epic British Stand on the Imjin River, Korea 1951* (London, 2009).

—— *Scorched Earth, Black Snow: Britain and Australia in the Korean War, 1950* (London, 2011).

Scheipers, S. (ed.), *Prisoners in War* (Oxford, 2010).

Song, H.-S., *The Fight for Freedom: The Untold Story of the Korean War Prisoners* (Seoul, 1980).

Tang, T. H., *Britain's Encounter with Revolutionary China, 1949–54* (Basingstoke, 1992).

Thomas, P., *41 Independent Commando Royal Marines: Korea—1950 to 1952* (Portsmouth, 1990).

United States, Department of the Army, *U.S. Prisoners of War in the Korean Operation: A Study of Their Treatment and Handling by the North Korean Army and the Chinese Communist Forces* (Fort Meade, Md., 1954).

—— *Communist Interrogation, Indoctrination, and Exploitation of Prisoners of War* (Washington, DC, 1956).

United States, Department of Defense, *POW: The Fight Continues After the Battle: The Report of the Secretary of Defense's Advisory Committee on Prisoners of War* (Washington, DC, 1955).

United States Senate, Committee on Government Operations, *Communist Interrogation, Indoctrination and Exploitation of American Military and Civilian Prisoners* (Washington, DC, 1956).

Vance, J. F., *Objects of Concern: Canadian Prisoners of War through the Twentieth Century* (Vancouver, 1994).

Walker, A., *A Barren Place: National Servicemen in Korea, 1950–1954* (London, 1994).

Wayper, L., *Mars and Minerva: A History of Army Education* (Winchester, 2004).

White, W. L., *The Captives of Korea: An Unofficial White Paper on the Treatment of Prisoners of War* (New York, 1957).

Wubben, H. W., 'American Prisoners of War in Korea: A Second Look at the "Something New in History" Theme', *American Quarterly*, 22 (1970), 3–19.

Wylie, N., 'Review Article: Prisoners of War in the Era of Total War', *War in History*, 13 (2006), 217–33.

Zweiback, A. J., 'The 21 "Turncoat GIs": The Political Culture of the Korean War', *The Historian*, 60 (1988), 345–62.

Index